CATHERINE OF SIENA

SIGRID UNDSET

CATHERINE
OF SIENA

Translated by
Kate Austin-Lund

IGNATIUS PRESS   SAN FRANCISCO

Original edition:
© 1951 by H. Aschehoug and Company (W. Nygaard) AS
Oslo, Norway

Original English edition
© 1954 by Sheed and Ward, Inc., New York
Published with ecclesiastical approval

Cover art: *Saint Catherine of Siena Receiving the Stigmata*
Domenico Beccafumi (1486–1551)
Coll. Moss Stanley, Riverdale-on-Hudson, New York
© Scala / Art Resource, New York

Cover design by Roxanne Mei Lum

Published in 2009 by Ignatius Press, San Francisco
ISBN 978-1-58617-408-8
Library of Congress Control Number 2009923626
Printed in the United States of America ∞

I

IN THE CITY-STATES OF TUSCANY the citizens—*Popolani*—businessmen, master craftsmen and the professional class had already in the Middle Ages demanded and won the right to take part in the government of the republic side by side with the nobles—the *Gentiluomini*. In Siena they had obtained a third of the seats in the High Council as early as the twelfth century. In spite of the fact that the different parties and rival groups within the parties were in constant and often violent disagreement, and in spite of the frequent wars with Florence, Siena's neighbour and most powerful competitor, prosperity reigned within the city walls. The Sienese were rich and proud of their city, so they filled it with beautiful churches and public buildings. Masons, sculptors, painters and smiths who made the exquisite lattices and lamps, were seldom out of work. Life was like a brightly coloured tissue, where violence and vanity, greed and uninhibited desire for sensual pleasure, the longing for power, and ambition, were woven together in a multitude of patterns. But through the tissue ran silver threads of Christian charity, deep and genuine piety in the monasteries and among the good priests, among the brethren and sisters who had dedicated themselves to a life of helping their neighbours. The well-to-do and the common people had to the best of their ability provided for the sick, the poor and the lonely with unstinted generosity. In every class of the community there were good people who lived a quiet, modest and beautiful family life of purity and faith.

The family of Jacopo Benincasa was one of these. By trade he was a wool-dyer, and he worked with his elder sons and apprentices while his wife, Lapa di Puccio di Piagente, firmly and surely ruled the large household, although her life was an almost unbroken cycle of pregnancy and childbirth—and almost half her children died while they were still quite small. It is uncertain how many of them grew up, but the names of thirteen children who lived are to be found on an old family tree of the Benincasas. Considering how terribly high the rate of infant mortality was at that time, Jacopo and Lapa were lucky in being able to bring up more than half the children they had brought into the world.

Jacopo Benincasa was a man of solid means when in 1346 he was able to rent a house in the Via dei Tintori, close to the Fonte Branda, one of the beautiful covered fountains which assured the town of a plentiful supply of fresh water. The old home of the Benincasas, which is still much as it was at that time, is, according to our ideas, a small house for such a big family. But in the Middle Ages people were not fussy about the question of housing, least of all the citizens of the fortified towns where people huddled together as best they could within the protection of the walls. Building space was expensive, and the city must have its open markets, churches and public buildings, which at any rate theoretically belonged to the entire population. The houses were crowded together in narrow, crooked streets. According to the ideas of that time the new home of the Benincasas was large and impressive.

Lapa had already had twenty-two children when she gave birth to twins, two little girls, on Annunciation Day, March 25, 1347. They were christened Catherine and Giovanna. Madonna Lapa could only nurse one of the twins herself, so little Giovanna was handed over to a nurse, while Catherine fed at her mother's breast. Never before had Monna Lapa been able to experience the joy of nursing her own children—a new pregnancy had always forced her to give her child over to another woman. But Catherine lived on her mother's milk until she was old enough to be weaned. It was all too natural that Lapa, who was already advanced in years, came to love this child with a demanding and well-meaning mother-love which later, when the child grew up, made the relationship between the good-hearted, simple Lapa and her young eagle of a daughter one long series of heart-rending misunderstandings. Lapa loved her immeasurably and understood her not at all.

Catherine remained the youngest and the darling of the whole family, for little Giovanna died in infancy, and a new Giovanna, born a few years later, soon followed her sister and namesake into the grave. Her parents consoled themselves with the firm belief that these small, innocent children had flown from their cradles straight into Paradise—while Catherine, as Raimondo of Capua writes, using a slightly far-fetched pun on her name and the Latin word "catena" (a chain), had to work hard on earth before she could take a whole chain of saved souls with her to heaven.

When the Blessed Raimondo of Capua collected material for his biography of St. Catherine he got Madonna Lapa to tell him about the saint's childhood—long, long ago, for Lapa was by that time a widow of eighty. From Raimondo's description one gets the impression that Lapa enjoyed telling everything that came into her head to such an understanding and responsive listener. She told of the old days when she was the active, busy mother in the middle of a flock of her own children, her nieces and nephews, grandchildren, friends and neighbours, and Catherine was the adored baby of a couple who were already elderly. Lapa described her husband Jacopo as a man of unparalleled goodness, piety and uprightness. Raimondo writes that Lapa herself "had not a sign of the vices which one finds among people of our time"; she was an innocent and simple soul, and completely without the ability to invent stories which were not true. But because she had the well-being of so many people on her shoulders, she could not be so unworldly and patient as her husband; or perhaps Jacopo was really almost too good for this world, so that his wife had to be even more practical than she already was, and on occasion she thought it her duty to utter a word or two of common sense to protect the interests of the family. For Jacopo never said a hard or untimely word however upset or badly treated he might be, and if others in the house gave way to their bad temper or used bitter or unkind words he always tried to talk them round: "Now listen, for your own sake you must keep calm and not use such unseemly words." Once one of his townsmen tried to force him into paying a large sum of money which Jacopo did not owe him, and the honest dyer was hounded and persecuted till he was almost ruined by the slanderous talk of this man and his powerful friends. But in spite of everything Jacopo would not allow anyone to say a word against the man; Lapa did so, but her husband replied: "Leave him in peace, you will see that God will show him his fault and protect us." And a short while after that it really happened, said Lapa.

Coarse words and dirty talk were unknown in the dyer's home. His daughter Bonaventura, who was married to a young Sienese, Niccolo, was so much grieved when her husband and his friends engaged in loose talk and told doubtful jokes that she became physically ill and began to waste away. Her husband, who must really have been a well-meaning young man, was worried when he saw how thin and pale his bride was, and wanted to know what was wrong with her. Bonaventura replied seriously, "In my father's house I was not used to listening to such words as I must hear here every day. You can be sure that if such indecent talk continues in our house you will live to see me waste to death." Niccolo at once saw to it that all such bad habits which wounded his wife's feelings were stopped, and openly expressed his admiration for her chaste and modest ways, and the piety of his parents-in-law.

Such was the home of little Catherine. Everyone petted and loved her, and when she was still quite tiny her family admired her "wisdom" when they listened to her innocent prattle. And as she was also very pretty Lapa could scarcely ever have her to herself; all the neighbours wanted to borrow her! Medieval writers seldom trouble to describe children or try to understand them. But Lapa manages in a few pages of Raimondo's book to give us a picture of a little Italian girl, serious and yet happy, attractive and charming—and already beginning to show that overwhelming vitality and spiritual energy which many years later made Raimondo and her other "children" surrender to her influence, with the feeling that her words and her presence banished despondency and faint-heartedness, and filled their souls with the peace and love of God. As soon as she left the circle of her own family, little Catherine became the leader of all the other small children in the street. She taught them games which she had herself invented—that is to say innumerable small acts of devotion. When she was five years old she taught herself the Angelus, and she loved repeating it incessantly. As she went up or down the stairs at home she used to kneel on each step and say an *Ave Maria*. For the pious little daughter of a pious family, where everyone talked kindly and politely to everyone else, it must have been quite natural for her as soon as she had heard of God to talk in the same way to Him and His following of saints. It was then still a kind of game for Catherine. But small children put their whole souls and all their imagination into their games.

The neighbours called her Euphrosyne. This is the name of one of the Graces, and it seemed that Raimondo had his doubts about it; could the good people in the Fontebranda quarter have such knowledge of classical mythology that they knew what the name meant? He thought that perhaps, before she could talk properly, Catherine called herself something which the neighbours took to be Euphrosyne, for there is also a saint of that name. The Sienese were however used to seeing processions and listening to songs and verse, so they could easily have picked up more of the poets' property than Raimondo imagined. Thus for example, Lapa's father, Puccio di Piagente, wrote verse in his free time; he was by trade a craftsman—a mattress maker. He was moreover a very pious man, generous towards the monasteries and to monks and nuns. He might easily have known both the heathen and the Christian Euphrosyne. Catherine was for a time very much interested in the legend of St. Euphrosyne, who is supposed to have dressed as a boy and run away from home to enter a monastery. She toyed with the idea of doing the same herself. . . .

One evening, when Catherine was about six years old, she was on her way home after visiting her married sister Bonaventura. She was with two small boys, one of whom was her brother Stefano—he was a year or two older than she, and presumably was often commissioned by their mother to look after his little sister. The children had come to a place where the street goes steeply downhill between garden walls and housefronts towards the valley, where Fontebranda's charming stone canopy shades the well where the local women do their washing, or from which they pour the cold clear water into copper urns which they then carry home on their heads. On the other side of the valley are the great stone walls of the abbey church of San Domenico, massive and austere, with no other ornament than a series of windows with pointed arches built into the gable-end of the choir.

The little girl looked over the valley—it is called Valle Piatta. And then she looked up, over the roof of the church. She saw a sight so wonderful that she could never have dreamed of anything like it: the Saviour of the world sitting on a royal throne, clothed in a bishop's robes, and with the triple crown of the Pope on His head. Beside Him stood the apostles St. Peter and St. Paul, and St. John the Evangelist. The child stood as though she were rooted to the spot. She stared enraptured at the vision "with the eyes both of her body and her soul". Our Lord smiled lovingly at her, lifted His hand and blessed the child with the sign of the cross, as a bishop does. . . .

Catherine stood motionless, while the love of God streamed into her soul, filling her whole being and transforming it—for ever. Up and down the narrow street the evening bustle of people, ox-carts and riders passed, and at the top of the street stood the little girl, usually so shy, with her face and eyes upturned, as still as though she were made of stone.

The boys were already halfway down the hill when Stefano turned and looked for his sister, and saw her standing there, right at the top of the street. He called to her several times. Catherine did not move. He turned and ran up to her, calling her all the time—presumably somewhat impatiently. But she did not notice him until he took her arm, and asked her what she was doing. Then she looked as though she had woken from a deep sleep. She looked down and replied, "Oh, if you had seen what I see I am sure you would never have interrupted me and taken such a sweet sight from me." When she looked up again the vision was gone. She began to weep bitterly, wishing that she had never turned from the heavenly vision.

When Raimondo of Capua had become her father confessor, Catherine told him that from that day she began to learn of the way the saints had lived, and especially of the life of St. Dominic and the Desert Fathers, though no one had taught her except the Holy Spirit. But a child of six can absorb a mass of knowledge without knowing where it comes from. The Dominican monastery with its fortress-like church lay at the top of the hill above her home. The preaching friars in the black and white robes of their order must have frequented the streets where the Benincasa children ran to visit their neighbours and married sisters. And in their house they had living with them a young boy who a few years later entered the Dominican Order—Tommaso della Fonte. He was the brother of Palmiero della Fonte who had married Niccoluccia Benincasa, and when Tommaso at the age of ten had lost his parents during the plague in 1349 he was given a home by his brother's father-in-law. The fact that Catherine had a foster-brother who wished to be a Dominican living in the same house may have affected her more than she understood at the time, or could remember later.

But the moment when Catherine had seen heaven and received the blessing of her Saviour in a vision had changed her for ever. She was still a little child, but everyone at home noticed that she suddenly became so mature and so extraordinarily sensible that she was more like a grown-up than a little girl. She had been initiated. The perky little Euphrosyne had seen a glimpse of the overwhelming truth which she had been seeking when she played her pious games—she had stepped into the boundless worlds of God's love and the love of God. Perhaps in a vague way she understood that her prayers and meditations had become a means by which she might prepare herself to receive a call—what it would be she did not know yet—which was to come one day from Him whom she had seen in a vision, and who had blessed her with His out-stretched hand. However she had learned of the lives and practices of God's saints, it is at any rate certain that Catherine now tried to imitate their vigilance and asceticism as well as she could. Quite unlike most growing children, she became quieter and ate less than before. During the day her father and the men in the house worked in the dye-works in the cellar, and her mother and the women were occupied in the big kitchen which was also the household living-room—a large room at the top of the house, with a terrace in front where small shrubs and potted plants edged the parapet, and a line of washing fluttered in the wind. In the meantime the bedrooms on the floor between were empty most of the day. Catherine sought the solitude of one of these rooms and secretly beat her thin shoulders with a little whip. But naturally the other little girls of the neighbourhood discovered this fairly soon— children never respect a person's need of being alone; and then they wanted to do what Catherine did, because they had got into the habit of imitating her. So they met in another out-of-the-way corner of the house and beat themselves, while Catherine said the "Our Father" and the "Hail Mary" as many times as she thought necessary. It was all delightfully secretive, and the little flock of small sisters of penitence must have felt highly edified and happy. It was also, as Raimondo remarks, a prologue to the future.

But sometimes Catherine longed to slip away from her play-mates, especially the little boys. Then, her mother told Raimondo afterwards, she used to go up the stairs so quickly that Lapa was sure she did not touch the steps with her feet—it was as though she floated. This terrified her mother, for she was afraid the child would fall and hurt herself. The longing for solitude, and the legends of the Desert Fathers about which she thought so much, made Catherine dream of a cave in the desert where she could hide herself and discourse only with God.

One beautiful summer morning Catherine provided herself with a loaf of bread and went out alone in the direction of her married sister's house near the Porta di San Ansano. But this time she went past it, and out of the gate, and for the first time in her life the little child of the city looked out over the quiet Valle Piatta and the green countryside. She was so used to her own world, with the houses close in on each other along the steep, narrow streets, and the swarms of people on foot or horseback, the donkeys, the ox-carts and the teams of mules, the dogs, and—ever-present members of all Italian families—the cats, that Catherine almost certainly thought that this green and peaceful world must be the desert. So she walked on and looked for a cave. Along the sides of the valley there were many grottoes in the limestone hills, and as soon as she had found one which she thought would be suitable she went in and knelt down. She began to pray as devoutly as she could. But in a little while an extraordinary feeling came over her—it was as though she were lifted up from the floor of the cave and floating under the roof. She was afraid that this was perhaps a temptation of the devil—that he was trying to frighten her out of praying. So she continued to pray even more devoutly and determinedly. When she awoke from her trance and found herself on her knees on the floor of the cave it was the time of Nones—three o'clock in the afternoon, the hour when the Son of God died on the cross.

It came to her as an inspiration from above that God did not wish her to be a hermit. He did not wish that she should chastise her fragile body to bear greater privations than were suitable for her age, and He did not wish her to leave her father's house in this way. It was a long way home, and she was tired, and afraid that she might have frightened her parents terribly—perhaps they thought that she had left them altogether. Again she prayed earnestly, this time that she might come safely home. And once again the strange feeling that she was floating came over her. When it had passed she was standing in front of the city gate. She ran home as fast as she could. But no one in the Benincasa household had paid any particular attention to the fact that she was not there; they thought that she was safely with her sister. And no one heard of her attempt to be a hermit before Catherine herself divulged it to her confessor many years later.

The visionary child saw how the grown-ups and other children round her were concerned with a whole lot of things in which she felt not the slightest interest. After a while she realised that it was these things which the Bible calls "the world". Her world—a world into which she ceaselessly longed to penetrate deeper and deeper—seemed to spread itself out behind and over all the things which she perceived with her physical senses. It was a heavenly world which she had been allowed to catch sight of for a moment when she saw Our Lord sitting royally among the clouds above the roof of San Domenico. Prayer was the key to this world. But the child had already discovered that one could enter it by a spiritual road also, without seeing or hearing anything with the outer senses.

Her mother and father, her sisters and brothers were all good Christians. But they were content to drink moderately of that spring which made Catherine more and more thirsty the more she drank of it. They prayed, went to Mass, were helpful and generous towards the poor and the servants of God, but at times they flung themselves head-first into those very acts which Catherine came more and more to consider as obstacles which prevented her from attaining the desire of her heart. And however carefully the Benincasa children had been sheltered from bad influences they could not help knowing something of the pride of the rich citizens, of the feuds and fights between hard and bloodthirsty men, of the vanity of worldly women. Catherine's heart burned to see them saved, all these poor souls who had cut themselves off from the love of God which she had experienced in such a way as to give her a foretaste of the bliss of heaven. She wished that she could become one of those who work to save the souls of men—for example the Dominicans, for she knew that their order had been founded with just this end in view. Often when she saw the preaching friars go past their house she noted where they trod, and when they had gone, ran out and reverently kissed the spot touched by their feet.

But if she were one day to be in a position to take part in the work of these friars and all the good people of the monasteries and convents, and escape being dragged from her secret life by the worries and pleasures which took up so much of the time and thoughts of her mother and her married sisters, she must remain a virgin always. This she understood. When she was seven years old Catherine begged the Virgin Mary to speak for her— she wanted so much to give herself to her Son, Jesus Christ, and be His bride. "I love Him with all my soul, I promise Him and you that I will never take another bridegroom." And she prayed both her heavenly Bridegroom and His mother to help her, so that she could always keep herself pure and free from stain in body and soul.

An Italian girl of seven in our own day is more mature than a child of the same age of the Nordic or Anglo-Saxon world, and in the Middle Ages children all over Europe grew up more quickly than they do now; even in Norway boys and girls of fifteen were considered ready for marriage. In *Romeo and Juliet* Lady Capulet reminds her daughter, who is not yet fourteen, that

> ... younger than you
> Here in Verona, ladies of esteem
> Are made already mothers. ...

Nevertheless when Catherine made her vow of chastity she could not have known much of the instincts of the body and the soul which she swore never to follow. The temptations of the flesh as yet meant two things for her: the appetite—the wholesome appetite for food of a healthy young girl during the growing years, for although she had secretly begun to practise self-denial Catherine was a strong and healthy young creature: and secondly, her fear of physical pain. The latter she had begun to fight against by disciplining herself with penitential scourgings more often than before. In order to master her appetite she would not eat anything but bread and vegetables. The large helpings of meat she was given at the family meals she smuggled to Stefano, who sat beside her, or to the cats miauwing under the table. Both the boy and the cats gladly accepted these extra rations. And the large family who sat round Monna Lapa's well laden table never seemed to notice what went on at the end where the youngest members sat.

But they could not help noticing at home that Catherine became more and more patient and calm. Many years later she came to call patience the very marrow of piety, and in view of the fact that grace does not alter our inborn nature, but perfects it, one must believe that this young woman who was later, with such awe-inspiring energy and whole-heartedness, to do all that her visions told her was God's will, must have been born with an unusual reserve of natural wilfulness. But she was always obedient to her parents, and received with patience her mother's scoldings—for Lapa had so much to do in the house, so many people always round her, that she was easily worked into a rage, and she gave her tongue free rein when she was annoyed. But at this time her family were still well pleased with Catherine's exemplary behaviour; they admired her because they thought her so much more sensible than one could expect at her age, and so pious and gentle.

It was probably because she knew that it gave her favourite child great pleasure to be sent on such errands that Lapa one morning asked Catherine to go to the parish church and offer a certain amount of candles and money on the altar, and ask the priest to say a Mass in honour of St. Anthony. St. Anthony was the gentle saint who during his lifetime had shown such great understanding and sympathy for ordinary women's troubles and sorrows that mothers and housewives had come to look on him as their special friend in heaven. Catherine went and did as her mother had told her. But she wanted so much to take part in this Mass that she remained in the church till it was over and came home much later than her mother expected—Lapa had intended the child to come home as soon as she had talked with the priest. Now she met her daughter with a proverb which was used in Siena when anyone was inexcusably late: "Damned be the evil tongues which said to me that you would never come back." The girl said nothing at first, but then she took her mother aside and said to her seriously and humbly, "Dear mother, if I have done wrong or more than you meant me to do, beat me so that I remember to behave better another time; that is just. But I beg you not to let your tongue damn anyone, whether they be good or evil, for my sake. It is unseemly at your age, and it hurts my heart." This made a deep impression on Lapa—she knew the child was right. But she tried to appear unmoved, and asked why Catherine had been away so long. She told her that she had remained in the church to hear their Mass. When Jacopo came home, however, Lapa told him what their daughter had done and said. Jacopo listened, silent and thoughtful, but in his heart he thanked God.

In this way Catherine grew up until she became a young girl and discovered that she was different, and that the world around her was also different.

II

It was the custom in Italian towns that once a girl was twelve years old she could not go out unless accompanied by an older woman. She was considered more or less of an age to be married, and her parents must now begin to look around for a suitable husband. When Catherine had reached her twelfth year, therefore, there came an end to running errands for her mother or slipping out to visit her married sisters. Her parents and brothers hoped that they would be able to find a husband for her who would bring honour and advantages to the whole family. Lapa was especially happy, sure that she would be able to find a really remarkable man for her darling, the charming and sensible youngest daughter.

But when Lapa told the young girl that now the time was come to try to make the very best of her beautiful appearance, arrange her lovely hair in the way that suited her best, wash her face more often, and avoid anything which could spoil her delicate complexion and white throat, she was bitterly disappointed. Catherine was not in the least keen to make herself beautiful for the sake of young men: on the contrary, it seemed as though she shunned their company and did everything she could not to be seen by them. She fled even from the apprentices and assistants who lived in their house, "as though they were snakes". She never stood at the front door or leaned out of the window to look at the passers-by and be seen by them.

Lapa sought the help of Bonaventura to make Catherine more amenable. Lapa knew how extremely fond Catherine was of her elder sister, and for a while it really seemed that Bonaventura succeeded in making the child slightly more obedient to her mother, so that she began to take more care of her appearance. According to what Raimondo says, Catherine was never a startling beauty, but young and vivacious as she was, slim, with a fair skin, beautiful dark eyes and an abundance of that shining golden-brown hair which the Italians have always admired so much, she must have been an extraordinarily attractive young woman.

However great or small were the concessions Catherine made to the fashions of the day under the influence of her favourite sister, she accused herself later with scalding tears and passionate grief for her fall from grace by giving herself up to sinful vanity. When her confessor Raimondo asked whether she had at any time wanted to break, or thought of breaking, her vow of chastity, Catherine answered No, she had never for a moment thought of it. Raimondo was a wise priest who had long years of experience as confessor among the nuns. He asked whether she had not perhaps decked herself out to make an impression on men in general or on one special man, in spite of the fact that she was determined to keep her vow: in other words, whether she had succumbed to the old Eve and flirted a little on the way from lesser to greater self-denial? But Catherine denied this too. Raimondo said then, that in that case she had committed no great sin in yielding to the wishes of her mother and elder sister, whereupon Catherine accused herself of exaggerated love towards this sister—it seemed to her that she had loved Bonaventura more than God. But still Raimondo refused to judge her as harshly as she judged herself: she had obeyed her sister without evil intent or excess of vanity, and it was surely not against the will of God that she should love her sister. But, complained Catherine, what sort of a spiritual director was this who excused her sins? "Oh, Father, how could this miserable creature, who without any struggle and without any merits has received so much grace from God, waste her time adorning this body which is condemned to rot away—adorning it so as to tempt other mortal creatures?" Then, as on so many other occasions, Raimondo the confessor bowed to Catherine the penitent because she had greater religious experience than he. What she said concerning absolute purity and undivided will must be right.

In the meantime there came a sudden stop to Catherine's little excursion into the vanities of this world, for Bonaventura died in childbirth. The younger sister was sure that her death was God's punishment because she had tried to tempt another soul from the service of God. But God revealed to Catherine that Bonaventura, who otherwise had been in every way pious, chaste and righteous, had remained only a short while in purgatory before she was freed to enter the bliss of heaven. But her sister's death made it even clearer to Catherine how futile were the vanities of the world. She turned with a new ardour to her beloved Master and begged His forgiveness. Oh, if only He would say the same words to her as He had said to Magdalen: "Thy sins are forgiven thee." She felt that St. Mary Magdalen must be her particular patron saint and example.

The death of Bonaventura made the question of Catherine's marriage even more pressing for Jacopo and his sons. For people in the Middle Ages the family was still the most powerful protector of the rights and welfare of the individual. In a time so full of unrest and disturbance, the protection a man could expect of the community—whether state or town—was at the best uncertain. But a group consisting of father, sons and sons-in-law who held fast together and faithfully defended their common interests, at least promised a certain amount of security. Niccolo was still a young man, and now that Bonaventura was dead he would soon marry into another family group. It now became Catherine's duty to obey her parents and let herself be married to a man who would be a substitute for the son-in-law they had lost.

When they discovered how absolutely unwilling Catherine was to comply with their wishes their admiration of her wisdom and sweet shyness came to an end. They threw themselves upon the child with a fury which makes one believe that after all Shakespeare did not exaggerate when he described the bitterness of the Capulets—the father and mother who shriek and swear at Juliet because she does not show seemly gratitude when they tell her that they have arranged a match for her.

It must be remembered that her family was completely ignorant of the vow she had made—Catherine had never dared to name it to them. If she had expressed a wish to go into a convent, Jacopo at least would have listened to her with understanding, even if he had not been willing to give his consent at once. But it seems that Catherine never said that she wanted to be a nun. Beyond the fantasies she had had when she was tiny—that she should become a hermit, or imitate the Blessed Euphrosyne and run away from home dressed as a boy to become a monk—we do not know that Catherine had at any time imagined a future other than that of a life of the deepest solitude—such a life as must be the lot of a virgin wedded to God, if she was to live at home in the midst of a large family whose other members were all engaged in the work and interests of the world. In the time of the apostles this had been the normal life for Christian women who had taken a vow of chastity. But the demands of practical life soon led to the foundation of convents where such dedicated women could live together under one rule. And an ordinary medieval dwelling house was not exactly suited to keeping, year in, year out, a daughter who refused to marry and did not think of changing home for a convent.

It was perhaps Jacopo who had the idea of sending for a Dominican monk who was an old friend of the family, in order to see if he could persuade Catherine to comply with the family's plans. It was Fra Tommaso della Fonte, who had once been brought up with Catherine. She confessed to him that she had already secretly promised Christ that she would be His alone as long as she lived. Fra Tommaso could only advise her to meet the hardness which her family showed her so resolutely that they would have at last to understand that she would never give in. And Fra Tommaso thought that if she were to cut off her hair, which was her greatest beauty, perhaps they would leave her in peace.

Catherine accepted this advice as though it came from heaven. She immediately fetched a pair of scissors and cut off her lovely golden-brown plaits close to the head. Then she tied a little veil over her shorn head. It was against the custom of that time for an unmarried woman to cover her hair, so when Lapa saw her daughter with this extraordinary head-dress she immediately rushed up to her and asked what it meant. The girl dared not tell her the truth and would not tell a lie, so she did not answer. Lapa tore off the veil, and when she saw her beautiful daughter standing there so disfigured she sobbed with sorrow and fury: "Child, child, how could you do such a thing to me?" Silently the girl put on the veil again. But when Jacopo and the boys came hurrying in, startled by Lapa's shrieks and tears, and heard what had happened, they threw themselves upon Catherine in fury.

To make matters worse for Catherine she had now a suitor, a young man whom the Benincasas were very intent on bringing into the family. So they abused her roundly. "You wicked girl, do you imagine that you can escape our authority by cutting off your hair? It will grow again, and you shall be married, even if it breaks your heart. You shall never have any peace or quiet until you give in and do as we say."

Now there was to be an end of the silly notions the stupid girl had of hiding at all sorts of odd times to pray and hold exaggerated devotions. She was no longer allowed to have her own little bedroom—she was told she could share a room with one of the others in the house. Catherine chose to share the room of her brother Stefano, who was still unmarried. In the daytime while Stefano was working at the dye vats in the cellar she had the little room to herself, and at night he slept like a log and did not guess that his sister lay awake for long periods in prayer and contemplation.

Lapa dismissed her housemaid and saw that Catherine had enough to do in the house the whole day long. She had to do all the washing, prepare the food, and wait at table. On top of this, the whole household teased and scolded her while they sent her running hither and thither. The idea must have been that the girl would be brought to see that it was better to be a housewife in one's own home than be chased like a slave in a large family. But Catherine was enough of a child still to be able to bring her games into the depths of spiritual life. She told Raimondo later that she used to imagine that her father was Our Lord Jesus Christ, her mother was His mother, the Virgin Mary—this must have been rather difficult for Catherine when Lapa was in one of her furies—and her brothers and the apprentices were the apostles and disciples. Then she could serve them happily and conscientiously, without being tired or sulky, so that her family, against their will, were bound to admit that she really was astonishing. This game made the kitchen a sanctuary for Catherine, and it filled her soul with happiness and sweetness to wait at table, for it was her Lord and Master she was serving.

The Holy Spirit had taught her how to build herself an inner cell, a place of refuge where she could pray and think of her Beloved, and from this no one could recall her; here no one could come and disturb her. "The Kingdom of God is within you": now she understood the meaning of these words, spoken by Him who is truth itself. Within us—it is there that the gifts of the Holy Spirit are poured out upon us to perfect our natural talents, to break down internal and external obstacles. If we passionately desire the true good, the heavenly Guest comes and lives within us—He who has said "Be of good courage, I have conquered the world."

Catherine trusted in Him, and felt that a cell, not built by human hands, was formed within her, so that she had no need to regret that they had taken from her the little cell of wood and stone. Later she used to advise her disciples when they complained of being so overburdened with the problems of the world that they never found quiet to meet God or to drink of the spring by which they lived: "Build an inner cell in your soul and never leave it." Raimondo admits that he did not understand these words of his "mother" at once, but "it is extraordinary to see how I and all who have lived near her understand all her actions and words much better now than in those days when we had her beside us."

One day Catherine knelt lost in prayer in Stefano's room. Her father came in to find something—she was strictly forbidden to lock her door. Jacopo discovered the girl kneeling in a corner, and on her head rested a snow-white dove, but when he approached it rose and flew out of the window. But when Jacopo asked about the dove Catherine said no, she had seen no bird in the room. Jacopo said nothing, but in his heart he mused over this and many other things he had noticed.

III

THE SISTERS OF PENITENCE of St. Dominic's third order origi-
nated from a brotherhood of laymen which St. Dominic had
founded and called the Militia of Jesus Christ. Besides under-
taking to say certain prayers instead of the daily Offices which
the monks read—many of these laymen could not read—the
brothers were also pledged to defend the possessions of the
Church. During the years when the heretics had been in power
in Southern France and Northern Italy, a large amount of the
Church's lands had come into the hands of layfolk who disposed
of them as though they were their own rightful inheritance. St.
Dominic chose a life of strict poverty for the first order, the
preaching friars, and the second order, the contemplative sisters. But the poverty of the plundered cathedrals and churches,
abbeys and convents had become a hindrance to the work of bishops and priests, and the same applied to the charitable and missionary work of the old monastic foundations. One of the objects
of the Militia was to try to regain for the Church what was hers
by right. The greater number of these brothers were married men
and therefore according to the Catholic laws of marriage could
not take any vows without the consent of their wives. Therefore
their wives had to vow never to hinder their husbands in the work
they had undertaken. In this way the third order came to consist
chiefly of married couples who lived together in a life of semi-
seclusion, in the world, but not of the world. As a sign that they
were attached to the Dominican order they were to wear clothes
of the order's colours, black and white, but nothing was prescribed regarding the fashion of their clothes. Towards the end

of the thirteenth century the order gradually lost its character of a militia but continued as the Sisters and Brothers of Penitence of St. Dominic's third order. When they became widows the sisters offered the rest of their lives entirely to the service of God. They remained in their own homes, but lived like nuns. They did not have their own churches or oratories, but used to meet in a chosen chapel, if possible in a church which belonged to the Friars Preachers. Here they took part in the Mass and prayed together. When, after a time, they were given a special costume—a white woollen dress with a white veil and black cape—they were called "le Mantellate"—the Cloaked Sisters.

In Siena there were many Mantellate. Married women and widows from every class of society belonged to this congregation, which had its meeting place in the church of San Domenico, in a chapel called Capella della Volte. Ever since childhood Catherine had had a special regard for St. Dominic and loved to slip out early in the morning to go to Mass in the church up on the hill above her home, so she must have seen the Mantellate gathered in devotion hundreds of times. Her sister-in-law Lisa, and an aunt, Jacobo's widowed sister, belonged to this sisterhood. At this time when her family was doing all it could to make this impossible daughter behave like a normal girl, sending her hither and thither, up stairs and down all day long, while they fumed over her obstinacy and almost as much over her patience and unfalteringly glad obedience in everything except the one thing which meant most to them—Catherine's soul was full of the longing which had woken in her dimly when she was a child: she longed to be allowed to become a Mantellata. Every day she prayed to her Beloved in heaven to bestow this gift upon her.

One night this servant of Christ dreamed that she saw before her many venerable patriarchs and fathers of monastic orders, and among them stood St. Dominic—she knew him at once by the beautiful white lily he held in his hand. All these saints told her to choose an order to which she could belong so that she might serve her Lord better than before. Catherine immediately turned towards St. Dominic, and he came to meet her. He showed her a robe like those worn by the Sisters of Penitence, and said to her, "Beloved daughter, take courage. Be afraid of nothing, for you shall surely be clothed in this robe which you desire." Catherine wept with joy and thanked Our Lord and His soldier St. Dominic, and awakened, bathed in tears.

But now that He had let His servant know what His will with her was, Catherine was sure that Christ would help her. She went to her parents and told them the reason for her incomprehensible resistance to the plans they had made for her future. She did this the very day after her dream. "I have already let you see so many signs that it should have been easy for you to understand, but out of reverence for my parents, such as God bids us show, I have never spoken out before. But now there must be an end of silence, and I will open my heart to you and confess that I have made a resolution, and that not recently, for I made it when I was still a child, and I have kept true to it ever since. In my early childhood I promised my Saviour, my Lord Jesus Christ, and His blessed Mother that I would always remain a virgin, and it was not out of childishness but for serious reasons that I promised this. I have promised them that I will never take another husband. And now that by God's mercy I have come to years of wisdom this decision is still rooted in my heart. It would be easier to melt a stone than to tear this holy resolution out of my heart. You only waste time in trying to fight against it. My advice to you is therefore that you break off these negotiations for my marriage, for on this point I shall never be able to obey you; I must obey God before men. If you will keep me in the house under these conditions let me stay here as your servant, I will gladly do everything to help you to the best of my ability. But if you chase me from my home because of this decision, so be it: it can in no way change my heart. I have a Bridegroom who is so rich and powerful that He will not let me suffer want, but will surely provide me with all I need."

When Catherine had spoken, the whole Benincasa family broke into loud lamentations; they sighed and wept, and no one could speak. They looked at this young girl who had always been so modest and quiet-spoken and who now spoke to them so boldly and seriously, and they understood that Catherine was ready to leave her father's house sooner than break her vow. There was no hope of making a good match for her. The Benincasas wept and wept.

But her father, Jacopo, soon mastered his emotion. When it really came to the point he was not greatly surprised. He answered her gently and kindly: "My dearest daughter, it is far from us to set ourselves against the will of God in any way, and it is from Him that your purpose comes. We have learned through long experience that you are not moved by the self-ishness of youth but by the mercy of God. Keep your promise and live as the Holy Spirit tells you to live. We shall never disturb you again in your life of prayer and devotion, or try to tempt you from your sacred work. But pray steadfastly for us, that we may be worthy of the Bridegroom you chose while still so young." He turned to his wife and sons and said, "From now on no one is to tease or annoy my beloved daughter or dare to lay obstacles in her way. Let her serve her Bridegroom in complete freedom and pray earnestly for us. We could never have obtained so honourable a marriage for her, so let us not complain that instead of a mortal man we have been given the immortal God-made-man."

The brothers were still sorrowful, and Lapa lamented loudly. But Catherine inwardly thanked her victorious Bridegroom who had led her to triumph, and she thanked her parents as humbly as she could.

They let her have her own room—a tiny little cell on the first landing. Like so many houses in Siena the Benincasa's home was built against a hill, so that Catherine's chamber at the back of the house was in fact on a level with the narrow lane which ran behind the building. The room was only three by nine feet. A few stone steps led up to the one little window, which was probably barred, as windows on the ground floor usually were. Some pictures of saints, a chest where she kept her few possessions, a bed of boards with a chunk of wood as a pillow—this was all her furniture. Catherine sat on this bed when she meditated, knelt upon it when she prayed, and lay on it, fully clothed in her woollen robe, to sleep. For a while she wore a hair-shirt next to the skin. But she was always meticulous about keeping herself clean—like St. Teresa of Avila there was only one form of corporal discipline which she never practised, the filth and lousiness which so many male saints have valued as a cure for pride. Later she changed the hair-shirt for a thin iron chain which she fastened so tight round herself that it bit into her flesh. She wore this iron chain right up to the time when her confessor commanded her to lay it aside, and this was towards the end of her life when she had become very weak.

Many years later Catherine wrote in her book *The Dialogue* what her heavenly Bridegroom had told her, when she was in ecstasy, about physical discipline: "What I demand of my servants is inner virtue and the struggles of the soul, not such external deeds as have the body alone as their instrument. These are means of increasing virtue, but are not virtues in themselves." And sometimes a soul becomes enamoured of such outward penitential exercise, and then it becomes an obstacle on the way to perfection. Complete trust in the love of Christ and a hatred of one's own ego; true humility, perfect patience, hunger and thirst for God's sake and the salvation of the soul—these were the signs of a pure heart which has killed sensual desire by the love of righteousness.

In the same way St. Benedict in the rules of his order forbade exaggerated corporal self-discipline: it is usually forbidden in the rules of the monastic orders for a monk or nun to exercise such discipline without first seeking advice from his or her confessor and spiritual adviser. But St. Benedict himself had in his youth practised extraordinarily rigorous self-discipline to cleanse his soul from the impressions he had received during the years he lived in Rome among corrupt men and women. Catherine, who was still extremely young, was certain that the self-discipline to which she subjected herself in solitude was inspired by the Holy Spirit. It was right for her, and so. . . .

It is not difficult to believe her when she later told Fra Raimondo that the sacrifice which cost her most when she was young was that of sleep. At first she spent the whole night in prayer and converse with her Bridegroom, and only when matins was being celebrated in the monasteries did she lie down to sleep for a short while. But after a time the soul triumphed over the demands of the body, until she was able to manage with half an hour's sleep, and this sometimes only every other day. As "her commerce was in heaven" she felt that the time she used in sleep was truly wasted.

For a long time now she had denied herself wine, which for centuries has been both food and drink to the Italians. First she mixed a little wine in the water she drank—just enough to colour it—so that she should not offend the others at table. It was several years since she had eaten meat—she told Raimondo later that the very smell of meat was unpleasant to her, a thing to be remembered when Catherine later of her own free will undertook all the housework which she had once been forced to do, and turned the spit and stirred the saucepans with the odorous meals of meat, vegetables and spices which are the masterpieces of Italian cooking. But it is not surprising that Lapa complained and even swore when Catherine also removed the good bread from her diet and wanted to live only on vegetables, and little enough of them. When Raimondo wrote his book on the blessed Catherine's way of life, he had good reason to emphasise the fact that this holy woman practised such strict self-denial as no one had heard of since the days of the Desert Fathers, and this not in the solitude of the desert, but in the home of a large and well-to-do middle-class family.

In order to imitate her spiritual father, St. Dominic, Catherine gave herself the discipline—scourged herself with an iron chain—three times a day: once for her own sins, once for the sins of all living souls, and once for the souls in purgatory. The blood often ran down her shoulders—as Raimondo says, she gave her Saviour "blood for blood".

Her poor mother had scarcely had time to accustom herself to the thought that her best loved daughter would never be a bride nor a mother, when she learned to her despair of these incomprehensible tortures which this incomprehensible child of hers was applying to herself. "Oh, my daughter, my daughter, you will die, you are killing yourself—Oh, who has taken my child from me? Who had brought this sorrow on me?" The wife of Benincasa shrieked and wailed until her voice resounded through the narrow streets around, filling the neighbours with alarm, and friends and passers-by rushed into the house to find out what new misfortune had befallen poor old Lapa.

As she was unable to make Catherine eat, she made up her mind to see to it that the girl at any rate got some hours of decent sleep each night. She walked into Catherine's cell, where she found her daughter kneeling on the planks of her bed, dragged her "by force" into her own room and compelled her to lie in her own bed, tucked warmly in between linen sheets and soft pillows. Catherine lay obediently beside her mother. She prayed silently and meditated until Lapa had fallen asleep and she could creep away and continue to pray as usual. But "Satan whom she had challenged with her steadfast determination, then wakened Lapa"—Raimondo was in no doubt that it was Satan who tried to use Lapa and her natural maternal love as his instrument to tempt Catherine from the way which would lead her to perfect union with Christ, even though the innocent and inoffensive Lapa of course knew nothing of this. Stefano Maconi, who knew through experience a good deal about the conflict between a vocation and well-meaning mother-love, contents himself with saying in his Italian translation of Tommaso Caffarini's Latin biography of St. Catherine that Lapa loved her daughter's body better than her soul. In order to pacify both her mother and her own conscience Catherine now smuggled some wooden planks in under the sheets in the place in Lapa's bed where she was to sleep. When her mother discovered her daughter's pious trick she was forced to let Catherine do "what the Spirit moved her to", even though Lapa muttered and moaned a good deal before she gave in.

Catherine often talked to her parents of her longing to belong to St. Dominic's order of Sisters of Penitence. This also made Lapa extremely unhappy. She dared not forbid her to mention the matter, but she hit upon the idea of making her daughter think of other things by taking her to the baths of Vignone, south of Siena. At that time this was a fine large watering-place, with a number of inns to accommodate the stream of visitors who came to the warm sulphur springs. Catherine agreed to her mother's plan obediently. But when they were about to begin their cure, she asked to be allowed to bathe alone. Lapa said she might do so—she did not know that instead of going to the pool where the water was pleasantly warm, Catherine went to the place where the sulphur water ran out of the pipes, scalding hot. The pain was awful, but she tried to imagine the torments of purgatory and hell, while she begged her Creator to receive these self-inflicted sufferings instead of the torments she deserved to suffer as punishment for each time she had offended God.

Lapa was bound to confess that she had lost the battle. And now Catherine implored her mother to go to the prioress of the Mantellate and ask whether her daughter could be clothed in the robes of the order. At last Lapa went, very unwillingly, and her heart was certainly considerably lightened when the sisters replied that it was against their custom to accept young girls in the congregation. As all the sisters had to live according to the rule in their own homes, ordinary prudence demanded that they should only accept women of ripe years who wished to offer themselves entirely to God for the rest of their lives.

But not long after, Catherine became seriously ill. She was covered with a kind of rash on her face and over her whole body, had violent pains and lay in a burning fever. Lapa sat by her bed and nursed her faithfully and tirelessly. She attempted to console her sick child with caresses and loving words, and did everything she could to make her well again. Catherine had but one wish, and Lapa was now willing to do anything if only she could save her child's life. She was therefore prepared to try once again to obtain for her daughter what her heart so passionately desired. After all, it was better that the child should become a Sister of Penitence here on earth than that God and St. Dominic could call her to themselves, for it seemed that they called her ceaselessly . . .

Her only sin had been that she had loved her child's health more than her soul. And now that she had made up her mind to atone for this, Lapa besieged the Sisters of Penitence with passionate determination and the full power of her rhetoric. The secret battles which she had silently waged for years with a husband who was too good for this world, and a daughter whose behaviour was an inexplicable riddle to her, had sharpened Lapa's wits and senses. She finally got the sisters to promise that they would think the matter over, as much for Lapa's sake as for the girl's. If she were unusually beautiful there could of course be no question of giving Catherine the robes of the order—Lapa knew well enough what cruel tongues were. She was cunning enough to tell the sisters to come and see for themselves. Poor Catherine, who lay there with her face swollen by the hideous rash, certainly did not appear to be a dangerous beauty.

The sisters chose three or four of the most experienced and careful among themselves and sent them to visit the girl and test her mind. Catherine looked almost ugly. But when they had talked with her for a while, they understood how ardently she longed to join them, how unusually pious, mature and understanding she was, and they went home happy and amazed to tell their companions what they had seen and heard. After they had received the consent of the brothers, the sisters met to vote on the matter. It was unanimously agreed that Catherine Benincasa should be received in the third order of St. Dominic as one of the Sisters of Penitence. When Lapa brought this news to her daughter, Catherine thanked her Bridegroom and St. Dominic, and wept for joy—they had kept their promise so wonderfully. Until now she had borne her illness with indefatigable patience, but now she prayed to be quickly well again, for she longed for the day when she should be robed. She recovered completely in the space of a couple of days. Lapa still tried to gain time. But she had to give in to her daughter's prayers, and so the day and hour of the ceremony were appointed.

Catherine was at home in her cell, praying and thinking of the moment when the desire of her heart should be satisfied. It was towards sundown; the narrow lane outside her window would soon be filled with a gentle dusk, and she would hear, in her solitude, the voices of people chattering and enjoying themselves after their day's work. And suddenly he who is the arch-fiend of God and all mankind threw himself upon the young girl who once again was to renounce everything she had been willing to renounce ever since she was a small child. She had met the devil and his armies before in her visions—in completely intellectual visions as well as in physical visions and apparitions. But until now she had never experienced anything but fear and aversion at the sight. Now the tempter came to her in the likeness of a young man, not to frighten her but to persuade. The beautiful youth unfolded in front of her all the wonders that the Italian weavers and embroiderers could create, and finally stretched out a garment towards her, a cloak heavy with gold and precious stones, more wonderful than she had ever seen in reality: "All this could be yours . . ." As though in a dream Catherine stared at these examples of earthly magnificence—symbols of the power and the joy the world can offer a young woman who is attractive and intelligent, with boundless possibilities of experiencing passion and love. . . . But then it was as though she suddenly awakened. Violently she flung the tempter from her. But the temptation remained.

She was a grown girl now, on the threshold of womanhood, and perhaps for the first time she really understood the nature of the earthly happiness which she was renouncing. However deeply convinced she was that earthly joy is an obstacle, however surely she knew that all these things which now seemed so tempting were in reality nothing—dreams which would vanish, which would surely change from happiness to pain and fear—nevertheless they were tempting.

She threw herself before the crucifix and begged her Bridegroom to come to her help. "You know that I love You, and only You . . ." But she felt no consolation, it was as though the Man on the crucifix were deaf and dumb however long she prayed. But suddenly another sight appeared before her—a woman clothed in radiance, the Queen of heaven herself. She offered Catherine a cloak; it shone like the sun, and pearls and precious stones gleamed on it. "Daughter, this cloak was hidden in the wound in the side of my Son as though in a golden casket. I drew it out of my Son's heart and sewed these pearls on it with my own hands." Humbly the girl bowed to the ground and Our Lady slipped the heavenly garment over her head . . .

Some days later at dawn Lapa and Catherine went up the hill and into the Dominican church. The Friars Preachers were assembled, and among them was surely Fra Tommaso della Fonte, who had once been brought up with her, and was now her confessor. In the presence of them and the assembled Sisters of Penitence Catherine Benincasa received the white robe and veil which stand for purity of body and soul, and the black cape which is the symbol of humility and death to this world.

It is not known on what day this occurred, and students of Catherine's life are not even in agreement upon the year. It is most likely that it was in 1366, and that Catherine was in her nineteenth year.

IV

DURING THE NEXT THREE YEARS the young Sister of Penitence lived a life of complete solitude in the little room at the back of the Benincasa house. She only left the house to go to early Mass at the Dominican church on the hill.

Spring and summer, autumn and winter, cast their changing colours over the lovely town and filled the steep and narrow streets with varying patterns of light and shade. The town is built on three hills; on the highest the slim spire of the town hall rises towards the sky, and the cathedral stands like a noble and imperishable crown. Proud Siena looks out from behind its city walls over the beautiful surroundings—those surroundings which the Sienese had so many times defended with force of arms. Siena and the Tuscan plain, and the hills which are spread round the town, seem like a magic world to us, a world where everything is filled with the dream-like beauty of the past. The town awakened no dream of the romantic past in the mind of Catherine—it was the world she lived in and prayed for, where passions and pride raged, and where precious souls struggled to love God or to turn from Him. For Catherine's countrymen, for her father and brothers, it was their own beloved town, the welfare and honour of which lay close to their hearts. It was so for Catherine too, in her own way. When at the break of day she climbed the steep streets towards the church she surely conversed with her Bridegroom and asked Him to bless her town and her people with His heavenly truth.

It is possible that she had already begun to remain in church for hours at a time after the Mass—a habit which came to annoy even the sisters of her own order and many of the friars. Once at home she retired to her cell and did not go out again until the next morning. The small amount of food which she ate—it was just a few raw vegetables with a drink of water—she had sent into the cell. Cut off from the world in silence and prayer, she never spoke to anyone except her confessor, Tommaso della Fonte, and her own family in so far as it was absolutely necessary. Yet she loved her family so much . . .

But now she could not see other people, or herself either, except in God, and it was only in God that she thought of herself and others. As Raimondo expresses it, with a simile which he takes from Catherine herself: "He who dives into the sea and swims under the water neither sees nor has contact with anything except the waters of the ocean and that which has sunk beneath them. He neither sees, feels, nor touches anything outside those waters. It is only when what is outside is reflected in the water that he can see it, and then only through the water, and as long as its reflection remains there. So it is with the right and proper love which we should have for ourselves and all other of God's creatures." Raimondo confesses that he was not sure that he had quite understood what Catherine meant by this simile. In the years to come Catherine was to show how limitless is the love possessed by a soul which has dived into the sea of heavenly love.

A favourite theme of the Italian painters towards the end of the Middle Ages and the beginning of the Renaissance was the so-called Holy Conversation—*Santa Conversazione*. A number of saints stand round Christ on the cross, or on a throne, or as a child at His mother's knee. This picture is an attempt to interpret the saints' experience of the presence of Christ, as Catherine now experienced it so that it filled her life in the solitary cell. The memory of pictures of this kind which she had seen affected the visual form in which her spiritual experiences were crystallised.

The first whom Catherine told of her spiritual experience in these early years of solitude was Tommaso della Fonte. He made a mass of notes of what she told him—several volumes full. They have disappeared, but were used by her biographers Raimondo of Capua and Tommaso Caffarini. Many of the conversations which she had with her Lord, and which filled her life in these years, she repeated and expounded in the book which she dictated towards the end of her life during several days of almost ceaseless ecstasy, and which came to be known as the *Dialogue of the Holy Catherine of Siena*. But the fundamental truth upon which she built her whole life was already revealed to her at this early stage.

One day while Catherine was praying, Jesus appeared to her and said: "Daughter, do you know who you are and who I am? If you know these two things you will be very happy. You must know that you are that which is not, but I am That Which Is. If your soul is possessed of this knowledge the devil will never be able to cheat you, and you shall escape all his snares and all his cunning without suffering. You will never consent to anything which is against My commands. Without difficulty you will attain all the gifts of grace and all the virtues of love."

God has created all life out of nothing, and if the mercy of God did not sustain its existence it would immediately return to nothing. If we are left to ourselves, without the mercy of God, we fall into sin, which is also nothingness. By ourselves we can neither think of nor achieve anything which is virtuous or good. It is therefore true that that which is created is in itself nothing.

But because God is the foundation and origin of everything, it is only He Who Is. As soon as a creature through the light of belief has come to understand this truth he may call himself blessed. For eternal blessedness consists of this: knowing God as He really is. As Jesus said to Catherine's namesake, the virgin martyr of Alexandria, when He visited her in prison: "My daughter, know thy Creator."

It seemed to Catherine that once a soul is possessed of this truth it ought to receive willingly and patiently everything which seems hard and bitter, out of love of the Highest Good who created us from nothing, and who from His boundless mercy offers us, whom He has raised from nothingness, eternal bliss in His own kingdom.

At times Catherine was tormented by the doubt that perhaps her visions were the work of the devil, for it is written of him that he can take on the likeness of an angel. In her humility she could not think that she was worthy to receive such special grace from God. But her Bridegroom understood her doubt, and promised to teach her how she could always differentiate between visions sent by Him and the mirages which the enemy of mankind could conjure up. "My visions are always accompanied at first by a certain amount of fear, but as they unfold they bring a growing feeling of security. First comes bitterness, but later come strength and consolation. The visions which come from the devil create at first a feeling of security and sweetness, but they end in terror and bitterness. My way is the way of penitence. At first it seems hard and difficult to follow, but the further you pursue it, the happier and sweeter it appears. The way of the devil, on the other hand, is sweet and happy to begin with, but as the soul pursues the way of sin it goes from bitterness to bitterness, and the end is eternal damnation. And because I am the Truth My visions always lead to a greater knowledge of the Truth, and it is of the greatest necessity that a soul gains knowledge of Me and of itself. This makes the soul honour Me and despise itself, and that is the meaning of humility. Visions which come from the devil make the soul which he visits proud, for he is the father of lies and of pride, and the soul is filled with vanity which is the core of all pride."

Later Our Lord taught her other axioms: "My daughter, think always of Me, and I promise to think of you." "Empty your heart of all other cares and thoughts, think only of Me and rest in Me. And be assured that I think of you, I who can and will provide you richly with everything you need."

Long ago the neighbours had jokingly called the little Catherine Benincasa "Euphrosyne", because she was always so happy and sweet-tempered. In the months and years of solitary days when the young girl "swam under the water in the sea of God's love" this natural happiness changed to the supernatural joy which was later to make such a deep impression on her children of the spirit. They found the most astonishing and delightful characteristic of their beloved "mother" was this joy which ceaselessly flowed from her, even when she had to bear an inhuman burden of work, apparent defeat and disappointment, terrible physical and spiritual suffering—the martyrdom which the holy Catherine of Siena had to suffer before her heavenly Bridegroom called His bride to Him.

As yet, Catherine had no idea that her Bridegroom would one day call her from this life of solitude and silence and send her out to fight His war on one front after another. But without knowing anything of the purpose which she was finally to serve, she submitted herself humbly and happily to His teaching. Again and again Catherine assured her confessors, who were amazed at finding such wisdom and insight into the secrets of the faith, such familiarity with the teachings of the Bible, in an unschooled young girl, that she had never had any teacher other than her Lord. All her knowledge had come to her from the Holy Spirit, from the lips of Jesus when He talked with His servant and bride.

At times her visions were completely intellectual—an insight into metaphysical reality which came to her without visions of sight or sound. When she knelt in the quiet cell while her physical ears were deaf to the noise coming from the house and the street outside her window, she heard the voice of her Beloved with the "ears of her soul", and answered, prayed, and asked Him questions without moving her lips. But at other times her visions were pictures which she saw and words which she heard; she saw Christ on the cross; or He appeared to her and walked in her cell while He talked to her. Sometimes He came alone, but at other times His blessed mother was with Him; or He came with some of His saints. Catherine had always had a special love for Mary Magdalen. Now she appeared in Catherine's cell with Christ, who said to His bride that He would give her Mary Magdalen as her "spiritual mother".

While she prepared herself for a fate of which as yet she knew nothing Catherine pondered over the two kinds of love— for she knew that "we cannot live without loving." There was the true and proper love of the Reality which is God, and the false love towards oneself and the world—love for things which have no real existence. She understood clearly that the pursuit of the first kind of love was a task which no one can complete as long as the soul is in the body, even though God may give richly of His grace. Therefore she prayed earnestly for strength. Her Bridegroom spoke to her in answer to her prayers. "My dear daughter, if you earnestly wish to win strength you must follow Me and imitate Me. It is true that I could have put My enemies to shame through My divine powers, but I would not do this, and did not fight against them with any weapons save those of the cross ... Therefore, my daughter, for My sake shall you let all that is bitter seem sweet, and all that is sweet seem bitter. Then you need be afraid of nothing, for you will be strong in all adversities."

A short time after this conversation Catherine was attacked by terrible temptations. She had seen and fought against the arch-fiend often before, but now the demons attacked her with a violence of which she had never dreamed. She was a grown woman now, with a strong and healthy body—Lapa's greatest joy was to tell her biographers how from the time she was fully grown Catherine had easily carried huge sacks of corn, such as one loads onto a donkey, from the front door right up to the loft. Now the flattering voices of demons whispered to her that she did herself wrong in choosing such a difficult and painful life. "If you continue in this way you will never manage to hold out to the end", they said to her. "You will simply bring yourself to an early death. God does not ask it of you; you cannot please Him with such suicidal self-discipline." They reminded her how many a saintly woman had won God's favour through virtues practised in marriage. Catherine knew this was true—but she knew too that God had ordained another way for her. She never replied to the tempters, but only tried to pray even more earnestly, and chastised her body with firm and strict discipline. Only when the evil spirit said to her, "It is impossible for you to hold out to the end", she replied, "I do not depend upon myself, but on my Lord Jesus Christ."

She was thereupon attacked by a crowd of sensual and unchaste thoughts, of abominable visions and devilish illusions. She saw before her men and women who openly before her eyes committed disgusting and infamous acts, while they tried with threatening words and touches to force her to join in their orgies.

During these dreadful sufferings she lacked the consolation of the visits of her Beloved. She prayed ceaselessly, but felt that her prayers were not heard. It seemed that He was not near her. She fled to the church, and remained there for hours after Mass was over—it seemed to her that the demons had less power there. But as soon as she came home to her own cell again it was as though the hosts of hell were let loose.

Patiently and bravely she continued to fight against them, and only blamed herself that she received no help from Christ—she believed that this had come upon her as a punishment for her sins. It was the unchastity in her own nature, a secret desire in her own mind, which brought this horror upon her. But she never relaxed in her devotions; she was on the contrary more persevering than ever. And one day a ray of light fell into her tortured soul from above. She remembered how she herself had begged her Saviour for the gift of strength.

But that meant that all these temptations which she had to resist had come to her with His consent, so that she might fight against them and gain strength. Once again her soul was flooded with the old supernatural joy. And when one of the demons, the most horrible and disgusting of them all, shrieked in her ear: "Miserable woman, whatever you may think, your whole life will be filled with these terrible sufferings, you shall never have peace, and we shall not cease to torment you until you bow before our will", Catherine answered "with holy temerity", as her biographer expresses it: "I have chosen these temptations as my refuge, and I say that I am happy that I may bear these and all other sufferings, from wherever they may come, out of love for my Saviour and my gentle Bridegroom, and for His honour, as long as He in His eternal goodness wills it."

It was as though the whole army of devils immediately took flight in wild fear. Before her she saw Christ on the cross, in a great light. He called her by her name, and said, "Catherine, My daughter, see what torments I bore for your sake; you should not think it so hard to suffer for My sake."

The vision changed—now the Saviour stood before her in the shape she was used to. He spoke in sweet words of the hard struggle she had had, and of her victory.

But Catherine was still so harrowed by the memories of the terrible nights and days of temptation that she murmured as St. Anthony in the wilderness had done: "My beloved Lord, where were You when my heart was filled with such terrible bitterness?"

"I was in your heart", answered the Lord.

Filled with amazement, Catherine asked how this was possible. He explained, "It was My presence which caused the sorrow and bitterness which I know you felt when the devils raged round you. And My grace guarded your heart so that you did not give in to the temptations of the demons. I would not that you should be spared these struggles as you wished, for I was filled with gladness to see how bravely you fought for your crown of honour. But when you offered so chivalrously to suffer every pain out of love for Me, you were immediately freed from these temptations of hell, because it was My will. And because you have fought like a hero, you have earned and won still more grace, and I will appear to you more often than before and show you greater confidence than before."

The vision disappeared, but Catherine was left full of indescribable happiness—chiefly because her Lord had called her "Catherine, My daughter" and promised to visit her more frequently than before.

Outwardly her daily life remained the same. Each day after the early Mass she returned to solitude and prayer in the little cell. But her old habit of praying aloud gradually gave way to silent prayer—it took too long for her tumultuous spirit to express in words all that poured into her soul. But she had nevertheless wished for a long time that she could read the breviary—the daily Office—a devotion which members of the third order were not bound to undertake because so many of them were unschooled men and women.

For a time Catherine tried industriously to learn her letters from a friend, presumably Tommaso della Fonte. But this method was too slow for her ardent temperament. And one day she decided to give up. "If my Lord wishes me to praise Him through the daily Office, then one day I shall be able to read. And if not I will content myself with saying 'Our Father' and 'Ave Maria' as other unschooled women do."

And then suddenly she could read. Catherine and her friends were convinced that a miracle had occurred—she had learned to read, too, from her heavenly Master. We who live in an age when all children have to learn to read and write find nothing miraculous in this. It is not so unusual for talented children to be able to read before they can manage to spell simple words. A woman with Catherine's intuitive genius may easily have been able to read fast and confidently from books long before she could manage the more painstaking work of spelling word for word. She was soon able to read any handwriting she saw, and some years later, after she had kept up a wide correspondence and was used to dictating letters to her secretaries, she tried one day to write herself. After her death there were rumours that there were some original manuscripts from her hand in existence. But as these have never been found some of her latest biographers are in doubt about the whole story of Catherine's ability to write.

The reading of the breviary opened a new treasure-chest of spiritual jewels for her—the Psalms of David, the liturgical prayers of the Church, so full of wisdom and profound poetry, and short sketches of the history of the Church and the lives of the saints. However much she understood by intuition and however deeply she was permitted through her visions to penetrate the essence of faith and the words of Our Lord—an ability which the Church has always considered she was granted by especial and supernatural grace—Catherine did not by any means think that she was above learning the essentials of her religion in the ordinary way. She submitted unconditionally to the teaching of the Church, and, at any rate according to her own opinion, to the advice of her spiritual directors. Filled with joy she repeated again and again the opening words of the breviary: "Deus in adjutorium meum intende; Domine ad adjuvandum me festina—O God come to my help, O Lord make haste to help me."

It happened sometimes that when Catherine was reading her breviary Our Lord appeared to her and read the responses "as when two monks read the Office together". And finally she received an answer to her repeated prayers that Christ in His mercy would grant the desire of her heart—to be one with Him in perfect belief and faith. Christ replied, "I shall make you My betrothed in perfect faith."

It was the last day of carnival. Everyone in Siena—bad and good Christians—prepared for the long and hungry weeks of the fast. The whole town was alive with frivolous young people revelling and rejoicing. At the same time good housewives like Lapa and her daughters-in-law prepared a luxurious meal of meat and cheese and all the good things which they were now to deny themselves for so long, for it would be a great shame if any of the food should rot or be wasted. So they urged everyone to eat, eat, eat, till dishes and plates were as clean as though they had been licked. Raimondo calls the carnival "a festival of the belly", and he is not usually censorious.

Only Catherine was alone in her cell, and prayed for the revellers—her life was already an uninterrupted fast. She was heavy-hearted, for she knew that during these days when people gave themselves up completely to the lusts of the flesh many of her townsmen would throw off the bonds which daily piety laid upon them and fling themselves headlong into gross sin. She prayed and scourged herself, while she begged her Lord to forgive all those who now offended Him. She received a princely answer: "For My sake you have thrown away the vanity of this world. You have regarded the lusts of the senses as nothing and chosen Me as the only joy of your heart. Therefore now, while all the others here in your house feast and enjoy themselves with good food and drink, I will celebrate the solemn marriage feast with your soul. I shall betroth you to Myself as I have promised."

Around Christ there now appeared His blessed mother, the apostle St. John the Evangelist and St. Paul, and David the poet-king bearing a harp upon which he played beautiful melodies. As is the custom at betrothals the mother, the Virgin Mary, stepped forward and took Catherine's right hand. She lifted it up towards her Son, and bade Him bind His bride to Him in faith as He had promised. Jesus put a beautiful ring on her finger; it was adorned with a brilliant diamond surrounded by four large pearls. He spoke the solemn words which the bridegroom says to his bride: "I here betroth you as My bride in perfect faith, which for all time shall keep you pure and virgin, until our marriage is celebrated in heaven with great rejoicing. My daughter, from now on you must undertake without protest all the works which I come to demand of you, for armed with the power of faith you shall triumphantly overcome all your opponents."

The vision disappeared. But afterwards the maiden could always see this engagement ring on her finger, although it was invisible to all others.

Jesus had betrothed her namesake Catherine of Alexandria to prepare her for her death as a martyr. The girl from Siena did not as yet dream of the work for which her Bridegroom had chosen and was training her. When it was revealed to her she drew back at first, weeping with apprehension, even though she obediently and patiently tried to follow her Master and be "obedient unto death".

V

A LITTLE WHILE AFTER her mystical betrothal Catherine again saw her Lord in a vision. It was at the time of day when the good folk of Siena gathered round the dinner table. Jesus said: "You are to go and seat yourself at the table with your family. Talk to them kindly, and then come back here."

When Catherine heard these words she began to weep—she was so completely unprepared to leave her cell and her life of contemplation and mix again with people in the world. But Our Lord was firm:

"Go in peace. In this way you shall serve Me and become more perfectly united to Me through love of Me and your neighbour, and then you will be able to rise even more quickly to heaven, as though on wings. Do you remember how the desire to bring souls to salvation burned in you while you were still a little child—and that you dreamed of dressing yourself as a man and entering the order of the Friars Preachers to work for this end?"

Although Catherine was more than willing to obey the will of God she tried to raise objections: "But how can I be of any use in the work of saving souls, I who am merely Your poor servant girl? For I am a woman, and it is not seemly for my sex to try to teach men, or even to speak with them. Besides, they take no notice of what we say", she sighed.

But Jesus replied as the Archangel Gabriel had once replied:

"All things are possible for God who has created everything from nothing. I know that you say this from humility, but you must know that in these days pride has grown monstrously among men, and chiefly among those who are learned and think they understand everything. It was for this reason that at another period I sent out simple men who had no human learning, but were filled by Me with divine wisdom, and let them preach. To-day I have chosen unschooled women, fearful and weak by nature, but trained by Me in the knowledge of the divine, so that they may put vanity and pride to shame. If men will humbly receive the teachings I send them through the weaker sex I will show them great mercy, but if they despise these women they shall fall into even worse confusion and even greater agony.

"Therefore, my dear daughter, you shall humbly do My will, for I will never fail you; on the contrary, I will come to you as often as before and I will guide and help you in all things."

Catherine bowed her head, rose and went from her chamber and seated herself at the table with her family. It is a pity that none of Catherine's biographers has described for us the amazement it must have caused Jacopo and Lapa to see their hermit daughter seated among them—not to speak of the reaction of her brothers and sisters-in-law and their children. But although Catherine had returned in the flesh to the bosom of her family, her thoughts were with her Saviour. And as soon as the Benincasas rose from the table Catherine fled back to her cell, filled with longing to continue her conversation with her Lord. For the young girl who was later to have such experiences as very few women have ever had, and who met these experiences with unyielding courage, this first return to the family circle after having lived outside it for three years must have been a terrible ordeal.

But she soon became accustomed to the new life. As her Bridegroom wished her to move among people, the girl considered that she must try to live among them as humbly and piously as possible, that she might be an example of Christian virtue. But she knew that if she was to achieve this she would need boundless humility, as no pride has such strong roots or is so cunningly hidden, none is so harmful both to one's own soul and to the souls of all those who come in contact with it, as the pride of "holy" people in their own holiness. The humility of the saints of God can often seem unreasonable to people of our own age, and there are many who do not believe in it and mutter the word "hypocrisy". For Catherine, with her deep insight into the life of the soul, the fight to achieve perfect humility was one of profound importance. The further her way led her from the first small circle of friends, the more she became renowned as a saint or slandered as an unfeminine trouble-maker continually meddling with what did not concern her. The more she was abused as a hypocrite or feted as a worker of miracles, the harder she fought to despise her own ego and to make herself less than the worst sinner, bowed in the dust before the feet of her Lord. Later, when her spiritual sons and daughters were upset because their adored "mamma" was slandered and persecuted, she said that she considered her human enemies as her true benefactors. It is unlikely that they understood what she meant—perhaps not even those who heard her cry on her deathbed, "Vanity? Never. The true praise and honour of God." From the day when Christ led the young Sister of Penitence out of her solitary cell and sent her into the restless world where He wished her to serve Him among people of every kind, until her last moment on earth, the fear of becoming self-satisfied must have throbbed like a wound in her inmost soul.

While she was still a girl she had learned to build a cell in her soul, and this became her refuge when she went back to live among her relatives. Soon she was to be dragged into the whirl of people in the streets of Siena, and finally over the roads and seas of the world to wherever her fellow-men had need of her.

Once—it seemed long ago to her now—her mother had made her work like a slave for the family in order to break her obstinate intention of living her own life as the Holy Spirit demanded of her. Now Catherine voluntarily undertook all this work, and even more. She had always been extremely fond of her family, and now that she had learned to sink her natural love for her parents and brothers and sisters into the sea of God's love, she was happy to be allowed to do all she could for them. Lapa had made sure of giving her intelligent young daughter a thorough training in everything concerning housewifery, and she did not need to waste much time on eating and sleeping; for years she had passed most of the night in prayer and meditation. Now she went round the house at night, collected all the dirty clothes, and washed them while the household slept; scrubbed the stairs and the floors and tidied up generally. In the daytime she prepared the food and baked bread, laid the table and washed up after meals. And although she did the work of an industrious servant, she also took upon herself the work of the other maid when she fell ill, and looked after the patient carefully and affectionately.

But it was at this time that she decided to receive Holy Communion more often than before. She felt that she needed to be united with her eternal Bridegroom not only spiritually but also physically, more often than before, now that she had to pray and meditate while her hands and feet were busy doing St. Martha's work in her father's house.

Members of the third order of St. Dominic were not bound to make the three usual monastic vows of eternal chastity, perfect obedience and personal poverty. Many of the brothers and sisters were married, some of them served masters in their work, some had property which they promised to administer like good Christians, while they themselves lived frugally and gave as much as they could to their neighbour. Catherine had made her vow of chastity while she was still a little girl. She had also promised Christ to be completely obedient to her spiritual director and to all others whom He might give authority over her. She maintained that she had never sinned against this vow of obedience. Although she was always ready to accuse herself of all kinds of greater and lesser sins she insisted that she had always been completely obedient. This obedience— the obedience of a penitent to her confessor, of an unschooled woman to priests and monks, of a child to her parents—was never meant to be the blind obedience of a deaf, dumb and unthinking object. Catherine obeyed humbly and patiently, but she felt that she had the right to protest whenever she was convinced that the rules her confessor wished her to follow were not right for her, and she felt that she was free to say so, when she realised that his advice would not benefit her soul. An extraordinary relationship grew up between Catherine and her confessors, especially Raimondo of Capua. The blessed Raimondo was many years older than Catherine, a learned theologian and experienced confessor of men and women, but he listened to his penitent and usually had to bow before her deeper insight into the spiritual life, and accept her advice like a son listening to his wise mother. He was her father in Christ, with the priest's authority over her; she was his spiritual mother, with an authority over him which she had by virtue of her greater understanding of the secrets of the faith—a bride of Christ to whom their beloved Master had entrusted greater knowledge than the average Christian possesses.

It was many years since Catherine had renounced the possession of worldly goods, except what was essential—one or two garments, the few things which furnished her cell, some books and a sewing basket with the necessary sewing materials. But now she had been sent out into the world again—and then as now the poor were part of the world. Beggars stopped her in the street or came to the door of the dyer's house; and then too there were the poor who tried to hide their misery because they were ashamed to ask for sympathy from their neighbours. For Catherine they were all people who were "sunk in the sea of divine love". Above them rolled the waves of the sea in which she lived.

Jacopo Benincasa was still a well-to-do master-craftsman, and when Catherine went to him and asked him in private if she could be allowed to take what she needed of his goods to help the poor he gladly gave his consent. She could help herself to whatever she wanted to help the poor, and was to take according to her own conscience and judgment. Not merely did he agree to this while they were in private, but said to the assembled members of the family: "No one is to hinder my beloved daughter when she gives alms, for I have given her authority to do so even though she gives away everything in my house."

It was he who was the master, and his wife and children had of course to submit to his will. But they soon discovered that it was a wise policy to keep one's private possessions under lock and key. Frequently when Catherine had to find something in a hurry to give to some poor half-naked creature, she just went into the room of one of her brothers and took a shirt or a pair of stockings for the beggar. Soon the whole underworld of Siena knew that the eccentric daughter of Benincasa, who was supposed to be a saint, gave away the goods of her old father with both hands to all who came and complained of their poverty. Occasionally they got an unpleasant surprise—Catherine was not to be fooled by swindlers, although her Christian charity did not judge of worthiness and unworthiness in exactly the same way as the world did.

She eagerly sought out and brought help to those who suffered poverty in secret. Once, as she lay in bed, so ill that she
could scarcely move, she heard of a widow who lived nearby;
she had been left, when her husband died, with no money
and a crowd of small children, and she was ashamed to beg.
When night came Catherine begged her Bridegroom to lend
her strength for a little so that she might take some food to
the widow's house. Immediately she felt well enough to get
up. She ran up and down stairs collecting in her cell a sack of
flour, a large bottle of wine and one of oil, and every kind of
food which she could find in her mother's pantry. It seemed
as though it would be impossible for her to carry everything
at once, but when she had divided the load evenly, with one
package under each arm, the sack of flour on her back and all
the small parcels hanging from her belt, she was given strength
to carry the whole lot—it must have weighed almost a hundred pounds, she guessed afterwards. She hurried off to the
widow's house before the first signs of daylight. It had often
happened before when she went on such errands of charity
and did not want to put the recipient to shame, that she had
as though by a miracle found the door open, so that she could
lay her gifts down inside and disappear without anyone dis-
covering her. This time too the door was not locked, but when
she was going to put the things down on the stone floor the
door creaked and wakened the widow. Immediately it was as
though all the strength ebbed out of Catherine's body—she
could scarcely keep herself on her feet, to say nothing of running away. Bitterly disappointed, she complained to her Lord:
"O You who have always been so good to me, why do You
betray me now? Does it amuse You to play with me, to leave
me standing here by the door? Soon it will be dawn and I
shall be an object of ridicule to all the passers-by." She begged
God to lend her strength to get home, but she had to drag

herself along by the walls of the houses. She escaped, but not before the widow had seen a glimpse of her visitor. She knew the costume of the Mantellate, and guessed who it was. It was not yet quite daylight when Catherine stumbled into her cell and collapsed on the bed, completely worn out and just as ill as she had been the day before. Later her companions were to discover that the continual attacks of illness which Catherine had did not seem to follow the laws of nature. In between paroxysms of the most horrible pain and extreme weakness she could get up, full of energy, as though borne on invisible hands, only to collapse again, ill and exhausted, when she had completed her task.

From the time when she began her life of active charity, her familiarity with the secrets of the supernatural world became more apparent to the world around her. When her soul rose upwards in prayer and contemplation, her body became as rigid, cold and insensible as a stone. It happened also that her companions saw the motionless, kneeling woman lifted from the floor "so high that one could put one's hand between Catherine and the floor"—they had certainly tried for themselves. At other times, and especially after she had received the Body of the Lord in the Blessed Sacrament, as she was withdrawn in ecstasy, it was as though her body were flooded with such heat that beads of sweat appeared all over her flushed face.

As the ecstasies came over her most often in church, the whole town was soon talking about her. For her friends, who were convinced that Catherine was a chosen vessel of God, these extraordinary attacks of unconsciousness were a source of awe and joy: when her soul had been lifted up to the presence of Divine Love it always returned bearing gifts for her fellows. Andrea di Vanni, the painter who once, while Catherine was in her twenties, made a sketch of her on a pillar in

St. Dominic's church, firmly believed that she was completely sincere, although it does not seem that he had at that time joined the circle of her nearest friends. He has given us the only authentic portrait we possess of St. Catherine. The lily which she holds in her hand, and the woman kneeling before her, were added after Catherine's death.

But for some of her townsmen Catherine became exactly what she had dreaded—an object for scandal. Poor Lapa was terrified when her daughter became as stiff as a corpse, and in desperation tried to force her out of this awful condition. She struggled to straighten out the rigid limbs and force up the bowed head. Catherine felt nothing of this while in ecstasy, but when she regained consciousness she suffered unbearable pains after these attempts to bend or straighten her limbs—she said it was as though her mother had tried to break her neck.

Many of her sisters in the order looked with extreme distrust upon this peculiar member of their community. Unconsciously and sometimes consciously too, many of these good and pious women envied Catherine the supernatural gifts of grace which were dispensed to her. For in the Middle Ages, people loved all kinds of wonders, not least those which were considered signs of holiness. Even those who did all they could to evade all contact with the supernatural world were desperately interested in stories of miracles and the miraculous, of saints who saw sights and prophesied. But this girl was not even a nun in a convent; she was the daughter of Jacopo Benincasa and old Monna Lapa; she lived at home with her brothers, who at that time were up to their eyes in the politics of the town; she ran about the streets of Siena considerably more than was seemly according to the good old rules of womanly modesty. No, all that was said about her visions and revelations could not possibly be true. She only wanted people to take notice of her, and these paroxysms of stiffness and blushing in church were obviously not genuine. Even among the Dominicans there were several who doubted, and in any case they did not like Catherine Benincasa disturbing the devotions of good and simple Christians with her extraordinary antics. If she must go to Mass each day let her keep to the back of the chapel.

Sometimes her ecstasies lasted right up to midday when the church was closed for a couple of hours, as was the custom while the whole of Siena took its siesta. Then the churchwardens took the unconscious girl and carried her outside and let her lie in the street in front of the church door. Passers-by, and those who thought that over-zealous Christians and exaggeratedly pious women were a public nuisance, would give her a kick or slap as they went by. When Catherine wakened again she had to limp home covered with bruises and spattered with dirt from the street.

But after a while the little flock who believed in Catherine's holiness grew. They gathered round this young woman whom they loved because she was always patient, cheerful and smiling; she talked to them of God's love so wisely and so beautifully, and she was so concerned for them, that they should all obtain eternal bliss. They asked her for advice whenever they had either spiritual or material difficulties, for they knew that her heart burned with love for all mankind. And those who were humble and broad-minded enough to accept her gentleness and tenderness without being jealous or envious of sharing it with their fellows, had already begun to feel a child-like affection which the young girl accepted with all the tenderness of a mother when they came and laid the troubles and anxieties of their lives in her hands.

Fra Tommaso della Fonte was still her confessor, and he brought several of his brothers in the order to Catherine; some

of them became her faithful spiritual sons and disciples—
among others Fra Bartolommeo de Dominici and Fra Tommaso Caffarini, who have both written about their "mother".
Bartolommeo tells us that when he first met Catherine she
was still extremely young, sweet and happy by nature, but
although he too was very young at that time, he never felt
embarrassed when he was with her as he would have felt if he
had been with other young girls. The more he talked to her
the more he seemed to forget all earthly feelings and passions.

Catherine too, who had once been as afraid of being with
young men "as though they were snakes", now met these friends
who were one with her in God's love, and talked as confidently and freely to them as a good sister. She sent them small
gifts, usually bouquets and crosses of flowers which she loved
to make. She was very fond of flowers, and although she seldom spoke of it, the beauty of her own Tuscan countryside
was a source of great joy to this saint with the soul of a poet.

Among her friends were a widow of noble birth, Alessia
Saracini, another Sienese lady, Francesca Gori, who was also a
widow and had two sons in the Dominican order, and Giovanna di Capo; these were the first to accept Catherine, who
was much younger than themselves, as their "spiritual mother".

At home, besides her father, she had at any rate one relation
who understood her. Lisa, who was married to her brother Bartolommeo, was a cousin of the Blessed Giovanni Colombini—a
rich merchant of Siena who one day turned his back on the
world, gave everything he possessed to the poor, and founded
the order of the Jesuati, a brotherhood of laymen who dedicated themselves to the saving of souls. We do not know whether
Catherine ever met Giovanni Colombini, as he did not live in
Siena during the last part of his life. But she must have known
of his work, both from what Lisa could tell her, and also through
the abbess of the Benedictine convent, Santa Bonda, who had

been a friend of Colombini, and now became one of Catherine's friends.

Lisa was also a Mantellata, and had belonged to the order some years when Catherine joined it. But she is not mentioned in the story of Catherine before the saint began her public life. Lisa presumably lived a life of retirement in her home, and served God by carrying out her duties as housewife and mother of many children. The Benincasa home was at this time full of grandchildren, some already almost grown-up, and some still infants. Like most Italians, Catherine was passionately fond of children, and once said that if it weren't for the shame of it she would have liked to spend all her time playing with and petting her small nephews and nieces.

Whatever other work and duties she took upon herself, Catherine continued to be just as industrious in her work about the house as long as she lived in her father's home. Although her open-handed generosity sometimes annoyed her less unworldly brothers, and although the fact that she was perpetually thrusting her hands into all sorts of dirt and sickness made Lapa furious with disgust and fear of infection, it seemed that a special blessing hovered over the pantry and the cellar when Catherine occupied herself there, drawing wine for the poor, or baking bread for the household. There was for example the story of the wine barrel—the contents of which were as a rule sufficient to slake the family's thirst for about a fortnight. It was unusually good wine, but to the greater honour of her Lord, Catherine always used to take the best she could find in the house to give to the poor. So each day she went down and filled several bottles of the best wine to give away, and the family too drew wine for the table from the same barrel. But when a month had passed and the barrel seemed just as full of wine, and a wine so delicious that her brothers and father confessed that they had never drunk better—they began to speculate upon this curious fact. Catherine was sure that she knew where this abundance came from, so now she gave away the good wine in every direction to poor people she knew; but the barrel remained just as full for another month, and the wine just as good. Then came the grape harvest, and all the people in the neighbourhood had to prepare their barrels to receive the new wine. The Benincasas' cellarer said that he would need the barrel in question: could they not transfer the wine in it to another vessel? They had just drawn off a large bottle, and the wine had been as clear and free from dregs as ever, but the next morning when they came down to empty the barrel, they discovered that it was already empty and quite dry. Then the family realised that He who had once turned water into wine to save a poor bridegroom from ridicule could still help His chosen friends in the trivial things of everyday life.

One day Catherine and Lisa were working together in the kitchen. Catherine was turning the meat on the spit over the fire when Lisa saw that her sister-in-law was withdrawn in ecstasy, her body stiff and motionless. Unperturbed, Lisa took over her work, and when the meat was ready carried it up to the table, and afterwards went down and attended to her own family, who were about to take their siesta. When she returned to the kitchen, she discovered that Catherine had fallen forwards into the fire-place, and was lying with her face in the glowing coals. Lisa screamed in fright, "Catherine has burned herself!" But when she dragged her unconscious sister-in-law out of the fire she saw that Catherine had come to no harm— her woollen robe was not even scorched, and there was not the slightest smell of burning.

It seemed as though fire could not harm Catherine when she was in ecstasy. Once in church, while she leaned against the wall, dead to everything around her, a candle fell down on her and wax and wick continued to burn on her head, without setting fire to her veil. Another time she fell into the fire as though an invisible demon had pushed her, but, as always, she came out unharmed. She herself only laughed at these attacks: "Don't be afraid, it is only Malatasca——", a name which they used in Siena for the devil because he went round trying to collect the souls of all those he had seduced in his ugly sack—"tasca".

The more her soul was allowed to fly into that kingdom which surrounds all that is visible, the more an aura of the supernatural seemed to surround her when she regained consciousness again and took up her daily tasks. Her Lord, in His power and majesty, seemed to permit even the most trivial things to be touched by the miraculous and the majestic when Catherine put her hand to them. There was for example the question of the beggars. Like St. Martin and St. Francis, Catherine saw her Bridegroom in the persons of all beggars— "Whatsoever you have done against one of these My brothers, you have done against Me." And like St. Martin and St. Francis, Catherine also saw in her visions how literally true were these words of Our Lord.

Once when she was in church a beggar approached her, a young man—he looked as though he were a little over thirty. He was so ragged as to be almost naked, and this was in the winter when it can be extremely cold in Tuscany. Catherine asked him to go to her house, saying that she would follow him immediately and find some clothes for him. But the beggar was insistent—he said he was dying of the cold. He looked so wretched that Catherine was overcome with pity. Carefully she slipped her hands under her gown, loosened her sleeveless undergarment and let it fall to her feet: "Take this——" But the beggar was not satisfied: "Thank you, but I must have a shirt too."

Catherine answered that in that case he must go home with her and she would find him something. She let the beggar wait at the door while she hurried in and ransacked the men's room, and came back with a shirt and a pair of stockings belonging to her father. But still the beggar was not satisfied: "There are no sleeves in the tunic you gave me, my arms are so cold."

Catherine replied politely, "Don't be annoyed at having to wait a little while, I will come back to you as soon as possible."

But this time she found nothing—until she discovered a dress belonging to the maid hanging on the back of the door. "With divine confidence", as Tommaso Caffarini expresses it, she cut out the sleeves and brought them to the beggar, who said "Now you have helped me generously, but in the hospital I have a friend, who is in just as bad a state as I; you must give me some clothes for him too."

Again Catherine searched the house, but this time she could find absolutely nothing except the maid's dress, and that she dared not take. But when she returned the beggar smiled, "Now I know that you are charitable, and I will not bother you any more—go with God."

The night after, as Catherine was praying, the Blessed Jesus appeared to her, dressed in her tunic, but now it glittered with ornaments. He spoke to her: "Daughter, yesterday you clad My nakedness with this tunic, and now I will clothe you", and out of His side He took a tunic, blood-red and gleaming like the light. "I shall give you this noble garment, invisible to all except you, and yet most useful and valuable, for it will shield you from the cold until the day when, together with all the saints and angels, you shall be clad in the eternal honour and glory of heaven."

From that day Catherine never wore more than one garment, but she was never cold. Even though it rained and blew and everyone else complained of the cold, she never felt any ill effects.

On another occasion she met a beggar in the street, who asked for alms. In vain Catherine asked him to follow her home—he was so impatient that she was forced to give him something at once. The only thing she could think of was the little silver cross which she had on her rosary. She took it off and gave it to the beggar. But at night Jesus appeared to her and held out a little cross covered with pearls and glittering jewels. "Do you recognise this?" "Yes, Lord, but it was not so beautiful when it was mine." Jesus said that He would keep this priceless cross for her until she came to Him in heaven.

Catherine only lived a few years in her father's house, industriously serving her neighbours, while her soul was lost in contemplation of her heavenly Bridegroom. But when, some years later, after Catherine's death, the Blessed Raimondo and Tommaso Caffarini collected reports of this part of her life, all the friends who had been near her during these years in Siena had such an inexhaustible collection of stories to tell of the miraculous happenings of this time, that it seemed they must have witnessed miracles every day while they lived near her. It seemed natural to them to group the stories of the miracles together according to their kind, as the monks used to do: how Catherine made lifeless objects serve her in her work of charity, how she cared for the sick, looked after the poor, and forced demons to release their hold on the bodies and souls of the possessed. They were not in the least interested in chronology, and we have no chronological indications to guide us until we come to the years in which Catherine's own letters were written. But it is certain that from the earliest days of her life as the ambassador of Christ among the Sienese, her care for the sick, which filled Lapa with such fear and disgust, led her to the city's hospitals and to homes where people lay suffering from all kinds of horrible diseases.

VI

THE TRUTH ABOUT the much slandered medical science of the Middle Ages is that it had probably advanced as far as was possible in an age when no one had as yet dreamed of the microscope, and sciences such as chemistry and biology were in their infancy. The medieval medical schools were built on the empirical knowledge of generations—in some cases on experience which went back to prehistoric times. But as to the efficacy of the various medicines from the vegetable, animal and mineral kingdoms, or the warm or cold springs to which people came to take the waters, the scientists of the time had more or less to guess. As they had no means of analysing the remedies they used, any understanding of their effects could only be based on mere theorising and speculation, and was often quite fantastic. The medical student of those days turned towards the theology and philosophy of his time to discover why disgusting things such as bones and entrails of animals or people worked as cures in certain sicknesses, or why one could make effective medicines of flowers and roots and decoctions of bark and wood. Organic therapy and the discovery of the part played by the hormones have to a certain extent rehabilitated some of the cures of the Middle Ages, which the doctors of the last generation regarded as the crowning stupidity of a superstitious age. But as no one knew anything of such things as adrenalin or the sex hormones, the learned men of the Middle Ages reasoned that as it is good for the soul to raise itself above such feelings as fear and disgust, the same must apply to the body; and as they thought in analogies they sometimes prescribed cures which were quite worthless, simply because they were bound to cause aversion among normal people.

They had no means of ascertaining which were the valuable ingredients in the medicines they made from herbs, but some of these still have their place in pharmacology to-day—not to speak of their use in patent medicines. The doctors of the Middle Ages knew enough about infection to institute quarantine for travellers who came from places where epidemics were raging, even though their ideas about the properties of infection were at times quite extraordinary, and they were far from sure which illnesses were infectious—a question which has also been widely discussed in our own time, and upon which the last word has not yet been said. They knew that it could be fatal if a wound were infected, but they had no other method of cleansing a wound than the red-hot iron of the surgeon or the method used in the Bible—bathing it in wine and covering it with oil. Sometimes by good luck the alcohol in the wine worked as a weak disinfectant, and oil poured over the surface of the wound gave it, at any rate, protection against infection from the air. Nevertheless the patient's lot was a hard one. Anaesthetics did not exist, although they had a few medicines which could dull pain to a certain extent, and besides these, generous doses of strong wine were prescribed.

But the will to alleviate the sufferings of mankind was as strong as at any time in the history of mankind. Much has been said and written of the cruelty of the Middle Ages. And it is true that when their passions were aroused men and women of those times could commit outrages and acts of cruelty against their enemies which are almost as horrible as those we know from our own time, with its totalitarian war, scientific torture practised by members of governments against people suspected of inimical attitudes towards the party in power, and the planning of the elimination of whole nations. On the whole the laws of the Middle Ages were nothing like so barbarous or unjust as those of the sixteenth, seventeenth and eighteenth centuries, when authoritarian states could, with icy ruthlessness, torture and condemn to agonising deaths those wretches who had infringed, or were suspected of having infringed, their rules. The Church, despite all the human weaknesses and sins of her servants, was a source of mercy, and at times, at the most unexpected moments and through the most unlikely spokesmen, stood up and reminded the powers of this world that justice should be tempered with mercy. But the ruling powers—in the city-states, the empires, the principalities— were often unable to maintain good laws against the evil passions of self-willed men. Catherine had seen too much of lawlessness and the expressions of human passion both at home in Siena, and later everywhere in her native Italy and abroad, for her to be surprised at anything.

But side by side with these expressions of violence, of outraged pride or desire which broke out in bloodthirsty revenge and rapine, every child was used to seeing men and women who had offered their lives to the service of the downtrodden and wretched—the victims of man's inhumanity to man as well as the victims of illness and catastrophe. Some of these messengers of divine grace had chosen this life of service while they were still in early youth, or even as small children; others had been hardened sinners who, in the very act of grasping at unlawful booty with bloody hands, had suddenly and dramatically been converted. There was a kind of universal consciousness that life was extremely uncertain in a community which could offer little protection to a man who did not belong to a family or a corporation, to whose accumulated strength he could add whatever strength he might have of his own. This laid the people of the Middle Ages open to sudden emotional reactions, which in certain circumstances could penetrate the very depths of the soul. Then the power of faith, all they had learned of religion, could suddenly break into their consciousness like fire which has been smouldering underground, and the conversion really be a new birth: the prince's royal garments, the knight's armour, the peasant's rough smock, clothed a man who was entirely different from the man he had been a moment before. The story of St. John Gualbert is not so very extraordinary, it is merely one of the best known of the kind. John and his men were lying in ambush on the hill near the church of San Miniato waiting to kill the man who had murdered John's brother. The enemy walked straight into the trap, and when he realised that he had fallen into the hands of a man from whom he could expect no mercy he threw himself shrieking into the dust of the road. Then John suddenly remembered that it was Good Friday: he leaped from his horse and fell on his knees beside his intended victim, took him in his arms and bade him go in peace. But when afterwards he hurried into San Miniato and fell on his face before the crucifix, then, according to the legend, Christ leaned down from the cross and embraced the young man who had forgiven as God forgives us. From his abbey in Vallombrosa St. John Gualbert seemed to send out silent waves of spiritual strength. He made peace between enemies and stilled bitter feuds and quarrels continually until his death in 1073.

The hospital of Santa Maria della Scala had flourished for at least two hundred years when Catherine Benincasa was a young girl. The friars and nuns who worked there had given everything they possessed to the poor and the sick. The republic of Siena had built the elaborate collection of buildings close to the cathedral, on one of the most valuable sites within the city walls. There were separate wards for men and women, lodgings for pilgrims, a house for foundlings, rooms where food for the poor was prepared and given out, storerooms and cellars. Brothers and sisters lived according to a monastic rule which had been adjusted to their vocation. As true sons of the merchant republic, the brothers had also worked out an extraordinarily effective system of book-keeping and administration of the revenue and expenses of the institution. It was made virtually impossible for a frail brother to enrich himself or his relations in the world at the expense of the heritage of the poor.

There were, however, several other hospitals in Siena, smaller and poorer, as well as a hospital for lepers, San Lazzaro, which lay outside the city walls, as was the custom at that time. The Mantellate and others cared for the sick in their homes. Catherine's mission in the world, as it had been explained to her by Christ Himself, soon led her to the hospitals of Siena and to the homes where women lay suffering from horrible diseases.

Catherine would sometimes spend the night in La Scala hospital, when she had been working in the wards after the time when it was safe for a young woman to go alone through the streets of Siena. She had been allotted a tiny room down in the cellars; it was shown in our own day to visitors—at any rate up till immediately before the last war. When she stayed the night at La Scala, it was also to take over the watch in the small hours—the cold and comfortless hours before dawn when the patient's life is at its lowest ebb and the nurses are worn out and without courage. Catherine's biographers tell us that she gladly took on herself the charge of hopeless cases and the most difficult and ungrateful patients. The good Sisters of La Scala were more than willing to let her take them over as soon as they learned her indefatigable patience and her unquenchable good humour and serenity.

There were in those days, too, a number of patients in the hospitals whom an angel from heaven could not have satisfied: it is the same in our own day, and will always be so. These became Catherine's patients, and she strove untiringly to do everything humanly possible to lessen their sufferings. She was always smiling and industrious, while the patients grumbled and swore at her and complained bitterly that she neglected them, was stupid, incompetent, and a hypocrite who went around pretending to be a saint. Old courtesans and superannuated prostitutes who had long ago been forced to retire from the life of pleasure to which they had belonged, found a bitter consolation in making the work of their young nurse as difficult as possible. Lying there in their hospital beds they were afraid: the aura of chastity and Christian charity which surrounded their nurse terrified them because they had offended God so continually, and they hated with their whole souls this woman whose help they could not forego.

A woman called Cecca who suffered from a revolting illness had taken refuge in one of the small hospitals when she could no longer be at home. The hospital was very poor, and Cecca possessed nothing, so the sisters could not give her more than the essentials of life. But her state grew worse and worse, and when it became obvious to everyone that she was suffering from leprosy none of them would nurse her as they were all afraid of infection. When Catherine heard of this she offered to nurse Cecca. She brought the sick woman medicine and food, prepared her meals and washed her whole stinking body, which was covered with scabs, before applying such salves as could to some extent lessen the irritation and smarting. But Cecca was a thoroughly unpleasant woman. Catherine promised to come to her every morning and evening as long as Cecca lived—and the poor woman perhaps found some miserable consolation for her own wretchedness in making this strong and healthy young girl as unhappy as she could. She soon began to treat Catherine as though she were her servant, and swore at her in a way that no decent housewife would ever dream of doing to her maid. Everything Catherine did for her was wrong. Sometimes when she had been praying rather longer in church she would come to Cecca later than usual. The old witch received her with oaths: "Welcome, noble lady, welcome queen and lady of Fontebranda—and where has the queen been all the morning? Isn't the queen a paragon, always with the brothers in the church the whole day long; it seems as though Her Highness can never have enough of the monks. . . ." She did her best to annoy Catherine, to see if she would make an angry reply. But Catherine only hurried to light the fire, put the water on to warm and hung the cauldron on the hook, while she begged the other's pardon: "Dear Monna Cecca, for the love of God do not be so angry, I shall have everything ready in a moment. . . ."

Quietly Catherine went about her duties for the leper, and Lapa's daughter was a competent nurse. Everyone admired her ceaseless care for the awful old woman with the poisonous tongue and stinking sores. Catherine's secret sorrow was for Cecca's soul, for the old woman was ill prepared to receive God's mercy, and she only became worse if anyone tried to talk to her of God. Catherine could only pray for her. Then Lapa intervened: "Wretched girl, you will be infected with leprosy. I forbid you absolutely to visit her any more!" Catherine, who trusted implicitly in God, tried to soothe her mother's anger as well as she could, and to persuade her that there was no danger of her being infected. But one day she could not help seeing it: her hands, which had touched the leper daily for so long, showed the sure signs of leprosy. The girl did not waver a moment. She cared nothing for what might happen to her body as long as she could do her Bridegroom a service which she knew would please Him. She knew by heart His words from the Sermon on the Mount—to fail Cecca now because she had these sores on her hands, would be the same as to fail Him.

Cecca died. It seems as though Raimondo believed that Catherine's sacrifice finally made sufficient impression on the old woman for her to listen to the consolation the girl whispered in her ears as she died in her arms. The corpse was horrible, and Catherine washed and clothed it and laid it in the coffin. And when the Mass for the Dead had been read she buried the leper with her own hands, for there was no one else who would do it. But when she rose from the new grave and looked at her hands, which were dirty from the last act of charity she could show Cecca, there was not a sign of the disease upon them. They were as white and beautiful as ever. Right up to her death, when terrible self-imposed agonies and ceaseless hard work, pain and sickness had ravaged her body, Catherine's hands remained unusually beautiful.

The patients in the hospital did what they could to try Catherine's patience, but for a very long time she had been absolutely convinced that those who tried to make life unpleasant for her were in fact her greatest friends, for her only wish was to follow in her Lord's footsteps, and His way on earth had been the way of suffering. He was misunderstood by the precious souls for whom He had been made man so that He might save them: they had slandered Him, betrayed Him and finally condemned Him to death as a criminal. A hard way? No, not for those who try to follow where He has gone before; has He not said "I am the Way"? So the whole way is Jesus Christ, who is love, light, sweetness and holy joy, and the way to heaven is like heaven itself.

Nevertheless, although Catherine steadfastly believed that it was a joy to be able to suffer for Jesus's sake, she could not prevent her heart of flesh from being hurt to the very core when her sisters in the order turned against her. Palmerina was a Mantellata, a rich widow who had given everything she owned to the Misericordia hospital. For many years she had lived a life of prayer and penitence. She was a very pious woman, but when the devil whispered to her that she was good and pious, she listened to him. . . . The whole town was now talking about this girl who was supposed to be a saint—a girl who was always gadding about the town, and was far too familiar not only with her women friends, but with a lot of young men too, not excluding some of the young monks, moreover. Palmerina could not rid herself of the thought that Catherine was not as holy as she made out, and all these supernatural gifts of grace, visions and ecstasies and all the rest—Palmerina had never experienced anything of the kind, and one must believe that God who is just would sooner have favoured Palmerina. . . . She fell ill and Catherine came and offered to nurse her. Palmerina had her chased from her door with taunts. Catherine was by now an experienced judge of souls, and could not help seeing that if Palmerina hated her it must be because she was jealous. She lay at her Bridegroom's feet and begged and prayed for the dying woman's soul: "It were better that I had never been born than that I should be guilty of the damnation of this sister of mine. O, gentle Jesus, do not let this soul which You have created in Your own image be lost for the sake of my sins."

Although Catherine was not called to the deathbed of this sister she was allowed to see in a vision that in her last hour Palmerina had repented of all her sins and received the Last Sacrament. Afterwards Jesus let His bride see this soul which she had saved by her prayers. Although Palmerina was not yet clothed in that glory which the soul receives when it sees God as He is—she was still in purgatory—she had regained that beauty which a soul receives at its creation and at baptism. But even that was a beauty so wonderful that, as Catherine said later to Raimondo, it was impossible to describe it in words. Jesus said: "Dear daughter, do you not think that she is lovable and wonderfully gracious? Who would not suffer all the torments in the world to win so glorious a creation? I who am perfect beauty, from which all beauty radiates, I loved the beautiful souls sufficiently to come down to earth and give My blood to buy them. How much more ought you to struggle to help each other so that such wonderful creations shall not be lost. I let you see this soul so that you may have an even greater longing to save everyone, and strive to draw others to this work, with the grace which I shall give you."

Catherine was so transported by this sight that she begged her Bridegroom to give her grace to see the beauty of the souls among whom she lived, so that she might be even more constant in her work for their salvation. The Lord promised her that because she had been so zealous to save Palmerina's soul He would in future enlighten her spirit to see the beauty or ugliness of the souls around her. "You shall with your inner senses understand the condition of these souls just as clearly as with your physical senses you can understand the condition of their bodies. And you shall be able to see not only the souls of those around you, but the souls of all those for whom you pray."

This was Catherine's explanation of the uncanny ability she had to see to the very bottom of the souls of others. Her children of the spirit were overcome with astonishment and awe each time their beloved mother—they soon came to call her by various pet names, "mamma" and "mammina"— seemed to be able to read their thoughts, and even the subconscious or secret movements of their minds. She always knew, as though by a sixth sense, what they had done or said at any given time while they had been away from her. She would say to them with a smile that they had read a certain book, or she would look at them with her large eyes full of affectionate anxiety and remind them that the last time they confessed they had left something unsaid, either because they had forgotten it or because they were ashamed to mention it. As by a miracle they would recover from some illness, or escape from some danger, and learn afterwards that their "mother" had seen that they needed help and had prayed to her Saviour with all the strength in her soul to save her beloved child from peril. Once she was reprimanded by her confessor—it was at that time Raimondo—because she let those who came to visit her kiss her hand. Catherine replied, in some astonishment, that she had not noticed it—the guest had such a beautiful soul that she had forgotten everything while she contemplated it. The sins of good people appeared to her as a stain on their beauty, but when she met people who lived in mortal sin, she became aware of a smell so awful that she needed all her self-control not to show how unwell she felt in their company. On occasions even her self-control failed—as once in Avignon when a beautiful and noble lady, the niece of one of the cardinals, came to see her. Catherine fled from her because she could not bear the smell of corruption which came from her: it appeared later that she had broken her marriage vows and had been a priest's mistress for years.

But when it was a question of some disgusting sickness of the body, Catherine never allowed herself to shirk any service of love because she experienced physical nausea. Ever since she was a child she had taught herself to remember that however strong and beautiful a human body may be as long as it blossoms with youth and beauty, it is fated to rot one day and become a thing so loathsome that it must be hidden as soon as possible in the earth. She was full of solicitude, too, for the physical well-being of her friends and her enemies, for the sick whom she nursed and for the pious men and women who asked her advice, and whom she guided with the forethought of a mother and with extraordinarily sound knowledge of human nature. She advised them against all kinds of exaggerated physical self-discipline which might weaken their health; she told them to eat, drink and sleep moderately, but sufficiently to keep strong in body and soul, so that they could carry out God's work in the way demanded of them by their position in the world. Though Christ had chosen her to follow Him in the way of suffering, and strengthened her with gifts and graces above what He gave to other Christians, she was the last to imagine that every person who loved God and tried to serve Him in the way which would lead them to heaven, was not just as precious to Him as she was. Perhaps even more precious, for if they let themselves be led by Him, they could achieve perfection, and she, in her own eyes, was so terribly imperfect. . . .

There was another Mantellata called Andrea, who suffered from cancer of the breast. The growth spread and ate into her flesh until almost her whole breast became one poisonous sore which smelled so abominable that people who came to visit her openly held their noses—a rather uncharitable way, one must agree, of approaching a sick person one has come to console. Catherine thought so too, and when she heard that there was practically no one who would visit Andrea or even enter the room where she lay, she offered to nurse her sister as long as she was ill, that is to say until her death. Catherine felt that God had given her this work, and to begin with Andrea was deeply grateful for her help.

So the young woman looked after the old widow and was like a faithful and affectionate daughter to her. The smell from the cancerous wound became worse and worse until it was almost intolerable. But Catherine never showed any sign of disgust, but breathed normally with open nostrils when she uncovered the rotting flesh. She washed and dried the sore, applied salves and put on clean bandages, gave the patient food, and helped her with all the necessities of life. Andrea appeared to be full of admiration for this girl who sacrificed herself with such fortitude for a miserable old woman, and who never seemed tired or depressed or repelled by the loathsomeness of the disease.

But even though Catherine's will never wavered, since she was firmly convinced that she was doing her Saviour's will, at times she came near to being overcome by her own senses. One morning when she took off the bandages and had to breathe in the awful smell, her whole stomach suddenly seemed to turn; she knew she was going to be sick. She was seized with a holy rage against her own body: "So you are disgusted with this sister who is saved by the blood of Christ—could not you too one day be the victim of a similar horrible illness, or even worse?" In a storm of feeling she bent her head over the revolting breast and touched the sore with her lips and nostrils until she mastered her nausea, while Andrea screamed: "Oh no, no, dear child, don't, don't, you mustn't poison yourself with this horrible decay——"

Catherine felt that she had won a great triumph over the old enemy of mankind who tempts us to stumble and waver on the way of the cross. But now Andrea's affection began to cool. Either the old woman thought that such exaggerated affection could not possibly be sincere, or Catherine's serene and happy nature got on her nerves—she knew that she must be an object of repulsion to normal people. Her secret ill-will soon turned to hatred. But she knew too that if Catherine ceased to attend her she would get no one else to nurse her, so she tried to hide her hatred. All kinds of hideous thoughts came to her, and the devil had a willing listener when he suggested to Andrea that when Catherine left her she almost certainly made up for this unpleasant work by seeking pleasure in shameful ways. Somehow or other these ugly thoughts soon spread from the room where the sick woman lay. And as people are what they are, and women have always been the same, Andrea began to receive visitors again. Soon the scandalmongers of the town were busy blackening Catherine's good name, and some of the other sisters of the order braved the poisonous smell which surrounded the bed of the cancer patient to find out what the poor thing knew about Catherine Benincasa. Catherine knew exactly what was going on, but "like a pillar of strength" she fastened her eyes on her crucified Bridegroom and continued to serve the widow unflinchingly.

But one day Catherine was called to a meeting with the prioress and the sisters. They piled insults on the girl and asked her straight out how she could let herself be seduced and throw away her virginity. Quietly and humbly Catherine answered: "In truth, my ladies and my sisters, by the grace of Jesus Christ I am a maiden." In reply to every lie and accusation she only repeated the same words: "In truth, I am a maiden. In truth, I am a maiden."

But deep within herself Catherine was terribly unhappy. The feeling of offence natural for an honest girl brought up by honest parents in a home where frivolous talk and unchaste behaviour had never been tolerated, was in Catherine mixed with horror for the feeling of outrage caused among Christian souls when they saw so many priests and members of the monastic orders living in sin. She knew enough now about such scandals to be terribly grieved over the attack on the Church of Christ which was being made by the Church's own servants. She prayed to her Beloved with bitter tears: "O, You who chose a virgin to be Your mother, You know how precious a good name is for all maidens. Help me, my Lord, my God, so that the serpent may not drag me from the work which I have undertaken out of love for You." Again she was granted a vision: the Saviour of the world appeared before her with a crown of jewels in His right hand, and in His left a crown of thorns. "Daughter, you must receive these two crowns, one after the other. Will you wear the crown of thorns while you live here on earth and have the crown of precious stones in eternity, or will you have the crown of precious stones here on earth—but then you must wear the crown of thorns hereafter? Choose which you will have." Catherine reached eagerly for the crown of thorns—she took it and pressed it onto her head so violently that the thorns pricked deep into her flesh. There was no visible mark from them, but afterwards Catherine could always feel the thorns about her head.

But then Lapa heard the rumours which Andrea had started, to humiliate Catherine. Lapa did not doubt her daughter's purity for a moment; but she was seized with a wild fury against Andrea, and some of her rage descended on Catherine: "What did I say? How many times have I said that you should leave the stinking old woman to her own devices? Now you can see the reward of your Christian charity!" Lapa screamed and shed floods of tears and told Catherine clearly and decisively, "If you don't stop nursing her, if I hear that you have so much as been near where she lives, I will never call you my daughter again."

Catherine fell on her knees beside her mother. "Mother, dear, sweet mother, do you not know that the ingratitude of mankind has never prevented God from pouring His mercy out on all sinners every day? Did Our Lord on the cross stop working to save the world because mankind had heaped shame and torture on Him? You know that if I stop going to Andrea no one else will nurse her and she will lie there and die, completely deserted.... Shall you and I be guilty of her death? The devil has seduced her, but God may still send her light so that she may understand that she has made a mistake." It ended with Lapa giving in and even blessing her daughter.

After a while Andrea really did begin to be sorry for what she had done—perhaps she was afraid that Catherine would leave her, and now more than ever she needed someone to pity her. Catherine came and went, just as friendly and concerned for her patient as ever. One day as she came in at the door Andrea saw that the girl was followed by a strange and wonderful light—it was as though she had been transformed into an angel. The old widow broke down completely; she sobbed and begged Catherine's forgiveness—"If only you will never fail me."

Quietly and patiently Catherine consoled her; she had never thought anything bad about her, and she knew that it was the devil who had put these bad thoughts into Andrea's head: "As far as you are concerned, dear mother, I ought to be grateful to you for watching so jealously over my virtue."

The sick woman now assured the guests who came to her that Catherine was an angel, a saint, and she told them of the mysterious light which she had seen with her own eyes and found so indescribably consoling. Catherine defended herself just as strongly against this new temptation, the temptation of letting Andrea proclaim her as something extraordinary and holy. She went about her work in the sickroom as quietly and competently as before. But it became more and more difficult to endure the smell of the decaying body. No flight of the soul towards other heights could prevent her physical senses from revolting at times, and she had to fight with all her might to avoid being sick. One day when she had washed the sores she knew that it was impossible for her to continue with this work any longer. Filled with anger against her own miserable flesh, she seized the bowl, which was full of the water she had washed the sores with, and pus from the sores: "By the Life of the Almighty, by the beloved Bridegroom of my soul, you shall receive in your stomach what you feel such fear of." She turned from the bed and drank the contents of the bowl. Later she confessed to Raimondo that once she had mastered her revulsion the horrible drink had seemed delicious. And from that time she never felt any reluctance about looking after Andrea.

The next night her beloved Jesus appeared to her. He uncovered the five wounds He had received on the cross: "My beloved, for My sake you have fought many a fight, and with My help you have always triumphed. But yesterday you won your greatest victory when you drank the terrible drink for love's sake, and trampled your own flesh under foot. Now I shall let you drink of a drink which is not often offered to human kind." He laid His right hand on the maiden's neck and bowed her face into His divine side: "Drink, daughter, drink My blood, and you shall taste a sweetness which will fill your whole soul; it shall even penetrate your body, which you have despised for My sake." And Catherine laid her lips to the very Source of life and was allowed to drink her fill—and was left both satisfied and changed.

People of our own time may consider the story of Catherine and Andrea more horrible than edifying, and feel that her ecstatic contemplation of the blood of Christ—a motive which recurs continually in her visions and her letters and her teaching—discloses an unhealthy love for the least attractive feature of Christianity. In our own lifetime we have learned to know the smell of rotting corpses on battlefields and in bombed towns; we know of the stinking sores and boils of prisoners from concentration camps, where dead and dying were made to lie on beds as wretched as the one Catherine had chosen for herself. We have poured out oceans of blood and tears, both of the guilty and the guiltless, while we hoped against hope that this blood and these tears could help to save a world reeling under the weight of its miseries. And how little have we achieved of the great things we dreamed! Yet we ascribe it to the confused ideas of the time she lived in and her own dark vision of Christianity, when Catherine intoxicated herself with the blood of Christ—that blood which would put an end to human bloodshed, if only we could agree to receive it as the redemption from our bloodthirsty passions, our insatiable lust for imagined gain for ourselves projected onto other nations or classes. Indeed, many Catholics think in this way. The strong-willed, brave and strangely optimistic girl who handled the powerful men of her time so masterfully, who had such an unusual understanding of the characters of the men and women among whom she lived, who really succeeded in making peace between many of her unruly townsmen, who in fact on one or two occasions prevented war, and on many put an end to bloody feuds—she would answer us as she answered her contemporaries in her letters and conversations and in the *Dialogue*: that the blood of Christ was the only source of her own courage and strength and wisdom, of her amazing and indomitable joy of living. She would say to us, Drink of it with the lips of your souls, as the saints in their visions seemed to drink it with their lips of flesh; assuage your thirst in the love which streams from God's holy Heart—then there will be an end to the vain shedding of man's blood by the hand of man. In her visions Catherine saw God's fire fall from heaven, like a rain of blazing light and burning warmth: can we really understand anything of her experience, we who have seen the fire of hate falling from the clouds, who fear in our hearts for the day when an even more destructive fire, invented by an even more bitter hatred and more violent passions, shall rain down over us and our children? For us, Catherine would have only the same message which she brought to her contemporaries, she would know only of the same remedy for our misery—the blood of Christ, the fire of God's love, which burns up self-love and self-will, and lets the soul appear, beautiful and full of grace, as it was meant to be when God created us.

VII

"THE LAWS WHICH THE SIENESE make in October are not valid in November", Dante had said with scorn about Catherine's birthplace—and with good reason. It is true that the poet from Florence was used to fights between different parties and continual changes of government, with the victors avenging themselves on the vanquished and arbitrarily banishing men whose loyalty towards their regime they doubted. But it seemed even more out of the question to create law and order, even for the shortest period, in Ghibelline Siena, the old enemy and rival of Guelphic Florence. The two dominating parties, the Gentiluomini—the nobles' party—and the Popolani—the citizens' party—were split into differing groups and cliques which constantly gave themselves up to their worst enemies because they were unable to agree. The citizens, the New Rich of the Italian city states, had made it their aim to break the power of the old feudal nobility, and throughout the latter centuries of the Middle Ages they worked for this end ceaselessly and remorselessly. It is true that the growing power of the aristocracy in the neighbouring countries and the gradual transformation of the technique of war which was beginning to do away with all that served the community in the feudal system, justified these attempts of the citizens. Its leading men were just as rich and just as cultured as most of the nobility, and after a while they asserted themselves as the most important element in the government of their own city state. It may be called a democratic movement—of a kind. But the situation developed as it always does; when a new class of the community has once got the power in its hands it uses and abuses this power in more or less the same way as its predecessors. "Unity makes strength, strength makes pride, pride goes before a fall", is a proverb which was just as true then as it is now or at any other time.

But when once in a while some group seemed to have the reins of government well in hand, then feuds between families and family groups, enmity between violent and wilful men, fighting in the streets and inns, filled the gutters of Siena with blood. There was war between the great families of Salimbeni and Tolomei; the Maconi family were on bad terms with the Tolomei; the Saracini and Piccolomini, Malavolti and Patrizzi had all inherited bloody feuds which they kept alive. Only a very outstanding man could assert himself as an individual; otherwise both the nobility and the citizens sought protection of their interests and their personal safety—as far as one could talk about personal safety—in their families or their guilds, and stood or fell with the group to which they belonged. Wise and just laws are not much help if no ruling power exists which is strong and stable enough to see that these laws are respected. The higher the waves of anarchy rose the more white-hot became people's passions—hate, fear, love for their own families or class. The murder of a relative, an attack upon a brother of the guild, had to be avenged, even if the duty of revenge became the inheritance of a child still in the cradle.

Priests and monks were born and brought up in this spiritual climate. The intense feeling for the solidarity of the family, which has always been an outstanding feature in the Italian character, did not die because a man or woman went into a monastic order. It was not everyone who was capable, as Catherine was, of sinking his deep affection for his own flesh and blood in the "ocean of Divine Love", or praying God to give such treasure as would make him rich in eternal life to all whom he loved. Worldly goods "are always bound up with so many evils, that I have never wished my relations that kind of riches", Catherine told Raimondo. Many monks and nuns felt as she did, but failed when real misfortunes seemed to threaten those whom they had left behind in the world. Some never even attempted such unworldliness; they remained members of their families first and foremost and were willing to use, quite openly and with no sense of shame, the power and influence they had gained in the Church or their order to protect their blood relations and advance their well-being. It is not strange, therefore, that the mentality of violence penetrated the very monasteries. Both the annals of Siena and chronicles from other Italian towns tell ugly stories of monks fighting and killing each other inside the cloister walls, of nuns letting their relations and the friends of their relations use the hospitality of the convent, until the intrigues and scandals stink to heaven.

In the autumn of 1368, when Catherine Benincasa's father died, there began a period of bloody fighting and rioting which was without equal, even for Siena. In 1368 Siena was ruled by a government of twelve members—"le Dodici"—all belonging to the citizens' party. The Benincasa sons belonged to this party, and Bartolommeo, the husband of Lisa Colombini, had been in the government the year before. But the nobles' party was ready to rebel—in their opinion the Government of Twelve lacked both experience and dignity, and their politics were based on gaining as many advantages for themselves as possible. In the meantime the small people of the town—Popoli Minuti—the poor, the craftsmen and shopkeepers, casual labourers and journeymen—were bitterly dissatisfied with the Government of Twelve. Unrest seethed among the lower classes. But even though they were threatened by revolution from below, the nobles and citizens could not manage to put aside their differences. On September 2, 1368, a group of nobles broke into the Palazzo Pubblico, the magnificent town hall of Siena, threw out the Twelve and organised a government in collaboration with a few men from the citizens' party whom they chose themselves. This Government of Nine—"le Noveschi"—lasted three weeks. Then came Malatesta Malatesta, the viceroy of the Emperor in Italy, and camped with his army outside the city. Even though Siena was a free and independently governed state it owed allegiance to the Holy Roman Emperor and payed tribute to him. The Ghibellines, who in the old days had supported the Emperor against the Pope and his Guelphs when the struggle between the Pope and the Emperor decided all Italian politics, had always been the ruling party in Siena. Now however the old party names, "Ghibellines" and "Guelphs", had lost something of their original meaning, and there were new difficulties which divided and split them.

On September 24 the Salimbenis rushed fully armed out of their palace, joined the party of the Dodici, and opened the city gates for Malatesta and the soldiers of the Emperor. But they had to fight their way from street to street and at last take the Palazzo Pubblico by storm. A new Government of Twelve was set up—"Difensori del Popolo Sienese"—the defenders of the people. Le Popoli Minuti had five representatives, the citizens four, and the nobles three. As a reward for the services they had rendered the "people's cause" the Salimbeni family was given "citizenship"—that is to say, any Salimbeni was eligible to enter the government, whichever of the Sienese factions was in power. Moreover they were given five fortresses outside the city of Siena.

A fortnight later the Emperor Charles IV came to Siena with his consort. They were received with jubilation and every mark of respect by the governing party. The Emperor, who stayed in the Palazzo Salimbeni, only remained a few days in the town, but promised to come back and celebrate Christmas in Siena. But before he returned the new Government of Twelve had been overthrown after a rising of the people, and the government was again in the hands of fifteen defenders, or reformers as they called themselves, from the Popoli Minuti. After still more battles, the citizens managed to get some representatives in the government, but the nobles were kept out, and most of the old families were banished from the town.

The Emperor returned on December 22nd, and again chose the Palazzo Salimbeni for his quarters; and now the Salimbenis hoped to be able to overthrow the reformers with the help of the Emperor's troops. To make the confusion in the town even worse, a papal legate had now arrived—the Cardinal of Bologna, and it was rumoured that the Emperor had decided to sell his authority over Siena to the Pope. On January 18, 1369, Niccolo Salimbeni rode through the streets with a following of fully armed men, shouting, "Long live the people! Woe to all traitors who plan to bring back the nobles!" The Sienese seized arms and streamed to the Campo, the square in front of the town hall—surely one of the loveliest public squares in the world. Here they were met by Malatesta and his cavalry, and while the great bell in the campanile rang, calling everyone to arms, the battle raged in the square. The Emperor tried to make a sortie from the Palazzo Salimbeni, but was met by Malatesta's cavalry, which were in wild retreat. Stones and missiles rained on the soldiers from the housetops, the Emperor himself only just managed to escape alive into the Salimbeni palace, but four hundred of his soldiers were killed and many more wounded.

Weeping with rage and fear, the Emperor Charles embraced and kissed any of the victors who managed to force their way in to him. He swore that he had been tricked by Malatesta and the Salimbeni. "Il Capitano del Popolo", the leader of the government, forbade, in the name of the people of Siena, that any supplies should be sold to the Emperor and his army. Charles promised to leave the town, but asked for a certain sum of money to cover the expenses of his departure. With obvious scorn the representatives of the reformers threw five thousand gold florins on the table before him, and the Emperor of the Holy Roman Empire withdrew humiliated from Siena.

Charles IV belonged to the royal house of Bohemia, and although he had been chosen as Emperor his heart remained in his little fatherland. He was not much interested in his empire, still less in his Italian domains, and the unheroic part he played during his stay in Siena agrees with his general policy, which was concerned chiefly with the well-being of his own country. He was an intelligent man who lacked all sense of heroism and always tried to prevent war and bloodshed. He succeeded to a certain extent in maintaining peace in at least one corner of war-ridden Europe, and this at any rate speaks in his favour.

After the departure of the Emperor, Siena fell into complete anarchy. The following summer something resembling peace was established; the banished nobles were allowed to return and the fifteen reformers managed to remain in power until 1385. The private feuds between the supporters of the Dodici and the Noveschi parties, between families of proud and embittered men, raged in the city in spite of the relatively stable government. It became more and more Catherine Benincasa's chief work to try to make peace. The daughter of the dyer had, through her prayers and self-sacrifice, through the power of her oratory and her diplomatic persuasiveness, become a power which was often successful in pouring the oil of Christian charity on troubled waters and overcoming the pride and bitterness of haughty nobles, arrogant citizens and worldly priests and monks.

Jacopo Benincasa was spared the sight of this wanton blood-shed and civil war. He died in August 1368, a day or two before the first revolution broke out, driving from power the party to which his sons belonged, and filling the narrow streets round his home with the clash of weapons and the smell of blood.

Catherine knelt beside his bed and begged her Bridegroom to restore her father's health. But in her soul she heard the reply—that Jacopo's pilgrimage on earth had reached its end, and that it was better for him to die now. (Did his daughter think of these words which her Saviour spoke to her, in the months which followed, when the fate of their beloved city and the dangers which threatened his sons would have cut the gentle and peace-loving old man to the heart?) From the talks which Catherine had with her father when they were alone she was convinced that the dying man had freed himself from all earthly cares and was happy to change this life for the life hereafter. But although Catherine knew what great gifts Our Lord had rained upon her, she still dared to beg for more—for her father's sake, her father who had been the best friend she had on earth. She prayed with all her might that Jesus might receive Jacopo's soul in heaven at the same moment that it left his body, for it was quite free from all graver sins. But the voice of Christ spoke within her and answered that it was true that Jacopo had lived a good and pure life as few men in his position in the world did, but his soul must go through purgatory to be cleansed of the dust accumulated by his small sins. Catherine would not give up: "Lord, I cannot bear that the awful flames shall sear my father's soul for even a moment. He has looked after me all my life, he has brought me up with ceaseless care, he has been my consolation as long as he lived, I beg You for the sake of Your infinite mercy, if my father still has anything to atone for, let me suffer for him."

And before Jacopo breathed his last Catherine knew that God had granted her wish.

When, after helping him in the last death-throes, she rose from her father's deathbed, she felt a violent pain in her side. She was aware of it as long as she lived; it was not always equally violent, but she felt it always, and she loved this pain which was a pledge that her Bridegroom had given her father eternal bliss—the sight of God as He is—the sight she herself so longed to see.

After Jacopo's death things did not go so well in the dyer's house at Fontebranda. The eldest son, Benincasa Benincasa, was now the head of the family. From letters which Catherine wrote to her brothers after they had fled from Siena and settled in Florence, it seems that Benincasa had difficulty in agreeing with his younger brothers and that his marriage was not of the happiest. But in the winter of 1368–1369 Jacopo's heirs still hoped that they could continue the family business in the same place, even though time after time they were in the danger-zone.

Once, when the people's rage against their party was at its worst, the brothers planned to flee to the parish church of San Antonio and seek asylum there, but Catherine did not think it would be safe and offered to take her brothers to La Scala hospital. Clad in her white veil and black cape she went with her three brothers through the town, which was in the wildest uproar; but no one made any attempt to molest them—which shows something of the position the holy young woman from Fontebranda already had in her own town. The refugees in San Antonio were dragged out and either massacred or thrown into prison, while the Benincasas came home unscathed when the danger was over.

Jacopo's death, the terrible things which she saw and heard around her, the constant anxiety for the lives of her sons, were too much for Monna Lapa, who was by now an old woman.

She began to fail, and after a while it became obvious to everyone in the house that she would never rise again from her sickbed. But Catherine prayed ceaselessly to her Lord that she should be allowed to keep her mother. Finally she was answered from above that Lapa was much more sure of salvation if she died now instead of continuing to live and experience all the sorrows which threatened her in the future. Catherine went to her mother and as tenderly and affectionately as she could tried to make Lapa understand how much better it would be for her if she would submit to Our Lord who called her to Him, and give herself over to the will of God without resistance. But Lapa was still bound to this world, which she was not willing to leave. She was terribly afraid to die and begged her daughter to pray even more earnestly that God might let her live—"never talk to me of dying."

However much it pained her, Catherine was bound to admit to herself that her mother was ill-prepared for death. She prayed with all the strength of her aching heart that God would not divorce her mother's soul from the body before it had submitted to His will. Lapa grew worse and worse, but still lived; it was as though God's maiden had thrown herself in front of her mother and protected her from death. But even though God seemed to listen to the prayers of the daughter, she begged her mother in vain to loosen her despairing grip on life and trust God to know best. Christ said to Catherine, "Say to your mother who to-day does not want to depart from the body, that a time will come when she shall call aloud and pray to die without being heard."

Nothing helped. And one day Lapa died—or so it seemed to all the women who stood round her bed. She had refused to confess and refused to receive the Last Sacrament, and Catherine lay over her mother's corpse and prayed and wept aloud: "O my dear Lord, is this how You keep the promise You once made me that none in this house should suffer eternal death? You promised me too that You would not take my mother from this world before she could leave it in a state of grace, and here she lies dead, without having confessed or received the Sacrament. My beloved Saviour, I call to You in Your great mercy, do not fail me! I will not go alive from Your feet until You give me my mother back."

Speechless and overcome, the women round the deathbed saw that life seemed to creep back into Lapa's body. She breathed faintly and made some slight movement. A day or two later Monna Lapa was on the way to recovery, and after a short time was quite well again.

Raimondo mentions by name the women who were witnesses of this miracle: the two Mantellate, Caterina Ghetti and Andrea Vanni, and Lisa, Lapa's daughter-in-law. He also tells us that Lapa lived to be eighty-nine. She lived to see the end of her family's prosperity and happiness, and the death of her daughters and most of her grandchildren. She had a little house near the Porta Romana, far from the place where she had lived as a busy, robust housewife in the midst of a large and happy family; and sometimes she complained: "I think God has wedged my soul crossways in my body so that it cannot come out."

VIII

IN THE YEARS 1369 AND 1370, while her home town was like a witches' cauldron bubbling with hatred, and the atmosphere in her own home must have been very strained on account of the uncertain future of her brothers, Catherine too went through a period of violent experiences. Outwardly her life was spent between her cell, the churches and the hospitals. But as rumours about her began to fly over Siena and to the neighbouring cities the solitude which had been so precious to her came to be a thing of the past. Her spiritual family demanded to be allowed to follow their beloved "mamma" wherever she went; crowds of people who wanted to talk to her forced their way into her little room; beggars and all kinds of unhappy and wretched individuals followed at her heels when she went through the city streets. Enemies, critics and scandalmongers were always busy retailing the latest gossip about Catherine di Monna Lapa, as she was often called after her father's death.

Tirelessly the young woman put herself at the service of all who came to her with their sorrows and difficulties. Always calm, happy and patient, she received visits from people who she knew came only to try to catch her in some heresy, or unmask her as a traitor. Monks came to lay traps for her or to abuse her—in a far from Christian spirit: Catherine thanked them seriously for showing such interest in the welfare of her soul. Young men about town who kept the whole of Siena talking of their mad pranks and wild life, broke into the solitary woman's cell to express their contempt for her and to rage at her for causing their friends to desert the gang and creep away to some dark church where they grovelled on their knees before confessors and crucifixes. The slender young woman in her coarse black and white robes met them with the friendliness and confidence of a sister; it was impossible to intimidate her. It often happened that after leaving her they went to find a confessor, and returned to Catherine to beg her to be their mother too, and support their faltering steps along the new road of life.

But to be alone, so that her soul could be free to raise itself towards the presence of That which was the cause of her power over men and women, the cause of all her joy and her ceaseless patience; to be able to pour out her burning love to the Origin of Life and to all she loved for His sake—this was a happiness which Catherine tasted now only when ecstasy overcame her soul, and her body lay still and lifeless. So it seemed only natural and in accordance with the economic principle of the spiritual world that her ecstasies became more and more frequent and of longer duration, and that the visionary was allowed to penetrate deeper and deeper into the secrets of the Faith.

When, after Catherine's death, the Blessed Raimondo of Capua was working on the biography of the saint who had been his penitent and his mother in Christ, he exclaimed in a sudden outburst: "O Lord, Your mercy is boundless! How good You are towards those who love You! How loving towards those who understand You! But what must You be for those whose thirst You quench so miraculously! Lord, I do not think that those who have no experience of such wonders can understand them—I know that I cannot. We only know them as the blind know colours, and the deaf, melodies. But in our attempts not to be entirely ungrateful we ponder over and admire the great gifts of grace which You give so generously to Your saints, and to the best of our ability offer our poor thanks to Your majesty."

It is of course futile to expect to understand the experience of the saints, unless one has seen a glimpse of the invisible beauty and majesty which they were allowed to contemplate while they were still divorced from it by the barriers of the visible world. Catherine herself had to give up when she once tried to describe in words to Fra Tommaso della Fonte what she had experienced while in ecstasy; she who had the whole of the lovely and rich Tuscan language at her disposal said, "It is impossible, it is like dipping pearls in the mud."

Descriptions by eye-witnesses of the miracles associated with the saints in their lifetimes are just as dependable and clear as any other evidence of historical events. There is no ground to reject them other than a dogmatic belief that there is no Almighty God who is able to alter the course of an individual life. No biographer has ever been more conscientious than Raimondo. He always gives the source of all his information—what he had heard from Catherine herself, what he himself had experienced, what he had heard from others, and who these others were and whether they were still alive. But after he had sifted the whole of his vast material and arranged it with immense care and love, he had to confess that it was beyond him to understand completely Catherine's inner life.

At the best, we can come to an approximate understanding of the way in which the inner life of a saint affected the saint's body. It is true that in our own day we know a little more of how mental conditions affect the physical functions of even quite ordinary people living quite ordinary lives, than did the old doctors who looked after the health of our grandparents. We know that blood pressure, indigestion and disturbances of the senses can be connected with depression or mental strain. We know that the consciousness of inferiority, of an inability to cope with a given situation, can create a physical illness which provides the patient with an excuse for escaping from the unequal fight. All such knowledge explains something of the fact that the mechanism of our bodies is to a very great extent subordinated to the movements of the mind, although of course it tells us nothing of the life of the soul—for example, of whether an immortal soul has any definite functions. We must take this problem to other sources and ask what a man *is*.

Like so many other saints Catherine was restrained by the insufficiency of human speech when she tried to bring her fellow-men the message which her Lord had entrusted to her. The accumulated knowledge absorbed by the senses involuntarily becomes the medium with which one tries to express the discoveries of the soul when the eternal reality which lies beyond the mortal realities of this world has been made known to it. The seer must use images and similes borrowed from the common experience of mankind. The visionaries had to speak analogously of seeing, hearing, smelling, even when their visions and the process by which mystical knowledge was poured into their souls was not accompanied by "shewings", as Julian of Norwich called her visions; or when God's voice in the soul did not take the form of audible words.

The object of Catherine's contemplation was God who became man and died on the cross out of love for the souls of mankind: it filled her mind with pictures of blood and fire which fell like cleansing rain on an earth scorched to barrenness on every side by the flames of unholy passions. Her firm belief that the source of eternal life flows perpetually from the wounded side of Jesus Christ caused her to receive with burning gratitude His invitation—that she should put her lips to this wound and drink of that drink which would make her invincible in the fight for the kingdom of heaven and for the Church which is the Mystical Body of Christ on earth. In order to make known to others how deeply she loved God, and at the same time how well she realised that such love as hers was but a tiny spark from the furnace of God's love for mankind, she had to use the language of human love—the love between man and woman, between a mother and her child—for all love here on earth is but a feeble ray from the sun of Eternal Life. Such rays may light up a soul until it mirrors God, as calm and clear water reflects the sky, or they may disappear like rays of the sun striking onto turbid marsh water. The natural talents of this Tuscan girl helped her to speak of indescribable mysteries in clearer and more lucid pictures than most mystics have used, but we can be sure that Raimondo told no more than the truth when he said that Catherine's spiritual life was unutterably more beautiful and ardent than she was able to reveal in the writings which became her gift to Christendom.

Because her soul rose ceaselessly beyond the barriers of physical life and returned from each flight into eternity bearing some new burden—some task imposed by grace and love, which she had to carry out with her miserable body as her only tool—it is only natural that Catherine Benincasa's life in the body was different from that which we consider normal for ordinary people. The lovely young girl whom her family had hoped to marry off so that they could all benefit from the match, had been strong and full of vitality. The spiritual tension of many years, the strict self-denial and the continual chastising of the body had given her a basis of physical toughness upon which supernatural grace could work, so that Catherine at the age of a little over twenty could achieve feats—whether it was housework all night, nursing the sick, or travelling on foot or on a donkey over the miserable country roads of medieval Italy—which few women in our own day could manage, even though they had done everything possible to ensure their good health. Right up to the last weeks of her life Catherine's wasted body obeyed her supernaturally strong will each time an inspiration bade her rise from her sick-bed and go out on some errand for her divine Master.

At this time—about 1370—she was completely unable to eat any solid food. For periods which became longer and longer she could take no nourishment except that of the Body of Christ in the Eucharist. "My Lord fills me at Holy Communion, I can eat no other food." Fra Tommaso della Fonte, who was still her spiritual director, was much worried about this extraordinary condition. He doubted whether this unnatural abstinence from food could really be what God wished; it might be a temptation of the devil, and ruinous for a sound religious life. So he told her to eat something every day, but before long he had to admit that she suffered so terribly when she tried to obey him that in the end he gave in to her. "Do as the Holy Spirit commands you." But Fra Tommaso had known Catherine since she was a little girl, and had had many opportunities of seeing that as a rule it was she who was right when she disagreed with him about the advice he gave her. She was a vessel which the Lord had chosen for a special purpose. Tommaso had only to look at the notes which he had made over the course of years on his penitent's daily progress to be convinced of this fact.

There were others who were not so easily dissuaded from their doubts about Catherine's much discussed holiness. And when the scandal-mongers of the town busied themselves with rumours that Catherine took absolutely no nourishment there were many excellent priests and monks who could not imagine what the point was.... Did she want to be more holy than Our Lord Himself—for everyone knows that He both ate and drank, and moreover in the company of both good people and those who were not so good. Had not many of the saints, canonised by Holy Church, warned against "peculiarities"? and this "peculiarity" of Catherine's was presumably nothing more than vanity. Some muttered that she probably fasted publicly and stuffed herself with food in secret. Later Catherine complained sometimes that she wished with all her heart that she could eat like other people, so that she could avoid causing annoyance. When it gave her the most terrible pain to swallow anything, and her stomach could not retain anything that she forced into it, she said that she believed it must be a punishment for her sins, and especially for the sin of gluttony, for she had been so greedy for fruit when she was little. . . .

Many took exception to the fact that she went so often to Communion. This was not usual at that time, for many were afraid that the devotion and awe due to the great mystery which is the Blessed Sacrament would be lessened if one received it too often. Even pious monks seldom received the Blessed Sacrament more than once or twice a week, and it had not yet become the custom for priests to celebrate Mass every day. Many of her sisters in the order, and also many of the Dominican monks, did all they could to try to lessen Catherine's desire to take Communion so often—partly because they thought that such a violent hunger for the Sacrament could not be completely sincere, and partly because they disliked the sensation caused by her ecstasies, which followed after she had communicated. The curious came to stare at the ecstatic virgin, the enemies of religion scoffed, and simple and pious people were disturbed in their devotions.

The fact that she met with so little sympathy among her brothers and sisters in the Dominican order worried Catherine's sensitive conscience. But whatever they said about her, and whatever they did against her, she refused to regard them as anything but her faithful friends or to see anything in their unfriendliness except concern for the health of her soul.

The evening before St. Alexis' day, July 17, Catherine prepared herself to receive Holy Communion the following
morning—that is to say, if she were allowed by the monk who
said the Mass, and by the sisters. As a reply to her prayer that
her heart might be washed clean, a voice in her soul replied
that to-morrow she should surely receive the Body of the Lord,
and when she prayed even more fervently to be made worthy,
she felt as though a rain of blood and fire streamed down
upon her soul and filled it with supernatural love and warmth.
It was as though it cleansed her to the innermost corners of
her being. But when the morning came she was apparently so
ill that no one thought she would be able to walk a step.
Catherine believed unconditionally in the promise which her
Saviour had given her when she prayed the evening before.
To the immense astonishment of all the friends who were with
her, she got up and went to church.

She had been forbidden to receive the Sacrament from the
hands of any other priest than her confessor. But when she
came to the Capella della Volte she saw no sign that Mass was
to be celebrated that day, and could see nothing of Fra Tommaso. He confessed later that he had not felt in the humour
to say Mass that day, and had no idea that Catherine had come
to church—he knew that she was at home, and very ill. Suddenly he felt that Christ touched his heart, and he was seized
with a burning desire to say Mass. When Catherine received
the Host from his hand, Fra Tommaso saw how her face glowed
and seemed to be covered with tiny drops of sweat and tears,
and the priest felt that her intense devotion pierced his own
heart with light. After Communion she lay long in ecstasy.
But even after she regained consciousness she was unable to
speak a word to anyone the whole day.

But when Fra Tommaso tried later to talk to her of what
she had experienced that day she said it was impossible to

describe. No, she had no idea what she looked like, whether she had been pale or flushed. No, human words could not express what she had seen and experienced—it would be blasphemy to attempt it. She could only say that she had tasted a sweetness so unutterable that all earthly things appeared as mud and offal, and not only physical things, but even the spiritual consolation for which she usually prayed. "I prayed that this too might be taken from me if I could be pleasing to my Lord and finally be able to possess Him. Because of this I bade my Lord take from me my own will and give me His will instead. He was so gracious as to reply to me, 'See, My dear daughter, I shall give you My will, and it shall make you so strong that nothing that may happen to you can ever touch or alter you!'" "And so it was", said Fra Tommaso, and he confirms that from that day Catherine was always happy and contented, whatever happened to her.

The same day Catherine was meditating over the words of the prophet, "Cor mundum crea in me, Domine", and as she prayed for God to take away her own heart, in which her self-will was rooted, she saw a vision. Her heavenly Bridegroom came to her, opened her left side, took out her heart, and carried it away in His hand. This impression was so strong and was accompanied by such a physical reaction that Catherine told Fra Tommaso at confession that she had no heart in her body. The monk could not help laughing, "Now, now, no one can live without a heart...." But Catherine was adamant. "But it's true, Father, I would have to distrust my own senses if I were to doubt that I now have no heart in my body. It is certain that with God nothing is impossible."

A day or two later Catherine had been to Mass in the Capella della Volte and remained in the church to pray long after all the others had left. Suddenly Christ appeared to her; in His hand He carried a human heart, deep red and sparkling with light. When Catherine saw how it shone she fell on her face. But again Our Lord opened her left side, and put the burning heart into her body. "My dear daughter, the other day I took away your heart. To-day I give you My heart, which will give you eternal life."

Her most intimate friends assured her biographer that they had with their own eyes seen the scar under her left breast where this exchange of hearts had taken place. From now on Catherine no longer prayed, "Lord, I offer You my heart", but "Lord, I offer You Your heart." And often when she received the Blessed Sacrament, the heart beat so violently and so jubilantly in her breast that those who stood near her heard it and were amazed.

Catherine also often saw when she took Communion how the Host was transformed when it had been consecrated by the priest: an unutterably beautiful Child was carried down from heaven by angels and laid in the hands of the priest; or else she saw a glimpse of a radiant Man's figure, or sometimes only fire which fell from heaven. It seems as though she saw these visions before she fell into ecstasy, while she wavered between consciousness and unconsciousness. When she had received the Body of the Lord she was always carried into that kingdom where no impression from outside could enter or disturb her in her company with the Beloved. She knelt as unmoving as a statue, while sometimes her friends heard that she whispered quietly "Vidi arcana Dei"—I have seen the secrets of God. Raimondo says that he heard this himself, but when, after she had regained consciousness, he asked her to tell him more, she begged to be excused—she could not. Even though she often talked with Raimondo about her mystical experiences—sometimes when he had not asked about them—this time she could not; this time it was impossible.

It was also during the critical summer of 1370 that once, when Catherine had come to the altar to take Communion, just as the priest approached her with the consecrated Host in his hand, and on behalf of the communicants said the usual words, "Lord I am not worthy that Thou shouldst enter under my roof", she heard a voice which answered, "But I, I am worthy to enter you." As she swallowed the Sacrament it seemed to her that her soul entered into God and God entered into her "as the fish is in the water, and the water is in the fish". This feeling of being one with God was so intense that she scarcely managed to return to her cell, and when she had sunk down on her hard bed, she remained lying motionless, while those who stood around her (it seems that at this time Catherine was never alone for a moment, at any rate during the day) saw that her body was lifted up and floated without any support. When she once again lay on the hard planks of the bed, they heard her whisper words of love to God, words so beautiful and so blissful that it was like a miracle to listen to them. A little later she began to pray for a number of people, and especially for her confessor. Fra Tommaso told Raimondo later that he had always known when Catherine prayed for him. He might be feeling indifferent or spiritually tired, but suddenly his soul would be filled to the brim with joy and love, and he always discovered later that at that exact moment Catherine had prayed for him.

It was during the same summer, while she was praying, that Catherine received the first of Our Lord's stigmata. She had begged Christ to promise her eternal life for Fra Tommaso and for all her friends, and He had replied that He would grant her this request. She asked Him to give her a pledge that He would save all whom she loved—not because she doubted, but so that she should always be reminded of the gift He had promised her. Christ said to her, "Stretch out your hand." The point of a glowing nail was placed in the middle of her right hand, and pressed into her flesh until it seemed that it pierced right through. There was no visible mark after this event, but the pain in her pierced hand was always with her.

Scarcely a day of the summer of 1370 passed without visions and revelations flooding Catherine's soul with supernatural love and desire to serve her Lord; and the more intense these spiritual experiences were, the more they seemed to wear out her body. Her consciousness of the eternal presence of Christ in His Church took the form of an almost continual vision—she saw Him and heard His voice in her heart. She saw His longing for the salvation of every soul springing up like flames, she saw His love to all mankind stream as blood from the wound in His side, she saw the glory of His heavenly majesty. Sometimes He appeared alone, sometimes with His blessed mother and some of the saints. Mary Magdalen and St. Dominic appeared to her: "Dominic's face is so like Our Lord's, oval, and full of tenderness; he has fair hair and a fair beard." While she described St. Dominic's appearance to Fra Bartolommeo de Dominici one of her brothers went out of the church, and Catherine turned a moment to look at him. Immediately the vision disappeared, and Catherine began to weep bitterly, full of self-reproach that she had allowed herself to be distracted from the vision granted to her by God.

But all these ecstasies seemed to take such toll of her physical strength that the moment came when her body could stand no more. Catherine had decided to go for the feast of Our Lady's Assumption to the Cathedral of Santa Maria, for the Mass for that day was always there celebrated with special solemnity, as Siena had long ago chosen the Virgin Mary as its patron saint. Catherine lay in her cell unable to move, but by a miracle she heard the Mass sung from the cathedral and was visited in a vision by Our Lady.

For many days she remained so weak that she could not move. But most of the time she was in ecstasy, and her friends who listened to her low whispering said afterwards that she seemed transported with bliss; she smiled and laughed softly, while her lips uttered expressions of love to her Bridegroom, talking of her ceaseless longing to be called to that heavenly home where Christ would be hers for ever and no separation could force her back to the world of the senses.

She was so tired of this body which shut her out from all she desired! But when her Lord said to her that she must not be selfish, He had still work for her which she was to carry out among her fellow-men on earth, she humbly bowed before His will. But she asked that she might be allowed to taste a little, only a very little—as much as she could bear—of the agony He had suffered in His body here on earth for the salvation of mankind. For she knew that then she would be more willing to suffer and bear all things for the sake of her fellows. She was granted this. But when in this way she learned how bitter His pains had been, how boundless was the love which succumbed to such suffering because His heart pitied mankind, then it was as though her own heart broke and the breath of life left her body. . . .

A message was sent to the church, to tell Fra Bartolommeo de Dominici that he must come at once to Catherine, for her friends were sure that she was at the point of death. Fra Bartolommeo and another Dominican, Fra Giovanni, had to elbow their way through the crowd outside her home, for people had streamed to the house when it was rumoured in the town that their holy virgin was dying. Round Catherine's bed knelt her nearest friends, weeping and lamenting. Fra Tommaso della Fonte, Fra Tommaso Caffarini, Madonna Alessia and Madonna Lisa and several others were there. The sorrowing Italians expressed their pain in violent weeping and loud cries, and it made such a deep impression on the consumptive young Fra Giovanni that he had a terrible attack of haemorrhage of the lungs. But full of confidence in God and His holy bride, Tommaso della Fonte took Catherine's hand and laid it on the breast of the sick monk. The haemorrhage stopped at once. A moment later Catherine opened her eyes, looked round her with an expression of deep disappointment—and turned to the wall and wept.

She wept unceasingly for many days. But little by little she told Tommaso della Fonte something of what she had experienced when she lay as though dead. She was quite certain that her soul had been freed from its prison of flesh and blood; she had seen a little of the pain and the burning desire of the souls in purgatory who know that the time will come when they shall possess God as He is, but as yet are cut off by their deeds and thoughts from that revelation which is blessedness itself. She had seen the agonies of the lost souls in hell, and for a moment she had tasted the joy of the blessed in heaven.

But at the gates of heaven Jesus had met her and commanded her to return to the world and tell what she had seen. But to explain these things as they really are is impossible for the human tongue—we have no words which can express such great mysteries. All she could do was to proclaim to the world how great was Our Lord's love to herself and all souls, how terrible are the agonies of hell, and how purgatory burns the souls which sorrow over their sins and long to be united with Him who they know is the only thing worth desiring. Many years later Catherine said to Raimondo that she loved her sufferings, for they would lead her to more complete unity with Christ.

Finally Christ had said to her: "There are many whose salvation depends on you. The life you have led up to now will be altered: for the sake of the salvation of souls you will be required to leave your native town, but I shall always be with you—I shall lead you away, and I will lead you back again. You shall proclaim the honour of My name to rich and poor, to clerks and laymen, for I shall give you words and wisdom which no one can resist. I shall send you to the popes and the leaders of My Church and to all Christians, for I choose to put the pride of the mighty to shame by the use of fragile tools."

It is not strange that Catherine asked her confessor at times, "Father, can you not see that I have changed? Can you not see that your Catherine is no longer the same?"

Some time in August 1370 three of Catherine's brothers, Benincasa, Bartolommeo and Stefano, left Siena to settle in Florence. There they were registered as citizens and continued the family's trade—dyeing—apparently with very little success. Some years later Catherine had to ask her Florentine friend Niccolo Soderini to help them with a loan. But it seems as though they were continually in debt. Catherine was forced to write to Benincasa that he ought not to ask their old mother for help: "She has given you your body, nursed you and suffered great pains and troubles for your sake and for all our sakes." It must have been a cause of great sorrow to Catherine that Bartolommeo's wife Lisa—the only one of her relations who after her father's death was really close to her—had to accompany her husband to Florence and take the children with her.

Those members of the family who remained in Siena—there was at least one brother and possibly some of the brothers-in-law who tried to continue the business in the old home—cannot have been lucky either. It was not long before they had to move from the old house in Via dei Tintori. It seems that from that time Catherine lived with various women friends until the time came which her Bridegroom had prepared her for during her mystical death, and she was sent out to wander by many strange roads.

But it was most probably while she was still living in her home at Fontebranda that her meeting with the Franciscan Fra Lazzarino took place. He was lecturer in theology at the college of his order in Siena, and a very popular preacher. Perhaps the old professional jealousy between the two mendicant orders had something to do with it—the Franciscan was at any rate professionally jealous of Fra Bartolommeo de Dominici, who was lecturer in theology in the Dominican monastery. Fra Lazzarino boiled with rage over all this nonsense about the Benincasa girl who was supposed to be so holy. He raged against Catherine in his sermons, and against the circle of friends who had collected round her—the "Caterinati", as the town had christened them. He was preparing for a last great attack on the charlatan—for that is what he was sure she was; and therefore he decided to go and visit her. He did not doubt for a moment that it would be an easy matter for him to unmask the ignorant young girl as a hypocrite or a heretic.

He was impudent enough to ask Fra Bartolommeo if he could arrange a meeting with Catherine. The unsuspecting Dominican thought that perhaps the Franciscan had begun to realise that he had done Catherine an injustice, so he gladly went with Fra Lazzarino down to the Via dei Tintori. It was late in the afternoon, but Catherine politely asked the Franciscan to seat himself. He sat on the wooden chest, Fra Bartolommeo on the edge of the bed, and Catherine sat on the bare floor at the feet of her guest.

Fra Lazzarino began with a stream of flattery. "I have heard so much about your holiness—about how Our Lord has breathed into your soul a deep understanding of Holy Writ, so now I have come to beg you to offer me words of consolation and edification."

No one on earth was less moved by flattery than Catherine. She replied modestly and calmly to the polite request, and begged the monk to talk to her, to strengthen and instruct her miserable soul. They continued to fence in this manner for some time. The Franciscan never managed to catch the young lay sister in any heretical or even suspicious utterance, and he had obviously not the faintest idea that the modest young girl saw right through him. When the church clocks all over the town began to ring for the Angelus, the two mendicant monks had to leave their hostess. Catherine followed them politely to the door, fell on her knees and asked Fra Lazzarino for his blessing, "and of your mercy, pray for me". The self-assured monk carelessly made some semblance of the sign of the cross over the kneeling woman, and mumbled absent-mindedly "and pray for me too, Sister".

That night Fra Lazzarino slept badly, and when he got up early to prepare his lecture, he felt extraordinarily sad and out of spirits. This feeling grew, and suddenly he burst into violent weeping. He detested all expressions of emotion and was terribly ashamed of himself—but he could not stop weeping. He had to cancel his lecture and stay in his cell, and as his tears continued to stream ceaselessly he tried to discover the reason for this unnatural attack of depression. Perhaps he had eaten and drunk too well yesterday evening—or perhaps he was going to start a very bad cold, for when he lay down to sleep the evening before he had forgotten to draw his hood up over his tonsured skull. Or perhaps this strange attack had been sent him from above to warn him that there was bad news on the way from his native town, Pisa; perhaps his mother or his brother was dead or in terrible danger? And last of all he began to wonder if, without knowing it, he had offended God in some way or other?

He remained in his cell the whole day. Towards evening it suddenly dawned on him—he remembered Catherine's bare little cell, and the young girl herself who had sat so modestly on the bare floor at his feet; he remembered how she had knelt and asked for his blessing ... And how coldly and proudly he had gesticulated and mumbled without meaning it "pray for me, Sister" ... and Catherine had prayed for him.

He looked round him. His cell was in fact two cells which had been joined into one, so that he could have a pleasant study, furnished with bookshelves, a good bed and comfortable chairs. Because he was not guilty of any of the obvious sins which so many of the town's clergy committed in the very faces of the faithful, he had considered that he was a good and upright monk. He had served his Lord and Master with his lips, but Catherine lived as he preached. Yes, she had love, burning love for God, and for His sake for all His creatures. She suffered for the sins of mankind, for his sins, too; she was poor as his father Francis had been, she was chaste, honest and holy. Now he saw her as she was.

And immediately the storm in his mind was stilled. He had acknowledged the truth about himself, and now he could look it in the face without unmanly tears. With the first light of dawn Fra Lazzarino hurried down to the house in the Via dei Tintori. Catherine came and opened the door to him, and when he threw himself on his knees before her she knelt also. They went into her cell together, sat on the floor and talked of their Master, and the monk confessed how up to now he had held the shell of faith in his hands, while she had the core. While Catherine talked to him, as tenderly and gently as to a son, peace fell upon Fra Lazzarino's soul. She reminded him of the vows he had made when young—vows of which his coarse cowl, the rope round his waist, and his bare feet were the symbol. "Follow your father St. Francis; his way is the way of salvation for you", said Catherine.

Fra Lazzarino went home and gave all his surplus possessions to the poor; he sold his books and gave away his furniture. He retained for himself only the most necessary clothes and one or two books for which he really had use. Of course he became the object of much scorn, criticism and ridicule—for now he did not know how to praise sufficiently the little Sister of Penitence whom he had scorned so heartily the day before. Fra Lazzarino was not perturbed by the scorn and ridicule. But some years later he retired to a life of solitude outside Siena, from which he occasionally emerged to preach, and his sermons were even better than they had been before. Catherine and Fra Lazzarino continued to be faithful friends ever after.

IX

Ever since she had given up her solitary life Catherine had been continuously busy with the corporal works of mercy. But from the day when her soul had left her body on its mystical journey through hell, purgatory and heaven, she knew that her call was first and foremost to practise spiritual works of mercy. When Christ chose her and Himself trained her, showed her such great confidence and gave her such unusual gifts of grace, He did this in order to forge her into a weapon which He could use in the battle for the souls of men.

It seems that the first of the miraculous conversions which Catherine achieved through her prayers, and which caused a sensation far beyond the city walls of Siena, was that of Andrea de Bellantis. He was an immensely rich young man of noble birth, and a complete scoundrel, so depraved that the whole town talked of him—and the good citizens of Siena were used to depravity among the young nobles. Andrea de Bellantis was a drunkard, a gambler, a perpetrator of violence, and a terrible blasphemer. He would not listen to a word about religion, and had had nothing to do with the Church since he became a man. In December 1370 he was suddenly taken very ill, but when the parish priest came, as his duty was, to visit him, Andrea drove him from the room where he lay with a flood of swearing and blasphemy. His family then sent for Tommaso della Fonte, but he was not able to move the young man to repentance either. Andrea told his relations that he intended to die as he had lived. Fra Tommaso then went to Catherine to beg her to pray for a soul which was about to die in mortal sin.

Catherine was in ecstasy when the monk came to her house, and the women who were with her told him that Catherine had also been in ecstasy that morning, and that then she had looked into heaven and seen how the hosts of heaven were preparing to celebrate the feast of St. Lucy, which was to take place the following day. Fra Tommaso gave the women his message and asked them to pass it on to Catherine when she regained consciousness.

Early the next morning Fra Tommaso heard that Andrea de Bellantis had died a repentant sinner, strengthened with the sacraments of the Church, and that he had made a will and disposed of his fortune as a good Christian should. Andrea had said to those who stood round his bed that he saw his Saviour standing in a corner of the room, and beside Him stood "the Mantellata whom they call Catherine". Christ appeared as a stern judge and said that Andrea's sins were so terrible that justice must take its course. But the maiden prayed for Andrea; she even begged to be condemned herself if only Christ would save this young man's soul. Andrea's stony heart was seized with repentance for his sins, he sent for a confessor, and died reconciled with his Creator.

Catherine admitted to Tommaso that this had really happened. While she knelt in her cell storming the gates of heaven with prayers for Andrea de Bellantis, in spirit she had been in the dying man's room with Christ, and she had offered to take on herself the punishment for his sins in eternity if only Christ would have mercy on Andrea. At first Fra Tommaso was not inclined to believe this story. But Catherine described the young man whom she had never seen, and the room where he had died, where she had obviously never been, but which Fra Tommaso knew all too well after his sad and vain visit to the sick man.

"No one should think it strange", she said later to Raimondo of Capua, "that I have such a great love for every soul, for I have truly bought these souls very dear, since for their sake I am willing to remain here on earth parted from my Lord."

But after the events of the eve of St. Lucy came a period of complete fasting—for several months Catherine was unable to take any form of food whatsoever. She lived only on the Blessed Sacrament, and was completely outside this world. Vision followed vision, and she returned to the world around her only when she had to carry out some task given her by her Lord. Although her physical strength ebbed from her and she often seemed so weak that her friends were afraid that she was dying, Catherine herself was sure that she would not be called away yet. Christ would always give her the strength she needed to carry out His wishes.

At the beginning of 1371 Catherine lived with her friend Alessia Saracini for several months. Alessia was a widow and had her father-in-law, Francesco Saracini, living with her. He was now over eighty, a hardened sinner and a fanatical hater of the clergy. Only once in his life had he been to confession, when he had been dangerously ill, but afterwards he laughed at his weakness and swore never to do such a thing again. There was a certain prior in Siena whom he looked upon as his arch-enemy: "If I ever meet the fellow I will kill him."

During the long winter evenings Catherine sat with the old gentleman and listened to him scoffing at religion and thundering against all priests. Catherine made no attempt to argue; instead she spoke to him of Jesus Christ, of His love towards mankind, His bitter death, and the saving power of His sacraments which He has put in charge of the Church, and which remain unchanged even though the priests who administer them may be bad and unworthy men. Finally she won; Francesco said he would be reconciled with her Lord

Jesus. Catherine said he would be forgiven all his sins if he forgave all who had offended him.

Early the next morning Francesco Saracini took his most precious falcon, and with the noble bird sitting on his wrist went to the church in the monastery where his enemy was prior. He decided that the first-fruit of his conversion should be the burying of his hatred, and as a proof of his sincerity he meant to give his most valuable falcon to his one-time enemy. But when the prior saw old Saracini, the poor man ran for his life—Saracini had to explain to the other priests why he had come and get them to go and fetch him back. When he had been assured that Saracini was unarmed, the prior, who was not outstandingly heroic, came to meet him, but he trembled with fear as he received the priceless gift from the penitent old man. Saracini returned to Catherine and told her what he had done—"and what must I do now?" She sent him to Fra Bartolommeo de Dominici to confess. For three days Fra Bartolommeo listened to the general confession in which Francesco Saracini admitted all the sins he had committed in the godless eighty years he had lived.

Obedient as a soldier to his young "mamma" Francesco went to Mass in the cathedral every morning, and afterwards said one hundred Pater Nosters and one hundred Ave Marias, with a rope with a hundred knots which Catherine had given him. He lived another year, and then died quietly and peacefully.

One morning during the same winter Alessia was standing at the window looking down into the street when she suddenly gave a shriek. "Oh, Mother, what an awful sight, right outside our door! They are driving two condemned men on waggons and they are being tortured with red-hot tongs...."

The men were two notorious robbers who had finally been caught and tried. The list of their crimes was so unbelievably horrible that they had been condemned first to be tortured and then put to death. This day they were driven round the whole town; they stood, each in his waggon, chained to a stake, while the executioner's apprentices pricked them with red-hot iron forks and tore the flesh from their limbs with burning tongs. Instead of shouting to the spectators for pity as most criminals did on the way to execution, these two shouted curses and blasphemed God so that all who heard them shuddered with fear.

Catherine looked out of the window for a moment—not out of curiosity, but out of pity. Then she retired and sought help in prayer. With the whole of her soul's burning desire she begged her Bridegroom to help these two poor wretches. "You saved the robber who hung on the cross beside You, even though he was justly condemned for his crimes; save these two miserable men who were created in Your image and redeemed by Your precious blood—or will You permit that they shall first suffer these cruel tortures before they die and then go to eternal agony in hell?" This, says Raimondo, is how Catherine prayed for mercy to Him whose will it is to be implored for help so that He may show His mercy. Catherine was allowed to follow in spirit the two condemned men on their terrible last journey.

The kneeling woman *saw* the waggons dragged through the streets to the place of execution outside the Porta della Giustitia. In the air round the two robbers devils swarmed like a cloud of mosquitoes, buzzing round the men and urging them to yet more violent hatred and yet wilder despair. But Catherine's soul also floated round the criminals; with all the ardour and tenderness of her soul she tried to move the two lost souls to repentance and trust in the eternal mercy of Jesus Christ. The unclean spirits which were gloating over their certain prey now turned in fury to Catherine—they threatened her with all kinds of horrors if she tried to take from them what was theirs by right; they said they would torture her until she lost her reason. Catherine only replied, "Everything which God wills I will too, and I will not fail Him because you threaten...."

The carts drove up to the gate, and under the shadowy arch stood Christ, crowned with thorns and bleeding from the scourging. Catherine saw Him, and the two robbers saw Him too. Full of sorrow He looked into the eyes and hearts of the sinners, and suddenly their defiance broke. They called for a priest; they wanted to confess. And the crowd which had followed the carts and gloated over the tortures of the two hated bandits abruptly changed over to shouts of joy when they saw that the condemned men were weeping from pure and honest repentance as they confessed their sins. Such sudden conversions were not unusual in those days, and even the most vindictive enemies of a man condemned to death could suddenly change and thank God that a soul had been saved. The ghastly procession continued on its way, but now the two men on the waggons sang hymns (how long could it be since they had last hummed those half-forgotten tunes?) and when the torturers seared their flesh with the glowing tongs they shouted that this was only what they deserved, or that they had merited even worse tortures. This change of attitude in their victims so moved the torturers that they laid down their instruments, and when they came to the place of execution the two criminals met death as calmly and happily as though they were going to a banquet.

The priest who had followed the condemned men told Fra Tommaso della Fonte of this extraordinary conversion, and Alessia informed him that at the very moment when the robbers died Catherine ceased to pray and awoke from her ecstasy. The Blessed Raimondo wrote later that he considered this the greatest of all the miracles she had worked, for, as St. Augustine and St. Gregory say, it is a greater miracle to convert such criminals than to restore them to life after they have been executed. (St. Eystein says the same in his book *Passio et Miraculi Sancti Olavi*, in the story of an obdurate sinner who was converted during the procession on St. Olav's day.) It is a line of thought common to all the biographers of the saints in the Middle Ages.

The fact that she caused the conversion of these two hardened sinners is, and always will be, a miracle, even though to-day, with our knowledge of unusual—some will say abnormal—psychic phenomena, it is to a certain extent understandable that Catherine, by concentrating the whole power and intensity of her soul on them, could convey what she was thinking and what she saw to the two criminals; in other words, the manner in which she carried out her miracle is partially explicable.

For her contemporaries this ability of Catherine's to affect people in their absence, so that they saw what she wished them to see and did what she advised them, was the most extraordinary of the many strange gifts of this young woman. Niccolo Saracini, another sinful old man, saw her one night in a dream. He told his wife that he was going to visit Catherine—just to see if she looked as she had in his dream: he was, of course, not interested in what the child might say to him! He left Catherine to go and confess, and, like his cousin Francesco, he became an honest and pious old church-goer.

The Tolomei were one of the great families who had given Siena a number of famous citizens and several holy men. They had always been leaders of the Guelph party, which supported the Popes against the German emperors. But young Jacopo Tolomei was feared far and wide for his brutality and his many cruel actions. Before he was twenty he had succeeded in murdering two men. His two beautiful young

sisters were the vainest women in the whole of Siena, and
thought of nothing but having a good time: if they were still
virgins it was because they were afraid of scandal in their
own circle of friends, not because they cared about purity.
Their mother, Madonna Rabe, went to Catherine and begged
her to pray for these children—the wild son and the frivolous daughters. Once again Catherine stormed the gates of
heaven with prayers, this time for the Tolomei.

The first meeting between Catherine and the two young
girls ended with their throwing all their powders and paints
down the lavatory. They cut off their lovely golden hair and
asked to be clothed in the robes of the Mantellate. Jacopo was
not in Siena when this happened, but when his younger brother
Matteo brought him the news, he went almost out of his mind
with rage. He thought, too, that Matteo's attitude was suspicious. "Take care", said Matteo, "when you come to Siena.
She might even convert you." "Never!" swore Jacopo. "I'd
sooner cut the throats of the whole bloody lot of sisters, monks
and priests."

Monna Rabe was terrified of her son's rage, but Catherine,
who seemed to understand the situation from A to Z, sent
Fra Tommaso to Jacopo. "You shall talk to Jacopo for me, and
I will talk to Our Lord about Jacopo."

Fra Tommaso took Fra Bartolommeo with him, and in Jacopo's fortress outside Siena the two Dominicans met the young
bandit. He was foaming with rage, but after a while it seemed
to Jacopo that his heart was changed. "I feel that I must do all
that Catherine wills." The beautiful sisters of whom he had
been so proud—it was right that they should now serve God
in the coarse dress of the Sisters of Penitence—and now he
too longed to confess and become the friend of Jesus Christ.

Jacopo Tolomei lived to be a very old man, a changed man,
an upright citizen and neighbour and a good husband and

father. Finally he entered the third order of St. Dominic. His young brother Matteo became a Dominican friar, and the two sisters lived and died as pious Sisters of Penitence.

Nanni di SerVanni was another of Siena's notorious evil-doers. Crafty and utterly depraved as he was there was none who dared to say a word against him, for although it had never been possible to prove any of Nanni's crimes—perhaps because no one dared to try to prove them—it was extraordinary how many of his enemies had been assassinated. Catherine very much wanted to meet Nanni and talk to him, for she hoped that with God's help she might make an end to all these enmities and violent deaths. But Nanni was as afraid of the girl "as the snake is of the snake-charmer". However, it appears that Nanni was not a priest-hater on principle—*he* was not afraid that any priest could make him change his ways; he lived exactly as it suited him. But one day he promised William Flete, a young English Augustinian monk, who lived in the monastery of Lecceto in the woods outside Siena, that he would go and visit Catherine—not because he thought of taking her advice, of course. . . .

Catherine was not at home when he came to her house— she was out on some errand of mercy. Fra Raimondo of Capua, who had now become her spiritual director, had also come to visit her. The friar received the man of the world, and they began to talk to each other. But suddenly Nanni shouted in terror, "O Almighty God, what sort of power is this—I want to leave, but I can't take a step. I have never known anything like it; some unknown power has triumphed over me." And when Catherine entered, he threw himself at her feet and sobbed: "Everything I have and everything I am I lay in your hands. Whatever you command me to do I will obey you, for only you, sweet virgin, can help my miserable soul."

Catherine spoke to him tenderly. She told him that she had spoken of him to her Lord and Master. Then she sent him to a confessor. Nanni was a changed man—but a short time afterwards he was taken prisoner by the podesta's men, and it was said in the town that he would be condemned to death.

Raimondo was deeply unhappy when he heard of this, and said to Catherine: "As long as Nanni served this world, everything seemed to go well for him. And now that he has turned to God it seems as though heaven and earth are against him. I am afraid he will break down with despair, for his faith is still weak. Pray that he may be led out of this danger."

But Catherine understood a man like Nanni better than this. "Do you not see how God has forgiven him and saved him from eternal torment? Instead he allows him to suffer temporal punishment for his sins. As long as he loved the world, the world loved him, and now that he is changed the world will hate and persecute him. Do not be afraid, He who has saved Nanni from hell, will also lead him out of this danger."

Surely enough Nanni was set free a day or two later, but he lost the greater part of his earthly possessions, Catherine only rejoiced the more over this, for she considered it a liberation from many temptations.

Nanni, however, still owned several fortresses in the surroundings of Siena, and he gave Catherine the deeds of one of them. She accepted the fortress with the intention of turning it into a convent for contemplative nuns of the second order of St. Dominic. It was a great joy for Catherine to be able to found this convent, but it was several years before she could get the consent of the government to turn a fortress into a nunnery, and she also had to obtain the Pope's ratification of her foundation. This she obtained in a bull from Pope Gregory XI, but it is uncertain whether the convent was completely ready before she died.

New sons and daughters continually joined the family of "the seraphic mother Caterina". The flock of Caterinati grew from month to month. Fra Raimondo and Fra Tommaso Caffarini found innumerable stories of her power over the souls of men when they collected material for their works. A host of witnesses appeared, eager to record what they knew of her wonderful life, of her charm, of her holy gaiety: everyone who knew anything about her burned to tell of the "Beata Popolana"— the blessed child of the people, as the Sienese loved to call the dyer's daughter from Via dei Tintori.

X

TIMES WERE HARD for the ordinary man in Italy. Towns and villages lived under the constant threat of being attacked and ravaged by the armies of the neighbouring republics or by some condottiere at the head of his mercenaries, either in the pay of some despot or temporarily unemployed and on the look-out for plunder. The vanquished became the victims of orgies of senseless blood-lust, torture, massacre and looting. In the wake of the soldiers followed plague and starvation. Men and boys who had grown up in this anarchy took to the woods or the mountains and became outlaws—murderers who neither gave nor expected mercy. It must not be forgotten that it was over wretched roads infested by such outlaws and soldiers of the enemy that Catherine and her followers made their journeys—as all travellers had to at that time.

The roots of these horrors were as many and as apparently ineradicable as those of a malignant weed—as the roots of all human miseries usually are. But one of the worst and the most deeply growing roots was the self-chosen exile of the Popes in Avignon.

The Popes of the Middle Ages had by no means always lived in Rome. The restless and self-willed people of Rome, and the Roman nobility, were all too ready to consider the Vicar of Christ, who was also their bishop, as their own property: rioting and anarchy broke out when they were displeased with the Pope's conduct, rioting and anarchy broke out during the papal elections, when armed mobs of Romans tried to force the cardinals to choose their candidate. The candidate put up by the Romans was often their favourite simply because he was one of the "Romani di Roma"—a native of Rome. German emperors had invaded Italy to force the Popes to acquiesce to their claim that spiritual power should be subordinate to temporal power; they had forced Popes to flee to Naples or Lyons, while a rival Pope supported by German lances took up his residence in the Lateran Palace. For several decades the Popes had preferred to live in Viterbo, but Anagni, Rieti, Perugia and other Italian towns had also served as residences for those Popes who wished to escape the eternal unrest and uncertainty of Rome.

But when Bertrand de Got, Archbishop of Bordeaux, was chosen in 1303 as Pope under the name of Clement V, he refused to leave his native France to live in Italy. Avignon, on the banks of the Rhône, did not belong to France, but was in the province of Venaissin, which belonged to the kings of Aragon until Pope Urban V bought it from Queen Joanna of Naples. But morally the Popes in Avignon had been the prisoners of the French ever since Bertrand de Got submitted to the influence of Philippe le Bel. King Philippe le Bel was a man without a trace of moral restraint; when he helped de Got to become Pope he was already guilty of both murder and sacrilege. One of the blackest chapters in the history of the Church of Christ is the story of how the weak and avaricious Clement V allowed himself to be persuaded to help the king when he dissolved the Order of the Templars in order to acquire the immense riches of the order for himself, and also because he feared the political influence of the Templars. Contrary to the principle which the Church had upheld for hundreds of years, according to which, though secular justice used torture as a legitimate means of obtaining evidence, in the eyes of the Church oaths and confessions obtained through torture were invalid, Clement V accepted the confessions of heresy and homosexuality which the French king's torturers had forced out of several of the knights of the order—some of them old men, now in their second childhood, who had belonged to the order since they were young boys. When the Church betrayed this long-standing principle it created a precedent which was later to become an excellent weapon in the hands of its bitterest enemies. For the people it meant that their strongest bulwark against the steadily growing brutality of temporal power was gradually undermined, until the Renaissance and Reformation gave the temporal lords almost absolute power in Europe, and the victims of their injustice became defenceless against organised cruelty to an extent only realised in our own time in the totalitarian states.

At his death Pope Clement V left a fortune of one million florins. His will shows how he had lent two Christian kings, those of France and England, money to make war against each other and ruin their own miserable countries.

His successor was also a Frenchman, Jacques d'Euse, who took the name of John XXII. He also lived in Avignon and continued the building activities of his predecessor, which made the papal city on the Rhône one of the most strongly fortified and mightiest cities in Europe. But the Franciscan order rebelled against the worldly and corrupt court of the Popes of Avignon, where simony and avarice spread shamelessly. The Franciscans coined the expression "the Popes' Babylonian captivity". The Pope replied with bulls of excommunication against the "Fraticelli, Beguines and brothers of Holy Poverty". For years the antagonism between the Popes of Avignon and the radical wing of the Franciscan order consumed the Church like an internal disease. The Popes condemned the Franciscans as heretics, and the Franciscans replied with bitter antagonism which often led them into heresies and into forming alliances with princes and despots who cared nothing whatever for the good or ill of the Church.

Meantime Dante accused the Pope of having married the papacy to France, saying that the Pope was no more than the King of France's chaplain. Petrarch also raised his voice in accusation against Avignon, the Babylon of the Apocalypse. It was all useless. A series of Frenchmen became Popes and in their turn created new French cardinals—often relations and friends of the reigning Pope. Some of these were upright and pious priests, but only a very small minority.

For the Church in France, too, the dependence of the Pope on French temporal power had unfortunate results. While the ceaseless wars with England ruined the country, both spiritually and materially, the people lost their love and trust in the Church of Christ since its power to lead souls into the right way and to heal the wounds of the exhausted people had been so sadly weakened. The morals of the clergy, both the higher and the lower, had in many places sunk so deep that the hearts of the faithful were filled with horror and grief. In many parts there was a terrible ignorance of religion; practically no religious teaching was given, men and women knew almost nothing of the faith which they officially professed. What they still retained of Christian tradition had become overgrown with a mass of superstitions—some dating back to pagan days, and some of recent origin.

The consequences of these unfortunate circumstances were felt throughout Christendom, though their influence diminished in relation to the distance from the source of the evil. But no place suffered from the absence of the Vicar of Christ from the old capital of the Church so much as Rome itself. The Papal States had now spread far over the Romagna to the borders of Milan, leaving the Tuscan republics like islands surrounded by the papal territories, and the Popes, who were also temporal lords, delegated their authority, both temporal and spiritual, to legates. Many of these were Frenchmen, without a trace of understanding or sympathy for the Italians; the

two so-called "Latin sister nations" had as little love and understanding of each other at that time as they have to-day. The
spokesmen for the Italian city-states, and the members of the
old ducal families who governed their small states as heredi-
tary rulers and vassals of the Holy See in a number of small
fortified towns, had equally little success when disagreements
occurred and they tried to come to an understanding with
the papal legates from Avignon.

In Rome itself there was no authority which could control
the aggressive members of the great baronial families, who
continually waged war on each other, supported by their friends
among the lesser nobility and the Roman citizenry. They had
fortresses inside the city walls, often built on ruins that had
come down from the Rome of the Emperors; and in the mountains round the Roman Campagna they had their castelli—
fortified castles surrounded by villages. Muratori's description
in his *Fragmenta Historiae Romanae III* is famous:

> Naked power had taken the place of justice, there was no respect
> for the law, no protection for personal possessions, no security
> for the individual. Pilgrims who came to pray at the graves of
> the apostles were robbed, peasants attacked outside the city walls,
> women were raped, injustice sat on the throne of justice,
> debauchery dwelt in the holy places and want in the bosom of
> the family. The churches of the holy land were in ruins; in St.
> Peter's and the Lateran cattle grazed at the foot of the altars. The
> Forum had become kitchen gardens, or lay unattended as a lair
> for wild animals. The Egyptian obelisks were overturned and
> smashed; fragments of them were buried among the remains of
> walls and rubble. As a result of the absence of the Popes, party
> war and enmity between small groups flourished unchecked. Gen-
> eral confusion and depopulation followed, and the great poets
> of the once proud Rome hung their harps on the willows and
> broke into the lament of the prophets: "How deserted is the town

which was once so full of people, the mistress of the peoples is become a widow."

But in spite of everything Rome was still the holy town of Christendom. Pilgrims still faced danger and exhaustion to come from distant lands to pray at the graves of the apostles, and to make the traditional visits to the holy places, within the city walls and outside in the lovely green Campagna, dedicated to the memory of saints and martyrs from the heroic days of the Church. They came home with indulgences they had won, with relics and pictures of the saints to be inherited by their children or their parish church, and with stories of how terrible everything was in the city of St. Peter and St. Paul.

Cola di Rienzi created an interlude which for a short time seemed to be the prelude to the re-birth of Rome. Niccolo di Lorenzo was of bourgeois descent, a man of outstanding gifts, eloquent, imaginative, high-minded, full of a burning love for his native town, whose great past he knew and admired. He dreamed that he had been born to bring back that past. In 1344 one of his brothers was murdered, and when Cola had tried in vain to bring the murderer to justice and judgment, he travelled to Avignon at the head of an embassy of spokesmen for the thirteen districts into which Rome was divided. The drastic picture which he painted of the miseries of Rome and the tyranny of the barons caused Pope Clement VI to send Cola back home as the notary of the Holy See. His great oratorical gifts soon brought the Roman people to his feet, and in 1347 he started his revolution. From the Capitol he proclaimed the constitution of the Roman Republic—Cola was convinced in his soul that it was the old republic which had returned from the dead. The people gave him the titles of Tribune and Liberator, and Clement was intelligent enough to accept the new situation and allow his representative, Bishop Raimondo of Orvieto, to co-operate with Cola. Law and order were again restored, the ruined churches were rebuilt, and warehouses built to store corn for use in the times of inflation and want which visited the city at varying intervals. The power of the barons was greatly curtailed, and pilgrims to the Holy City could wander unmolested from place to place both within and without the city walls. It seemed too good to be true. It proved too good to last. The fickle Romans turned against their Tribune and drove him from the city.

Most of what had been won through Cola di Rienzi's revolution was lost when the Black Death overran Europe in the years 1348 and 1349 and decimated the peoples of every country in a way which has never been equalled either before or since. It has been estimated that as much as one half of the population of Italy died during the plague. Everywhere people felt sure that this was God's punishment on a world which had rejected Him.

The chorus of voices which demanded that the world should do penance and the Pope return to the city which was the rightful home of the Holy See—most ordinary Christians of that time considered that this return was an inevitable condition for a re-birth of Christianity—was joined by a resounding female voice from Christendom's most northerly boundary. In vain poets, patriots and saints—for even in the blackest days the Church of Christ had never ceased to produce saints— begged the Holy Father to have mercy on his children and come home. In the jubilee year of 1350 a widow who has since become known as St. Birgitta of Sweden came to Rome with several pious Swedish priests and some relations and friends. St. Birgitta, prophetess and seer, commanded the Pope to leave

Avignon, and prophesied God's imminent wrath if he did not listen to her impassioned warnings.

Her contemporaries in Italy and many of her later admirers have called Birgitta Birgersdatter a Swedish princess. In a letter of 1347 Catherine speaks of her as "the countess who lately died in Rome". It is true that both Birgitta and her husband were related to almost all the great Swedish families which in Sweden's blood-drenched Middle Ages had worn and lost the crown. But they themselves actually belonged to the ancient aristocracy which, untroubled by titles and the like, could trace their family tree back to pagan times, shrouded in the mists of age, and which had for centuries ruled the districts where they lived as chiefs of communities of free peasants. At the same time there was nothing to stop their sons from allowing themselves to be knighted by their king, if they liked him and felt that they could follow him; but they rather looked down on the *parvenu* aristocracy of counts and barons and had no desire themselves for that kind of title.

Birgitta tells us how in one of her visions she was asked by the mother of Christ: "What do the proud ladies of your country say?" The saint replied: "I am myself one of them, therefore I am ashamed to tell you." Mary answered, "I know that better than you, but I wish you to say it." Then Birgitta said: "When they preached humility to us we replied 'We have inherited great estates and the customs and ways of chieftains from our forefathers, why should we not be as they were? Our mothers moved among the greatest women in the land, magnificently dressed—they had many servants and they brought us up to positions of honour and dignity in the world. Why should not I give all this in turn to my daughter whom I have brought up carefully so that she may behave with noble dignity, live happily and die honoured and admired in the eyes of the world?'"

But Birgitta had nevertheless been a pious child, a good and obedient wife to her pious and good husband, a loving and conscientious mother, a high-minded and wise housewife who ruled with care and competence over great estates. When her cousin, the young King Magnus Eriksson of Sweden, sent for her and asked her to manage his queen's household, Birgitta tried, without great success it is true, to lead the young couple from frivolity and vanity to the paths of Christian virtue. When her husband died she made a vow to live in poverty, chastity and obedience to her spiritual advisers, and she fought valiantly to bow her proud and passionate soul in perfect humility and love of Christ. She could not alter her nature: her great kindness towards all who suffered, and her princely generosity were natural to her. Grace does not alter our natures, it perfects them. Grace sanctified Birgitta and made her a prophetess and seer.

Before leaving Sweden Birgitta sent a letter to Pope Clement VI, in which she commanded him to make peace between France and England and return to Rome for the jubilee year. In the name of Christ she prophesied the terrible humiliations and misfortunes which would come upon the Pope if he did not begin a new life, if he did not think of what the Church had to suffer for his sake, while he took thought only for his physical well-being. "Search your conscience, and see if what I say is not true."

Two Swedish prelates brought this letter to Avignon. The Pope was deeply moved by the passionate language of the prophetess from the far North, which for the people of Europe seemed to be surrounded by a kind of mist of strangeness and romance—even though the connections between the North and Southern Europe were considerably more alive and intimate in Catholic times than they became after the Reformation. Moreover, Birgitta belonged to the royal family of her country, and she had been used to taking part in political life before she had turned her back on the world. But just at the moment Clement was in an usually difficult situation—in Germany Ludwig of Bavaria had quarrelled with the Curia, and consequently the Germans felt antagonistic towards the papal court at Avignon. In Spain the war between the kings of Castille and Aragon was raging, and the war between England and France had started again. In vain the Pope tried to make peace in a world where peace had become a stranger. The English accused him, and not without reason, of taking France's side. He only succeeded in bringing about an armistice for three years—and this armistice was broken before long.

When the Black Death came to Avignon, Pope Clement VI showed that he was not lacking in physical courage. In this time of disaster he tried to be a real father to his people. He was so shaken by the descriptions of the situation in Rome that he tried too to bring about a number of badly needed reforms—but he did this from Avignon. He refused point-blank to move to Rome. On the contrary, he strengthened the bonds between the Papacy and France, and created a number of French cardinals. When he died in 1352 Birgitta cried, "Blessed be this day, but not this Pope."

Cola di Rienzi returned to Rome like a meteor in the same year, and now he really came as the Pope's ambassador. Two years later the meteor was burnt out. In 1354 Cola di Rienzi was killed during a riot in Rome.

Birgitta had had great hopes of Clement's successor, Innocent VI, but she was sadly disappointed. She wrote to him, thundered, begged and threatened him with temporal and eternal punishment if he did not return to Rome. But he too died in Avignon without having set foot on Italian soil. After him came Pope Urban V, and in spite of protests and persuasion from the French cardinals and the French king in

1367 he sailed from Marseilles and landed in Corneto, where he was received by thousands of Italians, almost mad for joy. "It was the most beautiful and the most edifying sight that has ever been seen", wrote Blessed Giovanni Colombini to his friends at home—he had been there as representative of Siena.

In the autumn of 1367 Urban V made his entry into Rome, and the joy of the Italians seemed to outdo anything that had been seen before. The following year the new Emperor of the Holy Roman Empire came to Rome to be crowned. The Pope placed the imperial crown on his head. But soon after, Urban V left Rome after having been there only three years and three months. In vain Birgitta tried to persuade him to stay; she told him of the terrible revelations she had had, of the fate in store for himself and the Church if he failed in his duty. A short while after he returned to Avignon, Urban V lay fatally ill. He remembered the prophecies of the Swedish visionary and solemnly vowed that he would return to Rome and never again leave the Holy City, if God would spare his life. A day or two later he was dead.

Cardinal Pierre Roger de Beaufort was chosen as his successor. He was a nephew of Pope Clement VI, and at the court of Avignon had been well known for his deep piety and his pure life. When he ascended the papal throne under the name of Gregory XI all faithful Christians rejoiced. At last it seemed as though the most worthy man had been chosen as St. Peter's successor. The new Pope was a relatively young man, not forty years old, but he had poor health, and in spite of his many noble and excellent qualities his natural indecision caused him at times to waver and fluctuate.

Birgitta had seen in a vision the fate which awaited him if he failed in his duty and did not come to Rome, and she sent him a letter which made a violent impression on the emotional Pope. In his reply he sent her his apostolic blessing and a vow recording his determination to move to Rome. But when time passed and there were no signs of the Pope's making any preparations for his journey Birgitta wrote to him again and told him of a new revelation which she had had concerning him. If he let the love of his friends and relations and his native land of France prevent him from leaving, God would take from him the supernatural consolation He had always given the Pope. Moreover France would never enjoy peace and happiness if the French did not repent of their great sins towards Christ. With regard to the crusade which the Pope had planned, Our Lady had said to Birgitta that her Son would like it no better if the Pope sent hordes of godless warriors to His sepulchre than He had liked it when the Israelites in ancient times had offered their gold to make into a golden calf. . . .

It is very strange that Catherine later took a quite different attitude to the crusade in question. On the whole it seems as though the young Sienese Popolana saw political problems with a more realistic eye than the old Swedish aristocrat who was the daughter and the mother of warriors, and who from her youth upwards had been used to moving in circles which seethed with political intrigues. Both women knew that there was only one thing in the world worth living for—the love of God and all mankind for His sake. But Catherine was much more willing to hope that the best would triumph in all men, to take the world as she found it and to try to alter it with self-sacrifice, prayer and holy love, than the stern and passionate widow from Sweden.

Once again Gregory replied that his greatest desire was to move the papal residence to Rome. But just at the moment it was impossible. The war between England and France made it necessary for him to remain in Avignon. But in Italy too circumstances cried aloud for him to come, if only to save the Popes' temporal power in the Papal States. Most Christians of that time considered that this was a matter of great importance from the religious viewpoint also. In earlier days the fact that the Popes were princes of this world as well as being the Vicars of Christ had assured the liberty of spiritual authority as far as it is possible to assure it in a world where sinful men continually allow themselves to be led in any direction by their uninhibited lust for power. But the great Popes had defended the precedence and liberty of spiritual power against the German emperors and European princes who attempted to force the servants of religion into subjection to the lords of this world—an attempt which the Protestant Reformation some hundreds of years later helped the princes and monarchs to carry out.

The frontiers of the Papal States were threatened from the North by Bernabò Visconti, tyrant of Milan; and the Tuscan republics, which had seen with apprehension how the Pope's armies, under the leadership of the Spanish Cardinal Legate Albornoz, had vanquished the other Italian princes, wondered suspiciously whether their independence was threatened too. There were reasons enough, besides the chief one of all, to make it incumbent on Gregory to keep his promise to St. Birgitta and come to Rome. But the Frenchman still wavered.

In the meantime Christ had told Birgitta in a revelation that she was to go to Palestine. He would fulfil her old wish to offer her prayers at the holy places where He had been born of a Virgin, and had died for the salvation of mankind. She was not to hesitate from the fear that she was too old and weak to undertake the long journey.... So Birgitta left for Jerusalem.

Gregory had not yet come to Rome when Birgitta returned there, only to die a month or two later, on July 23, 1373. She was seventy years old. Birgitta and Catherine never met, but before Birgitta had closed her eyes in death the Sienese virgin had taken her work upon herself, and it was Catherine's destiny to carry it out. She was to be the master tool in the hand of God to bring St. Peter's successor back to his home beside the graves of St. Peter and St. Paul.

XI

AN EVER GROWING NUMBER of men and women, priests, monks and laymen, sought Catherine's advice and direction in matters of the conscience, although she had no other authority than her burning love of God and her zeal for His kingdom on earth. This meant, among other things, that she had a steadily growing correspondence.

She could not write, so she had to dictate her letters. It appears that at first Alessia Saracini and Francesca Gori managed her correspondence for her. But she was soon forced to take on more secretaries, and she never had any difficulty in finding the help she needed among her male disciples. All her secretaries have maintained that she was able to dictate two or even three letters at once, without for a moment losing the thread of each or confusing the different themes. As her mission as a peacemaker, and the reports of her holiness, spread beyond Siena, and men with power and influence among her countrymen in other parts of the land also began to consult her, Catherine must have understood that it was better for her letters to be written by a male secretary—she knew so well men's prejudice against women who mix themselves up in their affairs. . . .

It had gradually come about that Italian and European politics was one of the chief concerns of the Seraphic Virgin of Siena. The artificial division of religion and politics did not exist for the people of the Middle Ages. If they thought over the matter at all, they were completely aware that all the problems concerning the community—good or bad government, the welfare or misery of the people—are in the final instance religious problems. The fundamental question is, What do we believe a man *to be*? What is it he needs, first and foremost, so that he may be in a position to attain all his secondary needs—peace, justice, security, satisfactory relationships with his fellow men?

Catherine never had any doubts about the answer. A man is nothing by himself, has nothing from himself. His existence is in his Creator, everything he is and owns is from his Creator. United with his Creator, who is boundless Love, eternal Truth, Wisdom personified, man receives his share of the qualities of the Divine—within the limits of humanity. If a man loves God, he will be able to love his neighbour, to attain wisdom, and to be just and truthful. Because God is our eternal blessedness, a child of God becomes a blessing for his fellows. Love for one's own ego, for something which is in reality nothing, leads to an abyss of nothingness. The love of a selfish man is nothing, truth escapes between his hands, his wisdom will show itself to be foolishness, his justice injustice, and in the end a series of disappointments and mistakes will lead him to hell—to the devil who is the spirit of disappointment and barrenness. "Unless the Lord build the house, they labour in vain that build it." Catherine knew the truth of these words.

After 1370, Catherine's *Annus Mirabilis*, which she said had changed her to another woman, it looked at first to the observers as though her life continued more or less as before. Visions and ecstasies were her daily bread, and her body weakened only to show its miraculous resilience every time the love of Christ and her fellow-men forced her to rise and put her hand to the plough. The extraordinary manner in which she lived without eating was occasionally interrupted by periods when she could take a minute amount of nourishment—fruit juice or vegetables which she chewed, spitting out the solid parts afterwards, and a little water.

All the time the flock of her spiritual sons and daughters, the Caterinati, grew. Siena had seen with astonishment how one after another of the town's strong and sinful men were tamed by the little Sister of Penitence, and allowed her to lead them back to the fold. In fact it was perhaps even more astonishing how many of the young nobles, youths with a taste for intellectual refinements and aesthetic pleasures, became Catherine's disciples and daily companions.

Neri di Landoccio dei Pagliaresi loved poetry, and was himself no mean poet; his delightful poems were sung and read everywhere in Siena. Nervous and emotional, prone to attacks of melancholia during which he despaired of his life and doubted his salvation, he clung to his "mamma", whose divine joy no adversity and no physical pain could shadow. Catherine's genius was that her Christ-like heart had room for all her children of the spirit—perhaps she did not love them all with equal intensity, but at any rate she loved them in such a way that no glimpse of any jealousy among them has reached us. It is as though she loved each one in a special way, so that for each daughter and son she could be exactly what he or she needed. The theme of all her letters to Neri di Landoccio is always the same: be of good courage. But she also advised him solemnly to see through this world, to see how little its gifts are worth, to fill himself with the love of God, for His love for us will fulfil all our truest and holiest desires. In the precious blood of Jesus Christ was healing for his soul, which Catherine once compared with a leaf which trembles with every wind.

Neri worked for Catherine as one of her secretaries, and was continually with her. He brought many of his friends to her, and many of them became her disciples. Among them was Francesco di Vanni Malavolti, young, rich, sensual, avid for pleasure and distraction. His family had married him to a

young and beautiful girl of noble birth, but he had been a
sadly unfaithful husband who played the part of a Don Juan
among the girls and young wives on his family estates. When
he went with Neri to visit Catherine, he swore that if she
mentioned conversion and confession to him she would receive
a reply which would keep her mouth shut. No sooner did he
stand face to face with the young sister, looking into her shining eyes, and hearing the first words which she uttered with
her delightful voice, than he began to tremble. This was a
power he had never met before, and in his impulsive way he
immediately put himself into her hands, and asked to be allowed
to be her son.

He was sincere enough about his conversion, but it was not
easy for Francesco Malavolti to break with his former bad habits. Not long after she had received him as her son, he came to
see Catherine. She met him with a question: "My son, when
did you last go to confession?" Last Saturday, said Francesco
confidently, and on the following day, Saturday, he would go
again. But at this his "mother" turned her back on him, filled
with righteous anger: "My son, do you really think that I do
not know what you have done? Do you not know that I follow my children wherever they go? You cannot do or say a
single thing without my knowing of it at the same moment."
She told him where and when he had committed each sin.
"Go immediately and free yourself from such great misery."

It was not Francesco Malavolti's last fall from grace. Especially at times when Catherine was not in Siena the young
man would allow himself to be tempted back to the old sinful
ways. Catherine wrote to him and begged him tenderly to
come back to the fold. "I, your poor mother, wander around
distracted, looking for you. I wish I could lift you on the
shoulders of my unhappiness and carry you home. . . . You have
become poor, you are in need and your soul is about to starve

to death. . . . Comfort my spirit and cease to be so cruel towards yourself and your Saviour. . . . Dearest son, I must call you the child of my heart, for you have cost me many tears, bitterness and trouble."

Francesco came back, happy to be able to sit once again at the feet of his "mother". Again he went astray, until most of Catherine's friends gave him up—he would never be a dependable member of the flock. Catherine only smiled. She said she was sure that this wild bird of hers would not escape her in the end. But it was not until Catherine was dead and Francesco Malavolti had also lost his wife and his child and become a Benedictine monk that he really understood how bravely his beloved mother had fought to save his soul. He wrote the story of his conversion, which was to be published when she was canonised, and now he understood completely how he really had been her dearest child, even though she had had as great love towards many others: but how such things can be is the secret of those who have consented to have their hearts recreated to resemble the heart of Jesus.

But it was not only the young and frivolous, or the young and brutal, sinners of Siena's noble families who were captured by Catherine's intense personality. Messer Matteo di Cenni Fazi was quite another kind of man, a middle-aged citizen, when he went to visit Catherine together with another worthy elderly gentleman. They came out of curiosity, but the sight of the maiden kneeling in prayer, still as a statue, made such a deep impression on them that they attached themselves to her and became her faithful friends and disciples. Messer Matteo, who in his quiet and well-behaved way had been a very worldly man, gave everything he possessed to charity, and chose the arduous and exhausting work of serving the poor and the sick as rector of Casa della Misericordia, the second largest hospital in the town. Cristofano di Gano Guidini was also a citizen of ripe age, a hard-working notary, and he too joined Catherine's family and became one of her secretaries. Andrea di Vanni, the painter who had made a sketch of Catherine in her early twenties on one of the pillars in the Dominican Church, also joined the circle of Caterinati at about this time.

Messer Michele di Ser Monaldo was also a notary. He was a pious and just man, and with the consent of his wife he had taken upon himself to serve the nuns in the convent of San Giovanni Baptista in Siena. He let the nuns bring up his two little girls. But after a while the youngest, a child of eight, began to suffer from terrible attacks. She knew neither grammar nor Latin, but during these attacks she spoke fluent Latin and spoke of learned subjects as though she were an elderly doctor. Moreover she suffered from attacks of cramp, and the good sisters had no doubt that the small child was possessed of an evil spirit. She became so much worse, and her condition caused such confusion in the convent, that the nuns dared not keep little Lorenzina, but asked her father to take her home again. In vain the parents took the little girl to all the churches in Siena where miracle-working saints were buried, or where there were relics which could work miracles. Raimondo considered that the saints wanted Catherine to work this cure, and it was for this reason they would not help Lorenzina. Messer Michele and his wife took the child with them to Catherine and asked her to pray for her. But Catherine excused herself: "Ah, I am myself tortured every day by evil spirits, I do not need to take up the fight against other people's demons." She tried, moreover, to escape by a back door and hide herself from the despairing parents.

Her biographers are convinced that she did this from humility. But perhaps Catherine was really so beset with temptations from demons that she was afraid to have anything to do with Lorenzina's case. At a later date, too, she showed the same reluctance to deal with a woman who was possessed, although she finally overcame this fear of demons who tortured other people and indeed became famous for her power to cast out unclean spirits.

Messer Michele and his wife would not give up hope. Nothing could shake their confidence in Catherine, and as they knew that she was always obedient to her spiritual director, they took Lorenzina with them to Fra Tommaso della Fonte. He was sorry for them, and took the child to Catherine. He asked her to let the child sleep with her that night, and Catherine obediently received Lorenzina. She let the child kneel beside her when she prayed, and then Catherine fought the demon the whole night. At dawn he relinquished his victim, and Lorenzina lay down to sleep, apparently quite well and normal.

As soon as it was light Alessia hurried to Fra Tommaso with the good news. Together with Lorenzina's parents he went to Catherine, but when Messer Michele and his wife began to pour out streams of gratitude and delight Catherine replied seriously that it was best for the little girl to remain with her a few days longer. She taught the child to pray and instructed her in all kinds of devotions which would strengthen her soul. But one day Catherine had to leave the house for some hours. Before she went she said to her friends that they must on no account let Lorenzina be alone for so much as a minute.

Catherine left, but suddenly she said to the sister who was with her that they must put on their capes and hurry home. "I have a feeling that that wolf from hell has returned to torment and injure our little lamb." The first thing they saw when they entered was that the child was completely changed, had cramp and was raving. The zealous virgin immediately commanded the demon to depart: "Evil dragon, how dare you came back to torture this innocent little girl? I think that through the power of Jesus Christ you shall now be cast out in such a way that you will never return." The evil spirit threatened her: "If I am cast out of her I shall enter you." But Catherine replied, "If it is my Lord's will; for without His consent you have no power whatsoever."

Again the little girl became quiet, but the spirit had worked so violently in her throat that it was terribly swollen. Catherine made the sign of the cross over her throat and the swelling disappeared. Now it seemed as though Lorenzina was cured for good. A little while after, her parents were able to take her back to the convent, and when she grew up she became a good nun, who never showed any sign of being anything but healthy and normal. Both Raimondo and Fra Tommaso Caffarini knew Messer Michele and his wife well and heard the story from them.

But as rumours of Catherine's holiness and stories of the unnatural life she led spread through the neighbourhood of Siena, and even further afield, critics and scandalmongers outside the town also busied themselves talking about the dyer's daughter from Fontebranda. Fra Giovanni Tantucci, an Augustinian hermit, lived in the little monastery of Lecceto near a small lake north of Siena in the middle of a beautiful oak wood, and was much disturbed at the idea of this ignorant woman deluding simple and unlettered people with her alleged revelations and her arbitrary interpretations of the truths of the Faith. The Augustinian, who was a learned doctor of theology and a famous preacher, talked at great length of the affair to a friend who was also a doctor of theology, the Franciscan, Fra Giovanni da Volterra. The two experts agreed to visit Catherine and unmask her for what she was—a dangerous fanatic, and presumably a heretic too, although she probably did not herself understand this. . . .

They happened to come at a time when many of her friends were with Catherine. Besides Francesco Malavolti who has related this story, Fra Tommaso della Fonte was there—he was still Catherine's confessor—as well as Matteo Tolomei, Neri, and several other of her sons, Alessia, Cecca, and other Sisters of Penitence. The two learned doctors attacked Catherine "like raging lions", and bombarded her with the subtlest and most difficult theological questions they could invent. They were so abashed at her replies, given so clearly and wisely, that they wished they could withdraw from the whole affair, when Catherine suddenly took the offensive. She reminded them that they had once taken vows to live in poverty (the Augustinian hermits are also a mendicant order); but how had they kept these vows? They lived like cardinals, in spacious cells, with bookshelves, good beds and arm-chairs. "How can you dare to try to understand anything of the kingdom of heaven? You have thrown away the kernel and now chew the empty shell of faith. For the sake of Jesus Christ, stop living such a life. . . ."

The learned Franciscan offered Catherine the key of his cell—would she be so kind as to send someone there to empty the cell of all its superfluous contents and give them to the poor? Fra Giovanni Tantucci did the same. He later became one of Catherine's closest friends and accompanied her to Avignon and to Rome. When the Pope commanded that there should always be three priests among Catherine's following, so that they could hear confessions and give the sacraments to the sinners whom she converted, Fra Giovanni was one of the three.

Catherine visited the hermitage of Lecceto with Fra Giovanni and came to know the monks who lived there. One of them was the Englishman William Flete. He was a melancholy aesthete and dreamer who first and foremost sought spiritual joys for himself in his religion. He became a warm admirer of Catherine, exchanged letters with her, and after her death made her name and works known in England. But he refused very definitely to join the circle of a saint who combined the active with the contemplative life, as Catherine did. He was far too happy in his solitude in the beautiful woods, where he had experienced such wonderful hours in prayer and meditation.

Catherine Benincasa was both contemplative and active, and adulation and abuse made equally little impression upon her. She had been a mediator in controversies between individuals and between powerful groups; she had been a miracle-worker and a theological doctor. Her work in the world, which might seem exhausting to even the most robust of women, was interrupted for rest only during those moments when her soul escaped from her body into the embrace of her Bridegroom. Catherine received her spiritual energy, which few could resist, as well as the physical strength which allowed her to live a life completely independent of material things, from the words which He spoke to her soul, from His hands which held her up. Friends who were constantly with her saw how Catherine during her ecstasies seemed to be lifted from the floor where she knelt, and seemed to float, as though her soul in its flight upwards drew her body after it, instead of being bound to earth by the body.

Raimondo of Capua, who had had some mystical experiences himself, although they had been few and almost always seem to have occurred in connection with his penitent, tries with loving care in his description of her life to explain as much as he could understand of her strange way of life. When the soul is carried off to distant heavens and enjoys completely intellectual visions, it is made independent of the body, and in its longing to be made entirely one with what it sees—God—it passionately desires to be wholly free of the body. If God did not in a miraculous way maintain life in the body, it would disintegrate and perish. When the soul afterwards returns to the lower sphere, it seems like a humiliation; it is as though the soul in its knowledge of divine Perfection and its own imperfection drifts on outspread wings between two abysses. Confident and blessed, it has touched the shores of eternal life, but as long as it remains one with the mortal body it cannot have peace either in the hereafter or in this world. Raimondo believed that this was what St. Paul meant when he wrote to the Corinthians: "And lest the greatness of the revelations should exalt me, there was given me a thorn in my flesh", and further ". . . power is made perfect in infirmity."

The intense remorse which Catherine always felt for her sins came of her knowledge of what complete Purity, complete Love, really is. When she accused herself passionately for having slighted God because she let herself be distracted for a moment to see a brother go past in the church; when she reproached herself bitterly for her untruthfulness because she had politely said Yes to some Dominicans who invited her to come and see a monastery, when she had no intention of doing so—then the sensitiveness of her conscience may seem exaggerated, so that one can scarcely help wondering, was Catherine really quite sincere when she sometimes called herself the worst of all sinners? Even Raimondo of Capua had to confess that he had on occasion been doubtful. But in the end he learned to understand that Catherine measured perfection and imperfection with a yardstick which ordinary people do not know. Only God is perfect—this she had been allowed to see in her visions—and everything which is not God is imperfection. When she spoke as though she believed that her sins were the cause of the misery of the Holy Church and the whole world, she meant it with deadly seriousness. Obviously she knew that hundreds of thousands of other souls were also sufficiently sinful to bring the same miseries over the whole world and the Church. But it was not for her to judge them— she could only judge herself. This is the economy of the society of the blessed: just as the rewards of the blessed are collected in the treasure-houses of the Church, so that every poor and infirm soul may have its share of this treasure, so in a mysterious way the sins of the faithful impoverish the whole of Christendom. Our generation, which has seen how the horrors of war and the concentration camps have fallen alike on the guilty and on those who by human reckoning were the most guiltless, should find it easier than our forefathers, with their naïve belief in personal success as a reward for personal service, to understand the dogma of the Church that we all have our share in the rewards of all the saints and the guilt of all sinners.

When a volcano erupts, streams of red-hot lava pour out over the sides of the crater, while great pieces of rock and clouds of hot gases are thrown into the air. Sudden insight into the structure of one's own soul can come on one like the eruption of a volcano. But after a while the lava cools and stiffens, either to become fruitful earth in which forests and orchards may flourish, or to remain as a black and barren desert—all according to the circumstances. But for years after the eruption clouds of fine dust may float high up in the air currents— invisible except in certain strong lights. In the eyes of the saints the clouds of dust of small sins, which we scarcely notice, are always visible in the glow of the light from above.

XII

THERE HAD BEEN ENMITY between the papacy and Bernabò Visconti, the tyrant of Milan, ever since Bernabò came to power, even though there had been times, during strained truces in between the periods of open war, when both parties suspended further prosecution of their causes. When the legates from Innocent VI arrived in Milan in 1361 with the bull of excommunication, Bernabò forced them to eat it—parchment, seal, silken cord and all—and poured such abominable streams of abuse over them that the Archbishop of Milan attempted to admonish him—a thing which the prelates of his kingdom were extremely unwilling to do, for when Bernabò gave way to his wild rages he spared no one, priest or layman, man or woman. He roared at the Archbishop that here in his own land he was Pope, emperor and God Himself, for here God could do nothing without Bernabò's permission....

His contemporaries were hardened by the everyday sight of cruel punishment for both the guilty and the innocent, and by all that they heard of acts of violence and the injustice and vengeance of both greater and lesser tyrants: but in spite of this, Bernabò's cruelty seemed quite satanic. Bernabò was a great hunter, and had quartered his five thousand hunting dogs on his downtrodden subjects. Even the monasteries were compelled to take their share of the hounds. If the animals died he had the wretched keepers whipped or clubbed—sometimes to death. Any peasants or citizens who were suspected of having broken his hunting laws were tortured, blinded, or murdered.

He feared neither God nor man, but depended on his boundless cunning as a politician and his strength as a war lord, certain that he knew all the tricks and finesse of the art of war. His brother Galeazzo, lord of Pavia, was just as godless, but less talented. His wife, Beatrice della Scala of Verona, was worldly and almost as free from moral restraint as her lord and husband.

When Urban V was elected Pope, Bernabò sent his ambassadors to him with good wishes—this was merely a polite routine which all the Christian princes observed. But the Pope reminded the ambassadors that their lord was excommunicated and could not be received into the Church again before he had repented of his sins, and taken steps to repair the robberies and unjust actions he had carried out against the papacy. When Bernabò took no notice of the Pope's complaints, the Pope, as lord of the Papal States, declared war against Visconti and instituted a league against him. He invited the German Emperor, the Kings of Hungary and France and Queen Joanna of Naples to join him.

Bernabò Visconti counted on the smouldering resentment of the Pope's Italian subjects towards the behaviour of the French legates who were sent to rule the Papal States for him. In many places this resentment had become violent hatred—it would not be difficult to get the city states and provinces which were the vassals of Rome to rise and cast off a yoke which had become intolerable during the Pope's absence in Avignon. In 1371 the new papal legate, Pierre d'Estaing, had taken Perugia. The Tuscan republics, which were surrounded by provinces belonging to the Papal States, feared for their independence. Visconti was not exactly a pleasant ally, but if the coalition led by the Pope should succeed in vanquishing Bernabò Visconti, their own situation might become more than difficult.

At the beginning of 1372 Catherine wrote a letter to the Cardinal Legate, d'Estaing, who was at that time in Bologna.

"To the very dear and worthy Father in Christ Jesus, from Catherine, God's servants' servant and bondwoman, in His precious blood, who longs to see you bound by the bonds of love as you are bound by your work in Italy.... This news was a cause of great joy to me, for I am sure that you will be able to achieve much for the glory of God and the welfare of the Church ... I would wish to see you bound by the bonds of love, for you know that without love grace can achieve nothing." She writes earnestly to d'Estaing of the love which is the bond between the soul and its Creator, between God and man—that love which nailed God-made-man to the cross. Love alone is able to put an end to discussion, unite those who are divided, enrich those who are poor in virtue; for love will bring to life all the other virtues, give peace, put an end to war, give patience, strength and perseverance in all good and holy causes. "It never tires, cannot be divorced from the love of God and our neighbour, either by suffering or injustice, either by derision or injuries; it cannot be moved by impatience, nor by the joys and pleasures which this unreal world can offer us.

"I exhort you", the young Mantellata writes to the Cardinal, "to take upon yourself these bonds, this love, so that you may listen to the sweet Truth who has decided your destiny, given you life, form, and order, and has taught you the dogmas of truth." She commands him to work with all his might to clear away the disgraces and miseries of which the world is full, and which are caused by sin and offend God's name. He is to use the power given to him by the Vicar of Christ in the way she says: without love he cannot do his duty. But in order to love God with the whole of one's heart one must tear all self-love out of the heart, and with it, all submission to one's ego and the world. For these two kinds of love are opposites, so that self-love divorces us from God and our neighbour. The one kind of love brings life, the other death, the one light and the other darkness, the one peace and the other war. Self-love makes the heart shrink so that it cannot even contain its own ego; and certainly not its neighbour. It causes slavish fear which hinders a man from doing his duty, either from ignorance or from the fear of losing his position in the world. So Catherine advises the Cardinal to take courage and strength in Jesus Christ, to be zealous and to raise the banner of the holy cross. She signs this letter in the same way as all her other letters: "Dolce Gesù, Gesù Amore."

In another letter she writes of the same subject: "A soul which is full of slavish fear cannot achieve anything which is right, whatever the circumstances may be, whether it concern small or great things. It will always be shipwrecked and never complete what it has begun. Oh, how dangerous this fear is! It makes holy desire powerless, it blinds a man so that he can neither see nor understand the truth. This fear is born of the blindness of self-love, for as soon as a human being loves himself with the self-love of the senses he learns fear, and the reason of this fear is that it has given its hope and love to fragile things which have neither substance nor being and vanish like the wind. . . ." She begs him to learn from the spotless Lamb who feared neither the wickedness of the Jews nor the devil, neither shame, nor scorn, nor abuse—who did not flinch from the shame of death on the cross. "Seek for nothing but the honour of God, the salvation of the soul and the service of the beloved Bride of Christ, the Holy Church . . . Christ who is the Wisdom of the Father sees who receives His blood, and who, through his own fault, does not; and because this blood is spilled for all He suffers for the sake of all who refuse to receive it. It was this longing [the longing to save every soul] which was His suffering from His birth until His death, but when He had given His life this longing did not cease—but it no longer took the form of a Cross.... Take courage," she says, "act like a man: is it not a sad thing to see us at war with God through the countless sins which great and small people commit, and through rebellion against His Holy Church—to see us bear arms against each other, when all the faithful ought to volunteer to fight against the heathen and the false Christians?" Her last words to the Cardinal are "Peace, peace, peace, dearest Father, think of yourself and all others, and try to persuade the Holy Father to worry more about the destruction of souls than the destruction of towns, for God considers souls worth more than towns."

Pierre d'Estaing was one of the best of the legates who were sent to Italy, and he took to heart the advice he was given by the young woman whom people had come to consider as a saint, armed by God with special grace and powers. After vanquishing Bernabò Visconti he made peace with him, and he won the house of Este over to the Holy See, by acknowledging their sovereignty in Ferrara as vassals of the Pope, to whom they owed a yearly tribute. The peace with Milan however was not of long duration, and in 1374 Cardinal d'Estaing was recalled. Guillaume de Noellet was sent in his place, as legate to Bologna; and he was a much less worthy prelate.

While d'Estaing was still in Italy the country had been forced to receive yet another representative of the papal government, Gérard du Puy, abbot of Marmoutiers, and a nephew of Pope Gregory XI. He had known St. Birgitta. It seems as though he greatly desired to win the friendship of the Sienese prophetess. Catherine's letters to the Nuncio are written as answers to letters he has sent her. She begins by expressing her gratitude because he has remembered a creature so unworthy and miserable as herself, but then she continues by answering his question: "With regard to your first question about our loved Christ on earth [the Vicar of Christ], I believe and consider that he

would do good in the eyes of God if he hastened to right two
things which corrupt the Bride of Christ. The first is his too
great love and care for his relations. There must be an end of
this abuse at once and everywhere. The other is his exaggerated gentleness, which is the result of his lenience. This is the
cause of corruption among those members of the Church who
are never admonished with severity. Our Lord hates above all
things three abominable sins, covetousness, unchastity and pride.
These prevail in the Bride of Christ, that is to say in the prelates who seek nothing but riches, pleasure and fame. They
see the demons from hell stealing the souls which have been
put into their keeping, and are completely unmoved, for they
are wolves who do business with divine grace. Strict justice is
needed to punish them. In this case exaggerated mercy is in
fact the worst cruelty. It is necessary for justice to go hand in
hand with mercy to put a stop to such evil." Nevertheless she
is full of hope that the Bride of Christ will retain her beauty,
even though she may be persecuted, when she frees herself
from the abuses which shake her to the very roots. With regard
to herself, poor unworthy little daughter, she is willing to take
the burden of his sins upon herself. "We will burn your and
my sins together in the beloved fire of love which shall consume them." She advises him to repent sincerely of his sins,
and begs him to work not only for the temporal well-being of
the Church, though this is surely important too, but above all
to drive these wolves from the fold, these devils in human
shape who think of nothing but their own sinful pleasures and
their criminal love of pomp and power. Finally she begs his
forgiveness for her boldness, and asks him to pray for her.

But Gérard du Puy continued as he had begun, and drove
the Italians to ever-growing exasperation. He was an unpleasant example of Gregory's nepotism, which Catherine had chastised so openly in her letters. The helmet would have suited

him better than the mitre, but with his uncle's protection the Church offered him the best career. It was chiefly his fault that war broke out a little later between Florence and the papacy. He was made Cardinal in 1375, and in 1377, when the schism occurred, he took the side of Robert of Geneva against the true Pope and died a schismatic.

In the winter of 1373–1374 there was once again open enmity between the Pope and the Viscontis. Their attacks against the clergy and monastics in the archbishopric of Milan were so outrageous that the head of the Church was forced to intervene. But by then Catherine's influence in everything concerning religion and politics was so generally acknowledged that when Bernabò Visconti sent ambassadors to Siena to see if he could win the goodwill of the Republic in his dispute with the Pope, he gave them orders to make contact with the dyer's daughter, and if possible to get her support. Catherine sent him a letter in reply, penned by Neri di Landoccio. She addresses the excommunicated tyrant as her venerable father in the beloved Jesus Christ, and begs him to return and take his share of the blood of God's Son. Can any heart be so hard that it does not melt when it beholds the love which Divine Goodness has towards it? "Love, love, love, and remember that you were loved even before you were created. For God who sees Himself, passionately loves the beauty of His creation, and He created it because His love is boundless, to give it eternal life and to allow it to enjoy the indescribable blessedness which He Himself possesses." No power is worth having unless one has power over one's own soul. "This city [the city of the soul] is so strong, you are so powerful within it, that neither devil nor man can take possession of it without your consent." The soul is given this strength by the spotless Lamb, Jesus Christ—and Catherine with passionate eloquence reminds the tyrant of Our Lord's sacrifice for the whole of mankind upon the cross. But the blood of Christ is in the hands of the Church, therefore he who cuts himself off from the Vicar of Christ, or rebels against him, is a fool. "I beg you therefore not to continue in rebellion against him who is your supreme overlord. Do not listen to the whispering of the devil that your duty is to attack the bad shepherds within the Church ... Our Lord will not permit it." He alone has the right to sit in judgment over His unworthy servants—and we must continue to turn to them to receive the sacraments which God has given to His Church to administer for the sake of our salvation. Catherine, who was willing to offer herself to torture and death if God would receive her as a peace offering for the reformation of the Catholic Church, believed as firmly as St. Birgitta—and all other saints—that there is no salvation outside the Church.

To see the Bride of Christ regain her original beauty, to see the Church washed clean of all that its unworthy servants had soiled it with, became more and more the very core of Catherine's struggle to achieve perfect unity with Jesus Christ.

Her letter to Bernabò Visconti ends with a passionate exhortation to him to listen to the Holy Father's call to a crusade against the infidel. Gregory XI had called the Christian princes of Europe to a holy war against Islam, which had conquered all the one-time Christian lands of Asia Minor, Africa and even the south-west corner of Europe. The infidel now stood by the Bosphorus and threatened Byzantium—it seemed as though it was only a matter of years before the Constantinople of the Patriarchs would share the fate of the birthplaces of St. Paul, St. Athanasius and St. Augustine, and the crescent, which had fluttered over the birth- and burial-places of Christ for hundreds of years, advance further and further into the Christian world.

In the nineteenth century a certain school of historians had a tendency to write of the crusaders as bloodthirsty barbarians, whose superstitious beliefs and lust for plunder made them declare war against a more advanced culture. It is true that many of the Christian princes and knights who took up the cross and travelled over sea and land to fight the "infidel dogs" often behaved like barbarians. It is equally certain that the material culture of Europe in the Middle Ages was more primitive than the material culture of the Orientals—that is to say the culture of the upper classes in the oriental countries. The fact that these Eastern governments, in spite of their superiority in science, the arts and handicrafts, turned countries which had been well-populated and rich under the East Roman Empire into deserts, presumably meant as little according to these historians as it did to Catherine. For her they were only the enemies of the cross; wherever they had power Christian men and women were made slaves, both physically and spiritually. Birgitta of Sweden could deplore the fact that brutal and reprobate soldiers were sent to free the tomb of Christ: she had been the wife and mother of soldiers and knew from her own experience many of the conditions which the virgin from Siena had seen all her life, but would not allow herself to be intimidated by. She knew better than Birgitta of the ravages of the oriental pirates along the Italian coasts, and all the coasts of the Mediterranean; she knew the fate of the captured Christians enslaved by the Mohammedans. It seemed to Catherine that when some thoughtless soldier took the cross to stop this disastrous influx, this must be regarded as a step which, with God's mercy, might be the beginning of his return to God. As the flames of war consumed more and more of her beloved Tuscany and the whole of Italy, Catherine reasoned, somewhat simply perhaps, that as these men, princes, condottieri, and ordinary men-at-arms, seemed to love war, was it not better for them to march against the infidel and those who persecuted Christ and the Christians, than to wage civil war against their Christian brothers?

Catherine wrote also to Beatrice della Scala, Bernabò's proud wife. Again the Seraphic Virgin wrote of the unreality of all worldly things, which finally reduce one's own soul to nothing, and of the happiness of those who love the realities—God and the blood of Christ. It seems that Catherine had thought of visiting Milan to work for the salvation of this terrible couple. But nothing came of the idea.

In the spring of 1374 she was called to Florence. The Dominican order was to hold its Chapter General there at the beginning of the summer, and she was ordered to appear at it. Obviously rumours of the Sienese Mantellata had come to the ears of the highest authorities of the order—and the rumours were varied. Was she a saint, or was she a hypocrite and cheat? The Master General of the order, Fra Elias of Toulouse, had determined that he would see for himself what sort of person this Catherine Benincasa was.

XIII

CATHERINE AND HER COMPANIONS, who included some of the
Mantellate who were her closest friends, travelled through districts ravaged by war. The house of Salimbeni was waging war
against its own countrymen. The Sienese had taken prisoner
and executed one of the clan, the robber baron Andrea di
Niccolò Salimbeni, together with sixteen of his band. His relations took up arms against the justice which had dared to lay
hands on one of them, and the districts around Siena were
made to pay. The terrible scourge of the age, the bubonic
plague, had appeared again. The death rate did not reach its
highest point until later in the summer, but people were already
dying of the plague in Florence when Catherine and her companions arrived in the town about May 20.

About Catherine's reception by the Chapter General we
know very little, but it seems as though no accusations were
made against her. She made several friends in Florence—the
rich and powerful Niccolò Soderini, Francesco Pippino the
tailor, and his wife Monna Agnese with whom she afterwards
exchanged letters regularly. But the most important thing that
happened to Catherine during her first stay in Florence was
her meeting with Raimondo of Capua, for the most recent
investigation has shown that it was here they first met, although
Raimondo had naturally already heard a good deal about Catherine. To begin with he had listened to the stories about her
with a good deal of scepticism, and when they first became
acquainted he had obviously no intention of accepting everything she told him at its face value. He never doubted that she

was in good faith, but could a young and unschooled girl always differentiate between true revelations, her own imagination, and the work of the devil?

Catherine attached herself to Raimondo at once. She was sure that this was the spiritual director Our Lady had promised her. He was about to move to Siena where he was to be lecturer in the Dominican monastery. When the faithful Tommaso della Fonte ceased to be Catherine's spiritual director he handed his successor the four volumes of the journal regarding Catherine which he had kept ever since 1358. Without a doubt Raimondo, who was an older man and a man with greater insight, was better fitted to cope with a phenomenon like Catherine. Among other things he showed greater understanding of her need to receive Communion so often—Fra Tommaso had not dared to allow her to do so. It was also of importance for Catherine's missions between men and women who ruled over the fates of various countries and peoples that she could seek advice from a man with Fra Raimondo's background, even though it frequently happened that in such cases it was Catherine who, prompted by her inspirations, decided what she would do, and afterwards let Raimondo hear what his part in the matter was to be.

Raimondo delle Vigne came from one of the old aristocratic families of the kingdom of Naples. He was born in Capua about 1330, so according to the ideas of that time he was a middle-aged man when he first met Catherine. Even as a child he had been truthful, pure and devout, and had always had an especially tender love for the Mother of Christ. He was very young when he entered the Dominican order, where he became an example to his brethren, so that his superiors in the order allowed him to undertake several important tasks while he was still a very young man. In the meantime Raimondo had gained a thorough knowledge of theology and was known for his spotless life and deep piety. From 1363 he served as priest to the Dominican nuns in Montepulciano. While there he wrote a biography of Blessed Agnes, one of the sisters of the convent who had died in 1307, famous for the miracles she had worked both during her lifetime and after death: her unchanged body lay in the convent church. From Montepulciano he was called to Rome as priest of the convent at Santa Maria sopra Minerva, but after a short while he asked to be released from this position—he wanted to offer his life to the care of souls. In 1374 he was sent to Siena as lecturer, and as the Sisters of Penitence of the third order had always been under the leadership of the friars, Raimondo became Catherine's confessor. His lovable character, which is spoiled only by a certain anxiety and indecisiveness, shines from every line of the book he wrote about Catherine, the woman he loved as his mother and daughter in Christ, and honoured as the chosen bride of his beloved Master. Conscientious in the extreme, a learned and experienced spiritual guide, he submitted all the material he acquired to the most rigid tests, and made a thorough examination of its sources: he was determined to treat his subject in a manner worthy of Catherine herself. The result was that he came to give posterity one of the most fascinating stories ever written of a woman's life, the life of a rich and radiant talent developing in an exceptional way under the influence of divine grace.

The bonds between Catherine and Raimondo must have been strengthened considerably when they came back to Siena and were called to untiring self-sacrifice. They came to a town which had been attacked by the plague. Catherine's brother Bartolommeo had returned from Florence, either because he had given up the idea of becoming a Florentine citizen—it had certainly not been good business—or perhaps only because he wanted to see his aging mother and some of his children whom he had left with her. But Bartolommeo returned to his native town only to die of the plague. Poor Lapa also lost by plague a daughter called Lisa. Lisa must have been older than Catherine, but she was unmarried, and this is the only occasion when she is mentioned in the family history, so it is possible that she was defective either in body or mind. Eight of Lapa's grandchildren also died of the Black Death. As Catherine dressed the small bodies she sighed: "These children at any rate I shall never lose." She had good reason to fear that all was not well with her brothers. Stefano died in Rome about this time, and Benincasa, who was in Florence, seems to have grown bitter through adversity; from some words in one of Catherine's letters to him it seems that his family life was far from happy.

The plague devastated Siena—about a third of the inhabitants died of it. As so often during periods of common disaster the priests and monks showed their noblest side—even many of those who had been worldly and indifferent as long as they had been able to live a peaceful and comfortable life began to think of the responsibility laid on them by their calling, and risked their lives in surroundings filled with horror and despair to attend the sick, give the dying the last sacraments, and bury the dead.

Tirelessly Catherine went from hospital to hospital, in and out of homes where the sick lay, to nurse them, pray for them, console them, wash and clothe the corpses for burial. Day and night she moved among the victims of the plague, armed with a small lamp and a smelling-bottle which was supposed to be a protection against infection from the pestilential air.

The Dominicans worked bravely until they were on the point of dropping from exhaustion. Raimondo spent the whole day going from deathbed to deathbed, but once in a while he had to relax for a few brief minutes. Then he went to the Misericordia hospital, where he had found a good friend in the rector, Messer Matteo Cenni Fazi. Here he could rest for a while, though at the same time he was always ready if Messer Matteo fetched him to any of the poor wretches in the hospital who needed the services of a priest. But one morning when Fra Raimondo had gone out after the convent Mass and called at the hospital to ask how things were, he met some of the brothers carrying Messer Matteo, who looked as though he were already dying. Raimondo went with them, saw his friend put to bed and heard his confession. But it cut him to the heart to see in what terrible pain the sick man was, and the doctors said that his case was hopeless. Raimondo went about his work, but he was full of grief, and prayed silently that God might spare the life of a man who was of such great use to his fellows. As soon as he possibly could Raimondo went back to Casa della Misericordia—and met Catherine on her way out. Her expression was as usual happy and peaceful, and in his grief Raimondo turned to her with bitter reproach. "Mother, can you let this man die whom we are so fond of and who does so much good?" Catherine shook her head: "What are you saying? Do you think I am like God and can save a mortal man from death?" But Raimondo was no less bitter. "You can say that to those who may believe it, but not to me who know your secrets. I know well that you obtain from God all that you pray for with your whole heart." Catherine smiled: "Rejoice then, for he will not die this time."

Raimondo went in, and there sat Messer Matteo in bed eating a substantial dinner—vegetables and raw onions—not exactly the correct diet for a man who was on the point of dying of the plague. He then heard that Catherine had come, and while she was still in the corridor outside the sick man's room she cried loudly and gaily, "Get up, Messer Matteo, get up! This is not the time to lie and laze in bed!" Suddenly Matteo felt that he was free from pain and fever. He leaped up in bed, and immediately Catherine turned and fled, abashed because everyone was amazed and thanked her. When he had eaten his dinner Messer Matteo got up, well and strong, and immediately continued his work of mercy in the hospital.

This was not the first time that Messer Matteo had seen Catherine, as by a miracle, restore life and health to people who were apparently dying. But Raimondo experienced her strange power for the first time that summer when the plague was raging. There was an old hermit who went under the name of Fra Santo—Brother Saint. When he came down with plague Catherine had him moved from his solitary dwelling outside the town to Casa della Misericordia. Although he was very ill, Catherine said to him, "Don't be afraid. You will not die yet." But he seemed to get worse and worse, and she told all his friends to pray for him. She herself continued to whisper to him, "You will not die yet", and when the death throes began she murmured in his ear, "You will not die yet." The death throes lasted an unusually long time, but finally Catherine said to the unconscious Fra Santo: "I command you in the name of Our Lord Jesus Christ, do not die." Immediately it seemed as though the soul, which was fighting to escape from the body, came back; the saint sat up in his bed and asked for food. Later Fra Santo told his friends what Catherine had whispered to him, and that he was still alive only because she had commanded him in Jesus' name to live.

Carts rattled through the streets of Siena day and night full of blue-black corpses. People said that this time the plague was even more terrible than the time before. It struck people like lightning—a man might get up in the morning, apparently quite well, and be dead before evening. It was more infectious this time, too; the very air seemed to be full of it.

As the panic began to spread many of the priests and monks also lost their courage and escaped to the country. Raimondo and his faithful friends had to work even harder than before. But they were confident that "Christ is more powerful than Galen and the divine grace is stronger than nature", and continued to serve the sick fearlessly, for the soul of one's neighbour is more precious than a man's own life.

But one night when he wanted to get up and say his breviary after a few hours' sleep Raimondo felt a stinging pain in the groin. When he touched the place he felt a boil—the sure symptom of the plague. Horror-stricken he sank back on his bed and lay longing for the dawn so that he could go to his "mamma" for help. He became feverish and had a terrible headache, but he tried to say the Divine Office in spite of it. At last it was morning, and he called one of the friars, and with his help managed to drag himself to Catherine's house. She was not at home, and Raimondo, who could not go another step, was led to a bed, where he lay asking the people of the house to go and find Catherine. As soon as she came in she fell on her knees, covered his forehead with her hand and began to pray silently. Raimondo lay and looked at the ecstatic woman and thought, "She will succeed in healing either my body or my soul." He felt terribly ill, and thought that the moment was coming when terrible vomiting warned the victim of approaching death. But instead it seemed after a while as though something was dragged with force out of his body; the pains became less and shortly afterwards disappeared altogether. Even before Catherine had regained consciousness Raimondo felt quite well and strong. When she awoke from her ecstasy she told him to lie and rest while she went out and prepared some food for him. She returned and waited on him during the meal, and before leaving said seriously, "Go now and work for the salvation of souls, and thank the Almighty who has saved you from this danger." And Raimondo went back to his work as usual, while he praised God who "had given such power to a virgin, a daughter of man".

He was to be an eye-witness of many miraculous happenings which Catherine achieved through her prayers, both while the plague raged in Siena and in the years which followed. After a while the terrible disease began to disappear, but it was followed by famine. In Alessia Saracini's house Catherine baked bread which Alessia divided among the poor. But some of the flour was so mouldy and smelled so unpleasant that Alessia wanted to throw it away: when she gave to the poor she was used to giving the best the house could produce. Catherine protested: it was a sin, maintained the true daughter of Lapa, to throw away God's gifts. She began to bake with the mouldy flour, and made five times as many loaves as could reasonably be expected from the amount of flour—and it was delicious, fragrant bread. But later she admitted that while she was working in the kitchen Our Lady had appeared and helped her with the work—kneaded the dough and formed it into loaves which Catherine put in the oven. Pieces of this miraculous bread were later kept as relics by several of Catherine's spiritual children.

But at the end of the summer Catherine fell ill, presumably largely through overwork. Again she approached the fulfilment of her dearest wish, "to die and become one with her beloved Jesus Christ". On the day of the Blessed Virgin's Assumption Our Lady appeared again to Catherine and said that her Son wished her to live a little longer—He still had work which she was to do for Him on earth. The Virgin let her see in a vision the souls which she would save, and Catherine said afterwards that she saw them so clearly that she was sure she would be able to recognise them when she came to meet them again in this life.

A letter came to Catherine from Pisa, written by Pietro Gambacorti, who was more or less the ruler of the republic. The nuns in Pisa wanted her to visit them and sent their invitation through Gambacorti. In her reply Catherine sent the ruler of Pisa her usual warning against worldliness—the love of unreal things. She continually found new variations and picturesque expressions for this subject: a man who is bound to the rottenness of sin is as though in chains, he has handcuffs on the hands of his soul and cannot do the good works of Christ, his soul's feet are chained together so that they cannot bear him towards the good deeds which are the fruit of grace. Regarding her visit to Pisa she regrets that for the moment it is impossible. She is not strong enough, and moreover it would lead to "murmuring". But by the mercy of God she hopes she will be allowed to make this journey another time, in peace and without giving cause for any discontent, for she is always willing to do what the highest Truth commands.

Those who would "murmur" if she went to Pisa were the Riformati government in her native town. Relations between Siena and Pisa were, to put it mildly, strained; the Knights of St. John from Pisa had occupied Talamone, the port of Siena on the Tyrrhenian Sea. And while Pisa was still on the Pope's side, the government of Siena had not yet decided which side they would join. Catherine's presence in Pisa would also help to antagonise Bernabò Visconti, who was intriguing to get the republic over to his side.

But during the autumn Catherine left home to make a pilgrimage to Montepulciano. Presumably Fra Raimondo, who accompanied her, persuaded her to visit the grave of St. Agnes. Pilgrimages were the only form of holiday discovered by the people of the Middle Ages. The real reason for the pilgrimage was of course religious—away from the well-known everyday surroundings and the monotony of everyday life one could think of the welfare of one's soul with a fresh energy; the air of distant holy places blew away the dust of boredom from the soul, and strengthened one to pray with a new enthusiasm. But the journey, the changing landscape, the sight of new and unknown faces, brought relaxation for both body and soul. Catherine's intention was only to visit St. Agnes, a holy virgin of her own order, for whom she had great love, having heard so much about her from Raimondo. She looked forward to meeting Agnes in heaven. But it must have been very good for Catherine to get away from Siena for a while after all the strain of overwork and illness.

Catherine and the Mantellate who were with her arrived at the convent before Raimondo. She went to the church immediately to do homage to St. Agnes. All the sisters in the convent accompanied her, and they all saw how St. Agnes on her bier politely lifted her foot when Catherine knelt to kiss it. When Raimondo arrived the next day the whole convent was in an uproar over this miracle. As the provincial had given Raimondo complete authority over the convent he immediately called all the nuns to the Chapter to investigate the matter. All the women had witnessed the event, but they could not agree about what it meant. Some of them doubted whether it were a miracle—it might have been a deception of the Evil One. Others suggested that it might have a completely natural reason—the corpse had sunk deeper and the foot had tipped up. But Raimondo decided that in that case both feet would have been raised: God let St. Agnes lift up one foot only so that none could doubt that it was a miracle. When one of the nuns declared excitedly that St. Agnes had meant something else by this gesture Raimondo interrupted her abruptly: "My dear Sister, we do not ask you what St. Agnes meant to do; we know that you are neither her confidant nor her secretary. We only ask you, did you or did you not see the miraculous lifting of the foot?" "Yes", replied the nun—somewhat sulkily one may imagine. This event, which seems rather amusing to us, is described with heartfelt joy by Raimondo: that the two holy virgins of whom he was so fond should have expressed mutual reverence in this way must have caused his warm heart to glow....

Catherine visited Montepulciano for the second time some years later, with two of her nieces, Lisa's little girls, who were about to enter the convent as novices. On this occasion too signs occurred which witnesses took to be a proof that the two virgins, Agnes and Catherine, would be sisters in eternity.

It was a matter of the greatest significance for Catherine that Raimondo allowed her to receive Holy Communion much more often than her former spiritual directors had dared. It made no impression whatsoever on Raimondo that some of the sisters whispered among themselves, that some of the monks regarded her with scepticism, and that others complained of the disturbance caused by Catherine's ecstasies and tears. On the contrary, he assures us that he often felt the consecrated Host quivering in his hand when he was about to give it to Catherine—as though Our Lord in the Sacrament was impatient to give Himself to her who loved Him with all the strength of her fiery nature. Once, moreover, he was convinced that a piece of the consecrated Host had left the altar in a quite inexplicable way, and been brought to Catherine without the help of human hands.

He never doubted her burning love of God and her perfect sincerity. But at times he doubted whether she really had experienced all the visions and locutions which she described to him—were not at least some of them due to imagination? While they were together in Montepulciano, Raimondo said to her one evening that she was to gain full forgiveness for all his sins from her heavenly Bridegroom. He would not be satisfied with anything less than a bull of indulgence such as one receives from the Roman Curia. Catherine laughed softly and asked what sort of bull it was he wanted? The priest replied seriously that if he could experience a grief over his sins deeper than any he had ever known, he would consider this as good as the bull. Catherine nodded. After a short while they parted to go to bed.

But the next morning Raimondo felt so ill that he had to remain in bed. Another monk looked after and nursed him, Catherine was also ill and had a high temperature, but she got up to come and look after Raimondo. "You are even weaker than I", he said. "You should not have come." But Catherine sat down, and in her usual way began to talk of the goodness of God and the ingratitude of men. In the meantime Raimondo got up, rather embarrassed, but also encouraged by this visit of his "mamma". He sat down on a bench, and suddenly it was as though he saw a revelation: he saw all his sins naked before him, saw that he had deserved eternal punishment from the severe Judge—but he saw also the Judge's mercy and love, which had not only redeemed him and freed him from punishment, but had clothed his nakedness with His own clothes, warmed him and let him take his rest in His own bosom. Through His grace, and His eternal goodness, death had been turned to life, fear to hope, sorrow to joy, shame to honour ... Raimondo burst into tears and wept and wept as though his heart would break, and Catherine sat silently by his side and let him weep. Suddenly Raimondo remembered their conversation of the evening before, and it dawned on him: "Is this the bull I demanded of you?" "This is the bull", she replied and rose. For a moment she let her hand rest on his shoulder: "Remember God's gifts"—and then she left him.

They were still living in the convent, and Catherine lay in bed with a raging fever. Raimondo came to see her, and she began excitedly to tell him about her latest revelation. Raimondo openly confessed his own weakness: although he had received unusual grace in answer to her prayers, he still doubted: Yes, this is indeed very strange and extraordinary, but I wonder if everything she is telling me is true? He looked at the young woman's face, burning with fever, and suddenly it changed to the face of a man. The face of a man of about thirty, magnificently beautiful, oval, with fair hair and beard. He looked severely into the friar's face, and Raimondo began to tremble; he lifted his hands and called aloud: "Oh, who is it that looks at me like this?" Catherine's voice replied: "It is THAT WHICH IS." The vision disappeared; the face on the coarse pillow was again Catherine's. Writing of this event Raimondo ends solemnly, "Truly I say this before the face of God, before God Himself, Father of Our Lord Jesus Christ, who knows that I do not lie."

From that day Raimondo never doubted that Catherine had been chosen to act and speak as Christ's ambassador to her contemporaries. The new and deeper insight into things of the spirit which he obtained he attributed gratefully to Catherine's prayers and power. Their way here on earth parted after a few short years, but to the end of his days Raimondo of Capua lived on the inspiration he had received from his "mother", and never tired of praising God for His gift to mankind, His chosen messenger Catherine Benincasa.

XIV

APPARENTLY CATHERINE soon won the love of the nuns of Montepulciano, for she writes of the happiness she feels here among these contemplatives, where the peace and silence of the convent is only broken by services and singing in the church. But she was not given much breathing space before the complications of this world and the uncontrolled passions of mankind once again demanded her service.

The Riformati government in Siena sent for her—they desired her presence at home. To judge from the letter of reply she sent them it seems as though rumour, always busy with Catherine's comings and goings, had interpreted her visit to a strange town as unfaithfulness to her birthplace. Catherine does not defend herself against this interpretation—instead she tells the rulers of Siena that men who are to rule others must above all be able to rule themselves. How, she asks, can the blind lead the blind, or the dead bury the dead? "I have seen before, and I still see, that because you lack correct information you punish the innocent and let the guilty escape unpunished." Her advice is always the same: break the chains of sin, cleanse yourselves by confession, be reconciled to God—then you will be real rulers, for who can really be master if he is not master of himself, if reason does not rule his senses? She names a certain case in which a worthy abbot has been persecuted, and this, after the government leaders have complained so bitterly about unworthy monks. Is there any point in such behaviour? Regarding her return, she has still several things to do in Montepulciano, so it is not possible for the moment. She regrets that they have lent their ears to false accusations; certainly she loves them and prays with sorrow and tears that the Divine Righteousness may not send them the punishment which we all deserve for our ingratitude, and that truth may make us all free. "Let all do the work which God has given them, and not bury their talent, for that is also a sin deserving severe punishment. It is necessary to work always and everywhere for all God's creatures. God is not bound by places or people. He looks upon our honest and holy desires, which are the tools we must work with."

Towards the end of the year 1374 Catherine was home again in Siena, and here she was visited by Alfonso da Vadaterra, a Spaniard who had once been Bishop of Jaen, but was now a hermit of St. Augustine. He had been spiritual director to St. Birgitta of Sweden, and one of her best friends. The Pope had sent him from Avignon to give Catherine the papal blessing, and to ask her to support his plans by praying for Holy Church and for himself.

One of his plans was to call all Christian princes to a new crusade. It was now almost two years since his first summons, and the Christian princes were still only concerned with quarrels among themselves. Filled as they were with mutual distrust and the desire to increase their own power and lessen that of their neighbour, in whom they saw a potential enemy, they replied with excuses and evasions to the Pope's attempt to call them to arms against their common enemy, Islam. For Catherine this crusade now became a matter which was to occupy her for the rest of her life. For her it meant the liberation of Christians who were now the underdogs of infidel masters, the reconquest of the Holy Places where Christ had lived and died, and the apostles and martyrs had worked and suffered death. At any moment a wave of victorious Asiatics might flood the lands where Christians could still freely worship Him whom Catherine loved to call the Very Truth—the lands where nothing but the world, the devil and themselves hindered Holy Church from giving her children the gifts of the sacraments. If the war-hungry lords and peoples humbly armed themselves to fight for God's honour instead of for their own lust for power, a crusade would also put an end to the civil wars which ravaged the whole world as Catherine knew it; and it might do great good to the crusaders' souls. From this time on a stream of letters went out from Catherine's simple little cell to kings, statesmen and well-known military leaders in many lands. She advises them for the sake of their own souls to be converted to the true love of God and to arm themselves for the holy cause, the crusade. The Sienese Popolana writes to the powerful men of this world as one who has authority, conscious that she is neither more nor less than a tool in the hand of her Lord Jesus Christ: and as for the majesty of this world, Catherine did not believe in it. For her it was a mirage, which shines for a moment before it vanishes into nothing. This did not prevent her judgment of worldly affairs from being acute, and the advice she gave her correspondents full of sound common sense. But her advice was too straightforward and honest for people who dealt in cunning and intrigues—so they did not follow it.

It was at this time that Catherine wrote her first letter to Pope Gregory XI, and begged him for the sake of Christ's precious blood to "allow us to offer our bodies to every kind of torture". Catherine talks of martyrdom to the Pope, whose piety and warm-heartedness were spoilt by weakness and exaggerated love for his own relations and his beautiful fatherland of France; so that his will to take the necessary steps to put an end to corruption within the Church was powerless, and he never managed to do anything effective to prevent the lambs

whose shepherd he was from being led astray. Martyrdom, main-
tains Catherine, is the only means of giving the Bride of Christ
the beauty of her youth again. She was soon to show how
whole-heartedly she meant this.

By going to Pisa in February 1375 she would have the opportunity of serving the Pope's cause. Bernabò Visconti was still
interested in obtaining an alliance with the Tuscan republics,
Pisa, Lucca, Siena, Florence and Arezzo. Their adherence to
the Pope, that is to say the Pope as temporal prince of the
Papal States, lay in the balance—little was needed to tip it the
wrong way, especially as the French legates ceaselessly defied
the Italians. Catherine, and all faithful children of the Church
in Italy, knew of no other remedy for their country's misery
than the return of the Pope to Rome. But Catherine had not
yet come to the point at which she threw herself entirely into
this cause. But she started on the road which would lead her
to this when she accepted the invitation of the Pisans to visit
their town. Her presence there might for a time strengthen
their loyalty to the Pope.

Among those who accompanied her were Alessia, Lisa and
several other Mantellate. One of them was her mother, Lapa.
Some time before, she had let herself be clothed in the black
cape of the Sisters of Penitence, so now she too belonged to
her daughter's spiritual family. It is a pity that Catherine's first
biographers have not thought it worth while to describe Lapa's
conversion. One can only guess at the loneliness which the
old woman must have felt—she had lost so many of her children, and the child she was most fond of, her beloved Catherine, led such an extraordinary and terrible life. So she then
heroically decided to try Catherine's way of living to see if
this could help her to understand something of what was happening around her and lead her nearer to her own child. She
clung to Catherine, wanted to be with her wherever she went,

and was in despair each time it happened that Catherine could not take her.

Fra Raimondo, Fra Bartolommeo Dominici and Fra Tommaso della Fonte were also among the company. As so many were converted by Catherine's missionary work the Pope had ordained that there were always to be three priests among her company, to hear confessions and give absolution.

On their arrival in Pisa the sisters from Siena received a welcome such as people in the Middle Ages reserved for a guest who was generally considered a saint. The governor of Pisa, the Archbishop, and crowds of other prominent personages went out to meet Catherine, and the crowds cheered her as the crowds always, everywhere, cheer their favourite heroes, whether they be victorious generals, highly publicised leaders, popular football players or world-famous film stars. But in the Middle Ages it was chiefly saints who were popular heroes, even for people who themselves were very far from being saints, and had not the faintest desire to be saints because, as everyone knew, holiness demands heroism—heroism of an unusually severe and difficult kind.

Catherine and her companions stayed in the house of Gherardo Buonconti, a person of some importance in the town. Next to his house was a little church dedicated to St. Christina. Catherine went to Mass in this church every morning.

Sick people were brought to her and went away healed by her prayers and her advice to confess their sins and receive absolution. This of course brought even more people to her. It was while she was in Pisa that Raimondo saw for the first time that she allowed one of the visitors to kiss her hand. Raimondo did not like this and said so, but received the answer that she had the gift of seeing people's souls and therefore did not notice very much what people looked like otherwise, or what they did. . . .

But the most overwhelming event in Catherine's life while she was in Pisa was that she was marked with Christ's stigmata. Raimondo describes the event as he saw it.

On Laetare Sunday—mid-Lent Sunday—he celebrated Mass in the church of St. Christina and had given Catherine Holy Communion. She lay on her face for a long while afterwards without moving. Raimondo and her friends waited patiently—they hoped that when she awoke from her ecstasy she would have a message for them from the lips of her Bridegroom. Suddenly it was as though the outstretched figure was lifted up; she knelt with closed eyes and her face shining with supernatural bliss. She stretched out her arms, with the palms of her hands outwards, stiff and still: then she fell suddenly to the ground as though mortally wounded. A little while after, she recovered consciousness.

Some time later she called Raimondo to her and whispered: "Father, know that by the grace of Our Lord Jesus I now bear His stigmata on my body." Raimondo had guessed by her movements what had happened, but he asked her to describe the manner in which the gift of grace had been given her. "I saw Our Saviour on the cross lean down toward me in a bright light. And when my soul tried to hasten to meet its Creator, it forced my body to rise. Then I saw how five jets of blood came from the five wounds and streamed towards my miserable body. I cried out, 'O my Lord and Saviour, I beg You, do not let the wounds on my body be visible outwardly'—and while I spoke the jets of blood changed to shining light, and as rays of light they struck my hands, feet and heart."

In answer to Raimondo's question Catherine said the pains from the wounds, especially the wound in the heart, were so violent that it seemed impossible for her to suffer such agony and live, unless God worked another miracle. As soon as she returned to Buonconti's house she had to go to bed, and she lay there for a whole week unable to move; she looked almost as though she were already dead. Raimondo and her friends gathered round her and wept and lamented: they begged God not to make them motherless—how could they withstand the storms of this world if He took from them their mother and teacher, to whom they owed all they knew of the blessed way of virtue? They begged Catherine: "Mother, we know that you desire your Bridegroom Christ, but you are sure of your reward, so you must have mercy on those who must remain here without you in the storm and tempest, and who are so weak. . . . We beg you, pray Him to let us have you among us a little while yet." Catherine wept, but she replied: "With all my heart I wish you to be happy for all eternity, but I know that He who is your and my Saviour knows best how you shall be led. His will be done." These seemed terrible words for all those who loved her, for they took them to mean good-bye. They wept even more bitterly and begged God to let them keep their mother.

In this way a week passed, but then her children realised that they were not to lose her this time. On Easter Sunday Catherine was so well that she could get up and go to Mass and Communion at St. Christina's. It seemed as though her body had received new strength and energy, and when Raimondo asked, "Mother, do the wounds in your body still pain you?" she replied, Yes, but in some wonderful way these pains seemed to strengthen her and hold her up. As long as she lived, the stigmata were invisible, but on her corpse they showed clearly.

It was in Pisa, too, that there occurred another miracle— this time with a wine-barrel. Catherine was dreadfully weak, but as she could not swallow anything at all, Raimondo thought that it might perhaps refresh her if her wrists were bathed with a special sort of white wine. Buonconti had none of this wine, but thought they could obtain some from a neighbour. But the neighbour apologised—he had had a barrel of it, but it had been empty for a long while, and to prove this he drew out the bung. The wine poured out in such a stream that all three men were wet through. When rumours of this extraordinary event spread throughout the town it caused such a commotion that Catherine became greatly embarrassed and prayed for the stream of wine to cease. Those who came to get a little of the miraculous wine had to return disappointed—there was nothing in the barrel but a thick sediment.

There is an island called Gorgona which lies just outside Leghorn, the port of Pisa. On the island was a Carthusian monastery, and the prior and monks sent an invitation to Catherine to come and visit them. She finally had to accept and she and her friends took a boat from Leghorn to Gorgona. It was her first journey by sea—in fact the first time she had seen the sea. It would have been interesting to know what her reactions were, for the sea must have played a large part in her imagination; she so often used, to explain spiritual experiences, analogies such as "the fish in the water and the water in the fish", or based on things which have sunk to the bottom of the sea and are seen through the water.

The visitors were met on the jetty by the prior and some of the monks; Catherine and the women in the company were led to a hostel not far from the monastery while the men stayed in the monastery itself. The next morning the prior, followed by all the monks, came to greet Catherine, and the prior asked her to speak to them of spiritual things. At first she asked to be excused, but in the end she had to give in to their prayers, and she spoke to them of temptation and victory over temptation, "which the Holy Spirit caused her to speak of". Afterwards the prior said to Raimondo, "I am confessor for all my sons. But if Catherine had herself heard all their confessions she could not have spoken more clearly and more to the point—when she spoke of the difficulties and dangers of the monastic life each of my monks heard exactly what he most needed. There is no doubt that she is a seer and moved by the Holy Spirit."

Before leaving, Catherine took the prior aside and warned him: "The devil will try to cause trouble here in this monastery, but do not be afraid, he will not succeed." At his request Catherine gave the prior her cape. Some days later when a young monk suddenly had an attack of depression and tried to take his own life, the prior cured him by laying Catherine's cape on his shoulders. "I know that she prays for me", the monk said later to his brothers. "Without her prayers I should now have been damned."

Catherine's stay in Pisa was not exactly a holiday. In spite of visions which shook her soul to its roots, and in spite of physical overstrain, she worked tirelessly, using her influence with Pietro Gambacorti and his advisers to strengthen the bonds between Pisa and the papacy. She wrote letters to the Queen of Hungary and to Queen Joanna of Naples to win them to the proposed crusade.

Here too the doubters came to try to catch her in some heresy or charlatanism, but they were overcome by her wisdom and sound common sense. A poet from Florence wrote to warn her against misconceptions—he was especially afraid that her attempts to live without eating were a deception of the devil. Catherine replied very humbly and thanked him for his interest in her salvation; she was herself always afraid of the devil's snares, and as for the fact that she was unable to eat she asked him to pray for her to be like other people in this respect, but it seemed as though God had given her this extraordinary physical condition. Nevertheless she asked him to pray for her to be freed from it.

Then something happened which hit the whole of Italy like a streak of lightning. On June 7, a courier from Cardinal de Noellet, the Pope's representative in Italy, rode into Pisa with the message that the Pope had lately made a truce in Bologna with Bernabò Visconti.

The messenger bore an olive branch in his hand. It must have seemed like cruel scorn to the Pisans. In this truce they saw the first step towards a new league against the freedom of the Tuscan republics. The way to their small city states would now be open for the armies of both the Pope and Bernabò Visconti, and the Tuscans trusted neither of them. And the English condottiere Sir John Hawkwood, with his reprobate mercenaries, was at the moment out of work—he had been used by the Pope against Visconti. He would have to look round for plunder with which to pay his mercenaries, and it was most likely that he would turn to the small rich republics and the fruitful countryside of Tuscany. These republics were already examples of the advantages and disadvantages which follow democracy always and everywhere. Freedom had made the citizens rich, cultured and intelligent, their best men burned with patriotism and took their responsibility towards their countrymen very seriously. But these free citizens were also implicated in an endless series of private quarrels and political feuds—sometimes the enmity was caused by childish vanity or mean egotism, sometimes by serious conflicts between ideals and philosophies which led to differing opinions as to what is necessary to a good and just government. There were ceaseless encounters between men who cynically sought their own advantage or blindly believed in the infallibility of their own wisdom. People constantly changed sides in these quarrels, either because of their convictions or for the sake of what they could get out of it. Freedom had emptied its cornucopia over the beautiful Tuscan countryside and let its good and evil gifts rain down.

To make the prospects even darker the legate had forbidden all export of corn from the Papal States, and at the same time asked the Florentines for a loan of 60,000 guilders so that he might buy himself free of Sir John Hawkwood. If he did not receive them he refused any responsibility for what the con-dottiere might do.

The Florentines decided that sooner than lend de Noellet the money they would themselves hire Hawkwood and his troops. Hawkwood took what money he could from the Florentines and then began to force as much as possible out of the other Tuscan republics. As yet open war was not declared, but Florence, which was sure to be the first victim if an attack were made, gave the power to the Ghibellines and prepared for war. A government was formed of eight advisers—they were called "Otti della Guerra"—the eight war lords. There was no mistaking what Florence's policy was to be. When a conspiracy was discovered in Prato, a town which belonged to the Florentine republic—it was said that the conspirators intended to give the town over to the Cardinal—the plotters, one of whom was a priest, were brought to Florence and killed by a furious crowd who literally tore them to pieces and flung their flesh to the dogs. Now there was practically no hope of keeping the peace—and the Florentines were longing to fight for the freedom of their town. As a preparatory step to the war with the papal legate the Florentines made a five years' truce with Bernabò Visconti.

In the meantime Sir John Hawkwood, with some of his soldiers, desperate men of many nations who had turned their backs on their native countries and on all ideas of humanity and morals, came towards Pisa and camped not far from the town. From Pisa Catherine sent Fra Raimondo with a letter to the condottiere. "In the name of Christ Crucified and gentle Mary" she turns to the chief of the robbers and murderers and calls him and his accomplices her beloved brothers in Christ, asking them to consider what terrible pain and trouble they have suffered in the service of the devil. She advises them to be converted and take service under the cross of Christ. "I beg you in the name of Jesus Christ, because God and our Holy Father command us to attack the infidel, and as you are so fond of war and fighting, fight no longer against Christians, for that is a sin, but against our common enemies. Is it not a horrible thing that we who are Christians and are one, because we are the limbs of the body of Holy Church—that we should attack each other?" She is surprised that Hawkwood is thinking of making war here, as she has heard that he has promised to die for Christ in a crusade. (It is quite possible that the Englishman had made such a vow.) Such a war is a poor preparation to follow God's call to the Holy Places. He and his companions should prepare themselves by seeking the way of virtue and show themselves to be true and noble knights. She recommends Raimondo to Hawkwood and signs herself "Catherine, the useless servant".

For people of our time, perhaps the most astonishing thing about this exchange of letters between the leader of mercenaries and a young girl with no other power whatsoever than that she was considered holy, is that Fra Raimondo was well received in the condottiere's camp. Hawkwood promised, along with his captains, to join the crusade as soon as it took shape. He sealed his vow by receiving Holy Communion. It seems as though, at any rate for a moment, Catherine had managed to create a breathing space for Pisa, and Pietro Gambacorti and his advisers avoided a break with the Holy See, which would have been considered a terrible step for faithful children of the Church. They decided to try to keep neutral—always a difficult and doubtful policy.

In September Catherine was able to start on her return journey to Siena. She had received several letters from her native town impatiently demanding her return. Catherine had to reply and defend herself against the accusation that she was not loyal towards her own town: even some of her closest friends shared the doubts on this score. Among her friends in Pisa was a seventeen-year-old widow who was later to be known as Blessed Clara Gambacorti—the daughter of Messer Pietro.

Catherine's stay in Siena was short. The Pope did not yet seem to have any fear of the Sienese republic's forsaking him, and he now sent a message to Catherine that she should go to Lucca and see whether she could strengthen support for his cause in this republic—one of the smallest. Catherine travelled via Pisa, and it was presumably while she was in Lucca that she wrote a long letter to the Pope.

The letter is nothing less than a serious warning to Pope Gregory XI. If he did not shoulder his great responsibilities like a man, the terrible evils from which the Church of Christ was suffering could not be averted. As usual she begins her letter in the name of Jesus Christ and gentle Mary, and addresses herself to the Pope as her dearest and most worthy father in Jesus Christ. For herself she has chosen the title of God's servants' servant and bondwoman—it is reminiscent of the Pope's traditional signature, "the servant of the servants of God". She describes her longing to see him stand as a fruitful tree, loaded with noble fruit because it is planted in good earth. But if the tree is not planted in this good earth, which is self-knowledge— the knowledge that we are nothing, existing only in Him Who Is—the tree will wither. The worm of egoism will eat up the roots, for he who loves himself feeds his soul with mortal pride, the principle and origin of evil in all men, in those who rule and those who must obey. A man who has become the victim of self-love becomes indifferent to sins and faults among his subordinates, for he is afraid to annoy them and make them his enemies. Either he attempts to punish them so half-heartedly that it is useless, or else he does not punish them at all. In other words Catherine tells the Pope openly that in the last resort it is he who carries the whole responsibility for the terrible abuses which are draining the life of the Church, even though according to human reckoning he may be a fine person with many good qualities. Nevertheless it is he who is responsible for the bad shepherds and the treacherous monks whose shameful way of living is undermining the faith of believers. "If the blind leads the blind both fall into the abyss; doctor and patient hurry to hell together." The kind of mercy which is due to self-love and the love of friends, relations and temporal peace, is in fact the worst cruelty, for if a wound is not cleansed when necessary with the red-hot iron and the surgeon's knife, it festers and finally causes death. To apply salves to it may be pleasant for the patient, but it does not heal him. Love your neighbour for Jesus' sake, and for the honour and glory of His sweet name. "Yes, I could wish you were a good and faithful shepherd who was willing to give a thousand lives, if you had them, for the glory of God and the salvation of His creatures. Oh, my beloved father, you who are Christ on earth, imitate the blessed St. Gregory. You can do what he did, for he was a man as you are, and God is always the same as He was. The only thing we lack is hunger for the salvation of our neighbour, and courage. But to arouse this hunger in ourselves, who are nothing more than barren trees, we must graft ourselves to the fruitful tree of the cross. The Lamb who was slaughtered for the sake of our salvation still thirsts—His desire for our salvation is greater than could be shown by His suffering—for His suffering is without end, as is His love."

With regard to the unnatural children who have rebelled against the Pope, she says that Gregory shall have care for the things of the spirit, appoint good shepherds and good rulers in his towns, for it is the bad shepherds and the evil rulers who are the cause of rebellion. "Go forth and carry out with holy zeal the good resolutions you have made. Come back to Rome and start the great crusade.... Have courage, Holy Father, no more indecision, raise the banner of the holy cross, the fragrance of the cross is what will bring you peace." "Forgive me, Father, for all I have said to you. The tongue speaks of that which fills the heart...." Regarding the citizens of Lucca and Pisa, "Send them such fatherly words as the Holy Spirit will inspire you with. Help them as much as you can, and then they will stand fast and be faithful." She tells how she has used all her influence over the people in the two republics to prevent them joining with those who have been guilty of rebellion against the Pope. But they cannot understand why they get no help from him when their enemies press them so hard. Nevertheless they have as yet promised nothing... "Write at once to Gambacorti", is her advice.

Finally she talks of the forthcoming nomination of cardinals, and warns him that he must choose those men who are most worthy, otherwise he need not be surprised if God punishes him. For the Dominican order, which is to have a new Master General, she begs him to choose a pious and virtuous man, "for that is what our order needs". She ends by asking humbly for his blessing and forgiveness for all she has dared to write. "Sweet Jesus, Jesus Love."

This letter is a good example of those which she wrote to Pope Gregory during the following years. To this man, whose self-love was of the amiable sort which made him appear pure among prelates who openly gave themselves up to brutal and disgraceful vices, Catherine talks of holy love, love of God, and Christ's love of mankind, at the same time reminding him that he is Christ's vicar here on earth. And when Gregory at last overcame his egoistic love for his family, his beautiful Provence, and his French countrymen, who seemed so friendly and companionable compared with the stubborn and rebellious Italians, she started the fight against his other outstanding sin—his indecision when dealing with important matters. She cries aloud for manliness and courage. Although Gregory was less worldly than most of the leaders of his time, and much less revengeful than almost all his opponents, she exhorts him to fight for the Church's spiritual riches, and not for its temporal possessions, and advises him to show gentleness and loving forgiveness towards his enemies—towards his friends he showed all too much of both these qualities.

In order to get an idea of Catherine's almost uncanny ability to read the human soul, one has only to compare her letters to Gregory XI with those which she wrote later to his successor, the ascetic Urban VI, whose pure life was spoilt by his lack of mercy—a lack which, as the Pope grew older and his arteries hardened, developed into a psychopathic desire for revenge. She writes to him in quite another tone, begs him to forgive all his enemies, even the schismatics (whom she herself bluntly calls incarnate devils), if they are willing to return in obedience to the lawful head of the Church.

Catherine always wrote in Tuscan, her native tongue. It is impossible to give any proper idea of her style in translation—she has complete mastery over the music of the Italian peasant language, whether she is tenderly admonishing a soul whose welfare means just as much to her as her own, describing her heavenly visions, or threatening with the wrath of God; whether she is advising powerful lords or ordinary people, laymen or monks in cases concerning the fate of people and countries, or private people's everyday difficulties. But because her soul was filled with the love of Christ and belief in Him, her interest for everything human was bathed in faith; to use her own analogy, as the swimmer under the water only sees what is in the water, or what can be seen through the water, so she sees everything through her faith. But in our time and the language of our time the expressions we use for religious emotions and religious experience have become worn out and meaningless; words which in Catherine's language are as shining as new-minted gold, become, when repeated by us, worn-out coins, which have almost gone out of circulation. Catherine speaks of VIRTÙ, and for her the word retains its full weight; it means a vital and powerful pursuit of high ideals. "Virtue" in English has no connection in the popular mind with capability, capacity for goodness; we think rather of virtue as something slightly sour, weak and boring. Catherine's eternal *cri du cœur*, GESÙ DOLCE—GESÙ AMORE, is filled with very different associations from those which occur to us when we read "Sweet Jesus, Jesus Love." A sweet-Jesus, a lady-Jesus; Jesus-Love—a substitute or sublimation of sexual love. In Catherine's language, and when she lived, sweetness was also a name for strength, for all that is good and at the same time gentle and merciful. That goodness must also at times be hard and aggressive, no one knew better than Catherine. For her and her contemporaries, even for the hosts of people who in practice tried to forget or deny it, it was acknowledged that AMORE, love, is fundamentally an expression for the connection between God and the soul of man. Analogously one can speak of AMORE, love, between people—between children and their parents, between man and wife, between lovers, between brothers and sisters, between spiritual relations; and it can be a power of good or evil, according to whether earthly love is in harmony or disharmony with the will of Him who is AUCTOR VITAE—the origin of life. It is perhaps even more difficult for present-day people in Protestant lands to understand her attitude towards the two Popes whom she can in the same letter call Christ-on-earth, the immortal Peter whom Christ has built His Church upon, and advise, command and admonish for their human weaknesses; or she can turn to the Pope like an unhappy little girl to her father, calling him *Babbo*—"Daddy", in Italian baby talk. For her it was no contradiction, beyond the fact that all human relationships are full of contradictions, that Christ had set a vicar over His faithful as long as they live on earth, and that He demands we should show His vicar honour and obedience, even though the vicar may be unworthy to fulfil his mission. No one can know whether the Holy Father has been a holy man until his death—and as it has been put in the hands of men to appoint a man as the Vicar of Christ, it is only to be expected that the voters will all too often vote from impure, mean or cunning motives, for a man who will become an evil to the Church of God on earth. God will nevertheless watch over His Church, raise and restore again what mankind may ruin or soil; it is necessary, for mystical reasons which the saints have partly seen and understood, that the offence should occur. But woe to that person through whom the offence comes. . . .

In Lucca Catherine was received with enthusiasm and honoured as a saint. But the policy of the little state, threatened on all sides by dangerous and powerful enemies, was decided by other factors. Many new affectionate friends joined her circle. At least one—Monna Mellina Balbani—seems to have attached herself to her guest (Catherine had stayed with her) with an all too worldly affection. Catherine wrote to her later and reprimanded her for complaining that she had missed the company of her friend: "I do not wish you to be fond of me or any other person, if your love is not rooted in God." She begs her to take as an example the Very Truth who sought death on the cross, even though He loved His Mother and His disciples so greatly, and the apostles who divided and travelled separately to different parts of the world in order to work for the glory of God and the salvation of souls, although they loved each other and the Blessed Mary so much. Among all those who love God are to be found the bonds of real love, even though they may be separated in the flesh. She must love God and the crucifix, and then she will satisfy her natural hunger to love and be loved.

Here as everywhere where Catherine went, miracles occurred. Once when she lay ill a priest was to bring her the Body of Christ. She lay in bed, unable to move, when the priest came followed by the altar-boys carrying lighted candles, a bell, and all the usual requisites of the ceremonial. But the host the priest carried was unconsecrated—he had suddenly conceived the idea of seeing for himself whether this woman had supernatural instinct. The others who were in the room knelt and worshipped the Lord in the "sacrament", but Catherine made no move, and the priest corrected her because she showed no respect. Then she turned to him and said severely: "Are you not ashamed to come here with an ordinary bit of bread and try to lead all who are here into idolatry?" Overcome with remorse for his blasphemous trick the priest went away, convinced of Catherine's mystical gifts.

But in spite of all the respect and love which were shown to Catherine herself, the citizens of Lucca had presumably already decided that when it suited them they would give up the Pope's cause and attach themselves to Florence and the other rebellious republics.

In the autumn of 1375 John Hawkwood and his mercenaries were once again in the hire of the papal legate, and the Florentines took the offensive. The Florentine army marched into the Papal States and sent a proclamation to the towns which were vassals of the Pope, in which it was stated that Florence sought no advantages for herself, but only wished to help the Italians throw off the yoke of the cruel French lords who, in the name of the Pope, practised injustice and brutality wherever they had power.

In less than a month the whole of Umbria was in rebellion. Città di Castello, Viterbo, Gubbio, Forli, all declared for Florence. In Perugia a relation of the abbot of Marmoutiers had attempted to rape the wife of a distinguished citizen, who to save her honour threw herself out of the window and was killed on the spot. Raging with fury, the Perugians joined the rebels. In less than ten days eight towns were lost to the cause of the Pope.

Catherine had to make a short stay in Pisa on her way home from Lucca. Here she heard that her own Siena, where the Ghibellines had always been in power, had allied itself with Florence. When Fra Raimondo and another monk came and told her that Viterbo in the Romagna had also joined the rebels, she wept. When she saw how discouraged her friends were, she said to them: "It is too early to begin to weep. This is only milk and honey compared with what is to come." What could there be which was worse than the worst? Raimondo asked in fear—he believed firmly that Catherine could see into the future. "Shall belief in Christ be openly denied?" Catherine replied that now they saw how layfolk rose against the Holy Father, but it was not long before they would see the clergy do the same. "When the Pope really begins to reform the morals of the clergy they will rebel and split the Church of Christ." No, there would be no new heresy, there would be schism. And she said to Raimondo and his friend that they would live to see this horror.

But in spite of her dark misgivings, which really did foresee the Great Schism which took place some years later, Catherine wrote to the gonfaloniere (the general) and the elders of Lucca, a very long letter in which she did her best to strengthen their faith in the cause of the Church. She begins with her favourite theme—a man has to come to understand that his life depends on the fact that he believes in his Creator and loves virtue. "You know who said 'I am the Way, the Truth and the Life', and 'he who follows Me walks not in darkness but in light.' And the Church is His bride, the faithful sons of the Church are they who prefer to suffer death a thousand times than to leave it. If you reply that it looks as though the Church must surrender, for it is impossible for it to save itself and its children, I say to you that it is not so. The outward appearance deceives, but look at the inward, and you will find that it possesses a power which its enemies can never possess." God is That Which Is Strong, for all strength and virtue emanate from Him. This strength has not been taken from His bride, and nothing else possesses it. The enemies of the Church, who fight against her, have lost this strength and help; they are as rotten limbs severed from the body; so do not bind yourselves to these rotten limbs. She begs the government of Lucca to stand fast, to continue as they have begun, and to remember that they do not stand alone, they have their brother Pisans with them—and remember, if a father has many children, but only one remains true to him, he leaves all his inheritance to this child. . . .

The Pisans were still loyal. But the league against the papal legates included now the Queen of Naples, Bernabò Visconti and his brother, Florence, Siena and Arezzo; and beside them stood all the rebellious towns in Umbria and the Romagna. . . .

XV

CATHERINE CAME HOME TO SIENA just before Christmas 1375. On December 21 Gregory XI created nine new cardinals in Avignon. When Catherine heard their names she must have understood that her worst fears were to be fulfilled. Seven of the nine cardinals were French—three of them relations of the Pope; one was an Italian and one a Spaniard, Pedro de Luna, who later became the rival Pope Benedict XIII. This was a terrible blow for all the Italians who still remained faithful to the Church; it was chiefly French influence which had undermined all the attempts to get the Pope to return to Rome; and the major cause both of the corruption in the Church and the state of misery which reigned in Italy, was the Popes' "Babylonian captivity" in Avignon.

No new Master General was chosen for the Dominican order. Fra Elias of Toulouse continued in this office, and he ended by joining the rival Pope during the Great Schism. Catherine's wish was not fulfilled: the Pope did not give her order a "wise and virtuous leader". It was a long time since, as a little girl, she used to run out and kiss the paving-stones outside her father's house, where the mendicant monks in their black and white robes had passed. Long ago she had learned that the weeds grew plentifully among the good corn in St. Dominic's garden, and that here too there were far too many trees which never bore good fruit. A thorough weeding and pruning was sadly needed. But after Catherine's death the Dominican order was reformed by her spiritual children, Blessed Raimondo of Capua and Blessed Clara Gambacorti of Pisa.

Even though it had fallen to Catherine's lot to take an active part in the most important questions of the time, she was just as willing as before to do all she could to help every individual soul who asked for help. Some time early in the year 1376 one of her spiritual sons brought his friend Stefano Maconi to her. Neither the young nobleman nor his family had previously taken the slightest interest in the much-talked-of Popolana and her comings and goings. But at this time the Maconi family had become implicated in a quarrel with two families who were much more powerful, the Rinaldini and the Tolomei, and this young man had told Stefano di Corrado Maconi that if he laid his case before Catherine he was sure that she would be able to find a solution—she had already brought about so many reconciliations.

Stefano Maconi tells us that Catherine received him, "not shyly or fearfully like a young girl as I had expected, but like a loving sister whose brother has returned from a long journey". But with her ability to see into men's souls she had immediately discovered the latent beauty in this young man, who in spite of his light-mindedness and his craving for pleasure had kept himself free of gross vices from a natural sensitivity and pureness of mind. But Stefano too was deeply moved by Catherine, and listened with passionate interest to everything she said, seriously and tenderly concerned as she was for his true happiness. He was willing to go to confession at once, and wanted to try to be a good Christian. With regard to the quarrel between his family and the Rinaldini and Tolomei, she said that he must trust in Our Lord and she would do all that was in her power to bring about a peaceful conclusion.

She managed in fact to make Rinaldini and Tolomei promise that on a certain day they would meet Stefano and his father Corrado Maconi, in the church of San Cristoforo, so that they could be reconciled. But when the two Maconi arrived the others did not appear. They intended to insult the Maconi again. Catherine went up and knelt before the high altar: "If they will not listen to me, they will have to listen to Almighty God." She lay motionless in an ecstasy—and in a little while the Tolomei and Rinaldini slunk into the church through two side doors. It seemed to them that the kneeling woman before the altar was surrounded by a strange light. They laid the matter entirely in her hands and a reconciliation was soon brought about.

Stefano now became his "mammina's" dearest son. He spent as much of his time as he could with her, took over his share of her correspondence, and sang her praises to all who would listen to him—he cared nothing that his old companions laughed at him and his unearthly love for the little wraith of a Sister of Penitence. . . .

One day Catherine said to him: "My dearest son, I have good news for you. Your greatest wish shall be fulfilled."

"But, mamma mia," said Stefano, astonished, "I don't know what my greatest wish is——"

"Look into your heart", said Catherine, smiling.

"Really, dearest mamma, I don't think I have any wish except to be near you always."

"And that is exactly what you shall be", said his mother.

For in the meantime much had happened. Catherine knew that she would soon have to go to Florence, to see if she could arrange a reconciliation between the republic and the Pope. Whether she could see that she would continue her journey from Florence to distant Avignon, we do not know. But Stefano Maconi was to be among her travelling companions.

On March 12 Pisa and Lucca had joined the Florentine League, although with certain conditions: they were not bound to take active part in the war against the papacy. The Florentines even tried to get the Romans to desert the Pope, or at least to promise that they would not make further attempts to get him to return from Avignon. The Romans refused. Thereupon Gregory sent ambassadors to Florence in an attempt to reinstate peace. But so ingrained was the man's unfortunate habit of vacillation, and so great his lack of judgment, that at the same time he sent out a bull against the Florentines demanding that they should surrender all the members of the rebellious government into his hands—they were to meet him in Avignon before the end of March. Among those who were to be surrendered in this manner was Niccolò Soderini, who had been Catherine's friend since her first visit to Florence. He had been in the government about two months.

Catherine was forced to send the Pope a new letter. In it she writes to the head of the Church even more forcibly of the cause of peace. To her most holy and most honoured father in Christ his useless little daughter Catherine, God's servant and slave, directs her eloquent and passionate appeal—there must be peace between him and his children. It is perhaps necessary to defend and regain the Church's temporal goods, but it is more necessary to defend what is even more precious. The Church's treasure is the blood of Christ, and this treasure was not given for temporal riches but for the redemption of men's souls. First and foremost it is his duty to win back to the Church all the lambs who constitute the riches of the Church. It is true that the Church can never be poor, for Christ's blood can never be wasted, but it is about to lose all the ornaments which are given it through its children's virtue and obedience. But if he does his best, he will be innocent before God and men; he must win them back to the fold with the weapons of gentleness and love. He must show the desire for peace and then he will regain all his rights, both spiritual and temporal.

"My soul, which is united with God, burns with thirst for your salvation, for the reformation of the Church, and the happiness of the whole world. But it seems to me that God reveals no other remedy than peace. Peace, peace, for the love of Christ crucified, and do not let your children's ignorance, blindness and presumption hinder you." She repeats her warning: if the Pope allows himself to give his allies, in order to win their friendship, those prelates and shepherds they demand, instead of the best and most worthy, the reasons for war will be multiplied. "Oh, do not do such things, for the sake of Jesus' love and for the sake of your own salvation."

Catherine sent yet one more letter to Avignon—this time the bearer of the letter was Neri di Landoccio. Again she begs for peace, for good shepherds, for the correction of the evil ones who, like wolves, devour Christ's lambs. He gave His life for the glory of God and the salvation of the world, "and you, His Vicar, should do the same in His stead. Is it not the custom that the lieutenant follows his captain's example?"

After this she wrote a letter defending the cause of the rebellious Florentines: "I beg you from Christ crucified, and I demand that you do me this favour, overcome your wickedness by your goodness." More and more often Catherine's letters express her conviction that she, because she is the mouthpiece of her crucified Lord, is free to write: "I demand—" and that "you are to do as I advise you." "Oh, Father, we are yours, and I know that almost all of them realise that what they have done is wrong. Let us admit that there is no excuse for them, but it seemed to them that they could not act otherwise, because of all the injustice they have suffered and all the indignities they have had to tolerate at the hands of bad shepherds and rulers. They have been infected by the shameful way of life of these men (and you know well whom I mean)—these men who are devils in human shape, and they [the Florentines] fell as Pilate did when he condemned Christ because he was afraid of His power, from despicable cowardice. They have persecuted you to protect their cities. Mercy, Father, I beg for mercy for them. You must not look on their ignorance and pride, but draw your children to you with gentle love and kindness, with mild reproaches. Oh, Your Holiness, give us peace, we are your unhappy children who have gone astray. I say to you who are Christ on earth, from Christ in Heaven, do this without delay and without wrath, and they will run to meet you, full of remorse for their mistakes, and lay their heads on your bosom."

Remove to Rome, she says to the Pope, and raise the banner of the crusade, and you will see the wolves change to lambs. "Peace, peace, peace ... and if you consider that justice demands revenge, strike me and let me suffer all the tortures and agonies you wish—even death. I believe it is the infection of my sins which is largely the cause of this misery and anarchy, so punish your little daughter as much as you will. Oh, Father, I am dying of sorrow and cannot die."

Catherine had also written to Niccolò Soderini, and tackled the problem from the other side—exhorted the Florentine government to seek forgiveness from the Pope and be reconciled with him at any price. It is not our affair to judge the bad shepherds, God will reward them according to their deserts. And however corrupt they may be they have been consecrated to give us the sacraments. Catherine did not believe there was any salvation outside the Church.

On March 20 the army of the anti-papal league captured Bologna. But the following week the papal troops under Sir John Hawkwood took Casena, massacred the men and gave the women to the soldiers. At the head of a mercenary army of savage men aided by bloodhounds followed Cardinal Robert of Geneva, who later became the rival pope, Clement.

At the same time ambassadors from Florence appeared before the Pope in Avignon and declared, in the name of the republic, that the political leaders called by the Pope were unable to come, some of them being at the time in prison. And Florence was not willing to give herself up to the Pope unconditionally; the republic had already suffered too much injustice at the hands of the Pope's corrupt legates for that. The Pope replied by putting Florence under an interdict, and excommunicated the Eight War Leaders and twenty-one of the town's most prominent citizens—among them, Soderini. Donato Barbadori, one of the ambassadors, heard this terrible doom. He turned towards the crucifix hanging over the Pope's throne: "Look down on me, God of my salvation, and help me; do not forsake me, for my father and my mother have forsaken me."

In the Middle Ages, when a town was put under an interdict, its citizens became outlaws in all Christian countries. Competitors could take the opportunity to ruin its commerce, and to imprison or enslave its citizens, wherever they might find them. "Everywhere in the world the Florentines were seized by the governments and relieved of their property in the countries where they had business connections", writes Raimondo. "They had to seek reconciliation with the Pope through the intervention of persons whom they knew the Pope would listen to." He means Catherine.

Catherine was willing. In preparation for her mission she sent Raimondo and two priests of her spiritual family to Avignon with a new letter, in the same tone as those she had sent before. She demands reform within the Church—let the weeds be taken up by the root, the evil shepherds and rulers whose rottenness spread disease through the garden be thrown out, and pure, sweet flowers planted instead. She demands that the Pope should return to Rome, that the crusade should be started and peace made with the Christian rebels. Finally she recommends the bearers of the letter, her sons: "they are messengers from Christ Crucified and me."

On the night of April 1st she had a vision which she describes in a letter to Raimondo. Christ appeared to her and let her partake of His secrets in such a way that she did not know whether her soul was in her body or beyond it. And she was filled with an indescribable joy because she understood. She saw that it was necessary for Holy Church to suffer persecution, but she saw also that a new youth would follow afterwards. The Sweet Truth reminded her of these words in the Gospel: "It must needs be that offences come", but also "woe to him through whom they come." To rid His Bride of the thorns which stung her flesh and caused it pain, He had made himself a whip of evil men, as He had once made a whip of thin strings—with this He would drive out the unclean, greedy, miserly and proud merchants who sold the gifts of the Holy Spirit. But as her desire to see all mankind enter the wound in Jesus' heart spread like a great fire in Catherine, Christ allowed her to see that great multitudes streamed into the wound in His side, led by His saints. Among them she recognised her father, St. Dominic. Then Christ laid His cross on her shoulder and put an olive branch in her hand. "Go and say to them that I announce a great joy." "And I rejoiced, and said like Simeon, 'Lord, now lettest thou thy servant depart in peace.'" But what tongue can speak of the secrets of God? Not hers. So she can do nothing but seek God's glory, the salvation of men and the regeneration of the Holy Church, and by the grace and power of the Holy Spirit put up with this until death. "Rejoice therefore when you suffer affliction, and love, love, love each other."

Before Easter she wrote to the Florentines and offered to be mediator between them and the Pope. As Raimondo had sent news which gave them great hope, they joyfully accepted her offer. At the beginning of May Catherine and her companions came for the second time to Florence.

The Florentines accepted the interdict. No Masses were celebrated, a few priests were given authority to give the sacraments to the dying and to baptise babies, but otherwise there was an end of all pertaining to divine service. But the afflicted people went through a real religious awakening. Processions of penitents went through the streets scourging themselves while they sang Misereres. Some of the young nobles formed themselves into a brotherhood to devote themselves to works of mercy and good deeds. And Catherine was received as the only person who could bring them hope. . . .

The Florentines became so pious that their rivals said that the whole thing was merely an exhibition of humility by which they hoped to make an advantageous peace with the Pope. It is true enough that the material results of the interdict were so annihilating for the merchant republic that they had to find a solution as soon as possible. Before the end of May Catherine and her friends had already started on the long journey to Avignon. In the company were her faithful friends, Lisa, Alessia, Cecca and her "youngest son", Stefano Maconi, besides several others of her spiritual family. The Florentines promised to send ambassadors after her who should act on behalf of the town according to Catherine Benincasa's advice. The Signoria of Florence, the government of the proudest of the Italian republics, had given the power to decide all matters of vital importance for its future greatness and well-being to a young woman who was regarded as a saint.

XVI

CATHERINE ARRIVED IN AVIGNON on June 18. The last part of
the journey had been made in a little boat which carried her
and her companions up the Rhône. Among the great crowds
which awaited her on the quay were Fra Raimondo, Fra Giovanni Tantucci and her beloved son, Neri di Landoccio. But
neither Raimondo, who met her, nor Stefano Maconi, who
had travelled with her, has told us what Catherine thought
when she looked for the first time on the town of the Pope
beside a river in France. Avignon, behind its great walls, was
one of the most strongly fortified towns of the time; towers,
peaks and spires rose as though aspiring to heaven. Just beside
the cathedral, Notre Dame des Doms, loomed the great papal
castle, fortress and palace in one. To this day the old buildings
stand proudly in their beauty and their might, a gigantic mon-
ument to one of the darkest and most fateful interludes in the
long history of the Catholic Church.

But the Italians had seen plenty of beautiful and magnificent buildings in their own country. What seems to us to-day
to be the romantic inheritance of a time of terrible cruelty
and warlike passions, but also a time of creative activity and
love of beauty unequalled in the history of Europe, was for
Catherine the everyday background of her extraordinary life,
spent in intimate commerce with the invisible world and in
hard work in the world of men and women. Perhaps her large
and brilliant eyes dwelt on the buildings on the other side of
the Rhône with deep emotion; at the other end of the famous
bridge of Avignon the watch tower of the King of France

lifted its proud head. Yes, there was France; Villeneuve-lez-Avignon, the kingdom of the French king, lay in this country. The country of the enemy, since French influence had always been used to keep the Pope prisoner in this beautiful land of Provence. Some of the French cardinals lived there on the other side of the river.

The Italians were taken to the lodgings which the Pope had prepared for Catherine of Siena. They were in a palace which had belonged to a cardinal who had recently died. But Catherine could find herself a room which suited her ascetic taste, and there was an oratory to which she could retire to pray. In the course of the work which she now had before her she would need ceaseless support from her heavenly Bridegroom, who had led His bride far from the dyer's house in Fontebranda to the foot of the throne of His Vicar on earth. And the fragile and humble young woman was to speak to this Vicar with the authority of Jesus Christ.

Two days after her arrival in Avignon Catherine was received by the Pope. Raimondo was present to act as interpreter, for Catherine spoke only her native Tuscan language, and the Frenchman, Latin. Catherine understood enough of the language to be able to read the breviary, but she could not manage to conduct a conversation in Latin. But Gregory was so deeply impressed by the sound common sense and the deep spiritual insight of this woman who had sent him such outspoken letters, that before the conversation was over he had laid the whole matter of the Florentines in her hands. He asked her to realise that he too was filled with a deep longing to put an end to the terrible war, but "do not forget the Church's dignity."

But the ambassadors from Florence, who were to follow immediately after Catherine, did not appear. On July 26th she wrote to the Eight War Lords and advised them to prove that they really desired to put an end to the war with the papacy. The fact that they had recently put a tax on the clergy looked to her like a step backwards on the road to peace. "I have spoken with the Holy Father, and he has listened to me with great mildness. . . . He has shown that he truly loves peace and that as a good father he is willing to overlook the offences which his sons have committed against him, but it is necessary for the sons to humiliate themselves so that the father can forgive them completely. I cannot tell you how happy I was when after a long conversation with me he said that he was willing to receive his children and to do what I thought best." But she is astonished that the ambassadors have not arrived—nothing can be concluded without them. So they must come without delay.

Gregory said to her in one of their conversations: "The Florentines are making fools of both you and me. Either they will not send any ambassadors at all, or else when they come you will see that they have not the necessary authority." He was right. From July 6 a new government had ruled in Florence, and this government did not wish for peace. They sent three ambassadors merely to cover up their true intentions.

In the meantime Gregory too had succumbed to Catherine's power over the souls of men. He was completely convinced that this woman was one of God's saints. When she spoke openly to him of the abuses practised by priests and prelates, which caused such terrible ruin within the Church, she also condemned the luxury in the papal court and the vices which flourished under the very eyes of the Pope. Here where all the heavenly virtues should flower she smelled the stink of hell's putrefaction. Gregory interrupted her: "How have you, who have been here such a short time, got such knowledge of all that goes on here?" Catherine's attitude towards the Vicar of Christ was one of the deepest humility, but now she straightened up suddenly, looked him in the face, and spoke as boldly as one prince to another. "To the glory of Almighty God I am bound to say that I smelled the stink of the sins which flourish in the papal court while I was still at home in my own town more sharply than those who have practised them, and do practise them, every day here."

Rumours about the saintly Sienese woman naturally caused curiosity in the papal court. Among the most curious were the women who swarmed everywhere where they had no business to be—sisters and nieces of cardinals, distant relations and concubines. Some believed firmly in her and willingly allowed her to advise them so that they might become better Christians. Others made no secret of the fact that they were afraid of her influence. Still others made fun of the whole matter. Some simply thought it was all very exciting and crowded to her chapel to stare when she lay in ecstasy. The sister of the Pope, the Duchess of Valentinois, was so much moved by the sight that from that time onwards she honestly and truly tried to put the whole of her soul into her prayers. But young Alys de Turenne, who was married to the Pope's nephew, stuck a large needle in Catherine's foot to see whether it was true that she felt nothing. When Catherine regained consciousness the wound gave her such pain that she was not able to stand on the foot for several days.

Catherine had the gift (which some other saints have had) of recognising a soul which was living in mortal sin through the physical sensation of a smell of decay. Once a distinguished lady came to visit her; she seemed full of respect and godliness, but Catherine would not look at her and turned her face away each time the lady came near. Raimondo reproved her for being so impolite, but Catherine said to him: "If you had smelled the stink of her sins you would have done the same." A little later Raimondo learned that this "lady" was a whore and living in concubinage with a priest.

Three of the most learned prelates at the court came to examine and try to confound this ignorant woman whose influence over the Pope seemed so dangerous for French interests. At first they questioned her most arrogantly about her mission for the Florentines—was it really true that the government had sent her, as she made out? Could it be possible that there was no man who could act for them in such an important affair, and that they had to turn to an unimportant little woman like herself? Politely and patiently Catherine explained how it had come about that she had been sent, and against their will the prelates felt the influence of her charm. But they continued, asked her about her way of life, her visions, her fasting—and how could she be certain that it was not the devil who was ensnaring her? The discussion passed onto the most difficult theological questions, and Fra Giovanni, who was present, and who had himself taken a couple of doctor's degrees, tried to add a word here and there. The guests snapped at him: "Let her answer for herself, she does it much better than you." The discussion lasted from Nones until night fell, and by the time the learned gentlemen said good-bye to her they had become convinced that the "insignificant little woman" had clearer insight into spiritual things than any doctor of theology. As they were upright and really learned men they went to the Pope and told him what had happened.

She made other friends among members of the Roman Curia. One of them was Vice-Chancellor Bartolommeo Prignano, Archbishop of Acerenza. He was a model of virtue and righteousness, passionately desirous of weeding out the corruption and luxurious way of living in the Church. An excellent man in a subordinate position—his hardness and lust for revenge only became a menace to his honest attempts at reform when he succeeded Gregory XI as Pope Urban VI.

While the Florentine ambassadors still failed to appear, Catherine was received several times by the Pope and had plenty of opportunity of talking to him of the things which lay nearest her heart—his return to Rome and the call to the whole of Christendom for a new crusade. Gregory had occasionally talked of his longing to move the Holy See back to the town of St. Peter, and those who surrounded him saw with horror that he became more and more convinced that the Holy Spirit called him through the mouth of Catherine. The Pope is also Bishop of Rome, and they remembered that a little while before, when the Holy Father had reproached a bishop for his absence from his bishopric, the bishop had replied, "And you, Most Holy Father, why do you not return to your bride who is so rich and so beautiful?" The Pope had appeared greatly moved.

But Catherine, who could see into men's souls, knew more. Once when the Pope, who was extremely nervous, had asked her opinion on the matter—as though he did not know it from her letters—she replied humbly that it was not seemly for her to give advice to the Vicar of Christ. He answered, extremely irritably, that he did not ask for her advice, he asked her to tell him God's will. Catherine replied: "Who knows God's will so well as your Holiness, for have you not bound yourself by a vow—" Greatly shaken, Gregory stared at the young woman. He had made a vow that he would return to Rome if he were ever chosen to be Pope—it was while he was still a cardinal. But he had never told a living soul. From that moment he knew that he would have to leave Avignon. But he knew too how many hindrances he would have to overcome before he could do so. It was an agony for his nervous nature, which was so afraid of wounding the feelings of his friends and relations.

From Villeneuve-lez-Avignon, where Catherine had been persuaded to make a short visit to the wife of the Duke of Anjou in their castle, she wrote to Gregory and begged him not to listen to the cardinals who tried to prevent him from going to Rome. "I beg you from Christ crucified that it may please Your Holiness to act promptly. The more quickly you do it, the less you will suffer.... If God is with you none will be against you."

At length the Florentine ambassadors arrived. But when Catherine, in the presence of Raimondo, told them that the Pope had appointed her to negotiate with them for peace they replied shamelessly that they had no authority to treat with her, they had come to Avignon to speak with the Pope, not with a woman.... Nevertheless Catherine tried still to intercede for the Florentines. The Pope appointed two French cardinals to negotiate with them. But in spite of the terrible consequences of the interdict on the commerce of the republic, the ambassadors were not sent in good faith. The negotiations broke down, and in September the Florentine ambassadors were asked to leave Avignon. Home again in Florence they gave an account of their mission from their own point of view, and Florence's Signoria decided to continue the war to suppress the Church's temporal power. They now tried to strengthen the anti-papal league by winning the support of Venice and Genoa.

So now Catherine's sole work was to get the Pope to remove to Rome and start the crusade. She had won the Duke of Anjou over to the cause, so that he had promised to be one of the military leaders if the crusade were set on foot; and from his castle she wrote also to his brother, King Charles of France, to persuade him to join.

A final attempt was made to get the Pope to change his mind; the French cardinals induced a person who was considered a saint to write and warn him that if he went to Rome he would certainly die. Gregory sent the letter on to Catherine, who called it the work of a devil in human shape, and with regard to the danger of being poisoned if he came to Rome, she remarked rather tartly that poison can be bought everywhere—"there is certainly just as much poison in Avignon as in Rome."

On September 13, a day or two after Catherine had started on her journey to Italy, Gregory left Avignon—for ever. He had taken Catherine's advice and left suddenly, taking with him all the cardinals except six. The French cardinals in his retinue wept, and his relations who remained behind wailed and lamented. The Pope's old father, Count Guillaume de Beaufort, knelt at the city gates, in despair at the departure of his son. Pope Gregory passed him without a word. . . .

On October 2 he went on board the ship which was to take him from Marseilles to Genoa. The Pope wept, his French followers wept and lamented, but there was no way back. Jesus Christ's words to Catherine many years before, when He said to His bride that He would use weak women as his ambassadors to the proud and powerful men of this world, had come true in a manner which makes Catherine of Siena's destiny astonishing in the history of the world.

XVII

CATHERINE AND HER COMPANIONS appear to have done most of the journey on foot. But each time she came to a town and stayed the night the people crowded to see this Sister of Penitence who had got the Pope to break out of his Babylonian captivity. Raimondo tells us that they were mobbed in Toulon by crowds who could not contain their curiosity, but also by people who hoped that she might be able to help them. An unhappy mother broke into Catherine's room in the hostelry and laid her dying baby on the virgin's lap. It recovered instantly.

But when she finally set foot again on Italian soil, it seemed as though the holy joy which Catherine's friends speak of so often was coloured by a natural human feeling of happiness: she shouted with joy at the sight of the earth covered with red flowers, or the milling life of an ant-heap. Everything our Creator has made is equally wonderful. "These tiny ants have proceeded from His thought just as much as I, it caused Him just as much trouble to create the angels as these animals and the flowers on the trees." Passionately as Catherine longed for the salvation of every human soul, she loved her own town of Siena and all the lands where her own Italian people lived, with a healthy, uncomplicated passion.

North of Genoa she went through a little town called Varazze, which had been almost depopulated during the plague. Varazze had been the birthplace of Jacopo de Voragine, the author of *The Golden Legend*, which was the favourite book of the Middle Ages. Catherine advised a handful of the citizens who had survived the epidemic to build a chapel to his honour; they would then be freed from the plague. They did so and since then the plague has never returned to Varazze.

The company of travellers was forced to remain a while in Genoa as one after another of them was taken ill. Madonna Orietta Scotti received them hospitably in her palace and had the best doctors of the town brought to those who were ill. But Neri di Landoccio had a very bad attack; he had high fever and such terrible internal pains that he could neither lie down nor sit, but crept on all fours from one bed to another "as though he were trying to escape from his sufferings". Stefano Maconi and Neri had become close friends—another proof that egoistic jealousy did not exist among those who loved Catherine. Stefano was terribly worried, and begged their "mamma" not to let Neri die so far from home and be "buried in a strange land". But it seemed as though Catherine intended to leave Neri in the hands of the doctors, and they gave no hope that he would live. So Stefano went to their mother again, and Catherine promised to pray for Neri the following morning when she went to Communion. And when she wakened from her ecstasy she could tell Stefano, with a smile, that God had promised to make Neri well again. But when, the following day, Stefano himself lay in bed with a high fever and an unbearable headache, Catherine came to his bedside at once and simply commanded the fever to depart. Immediately the fever left him.

We learn from a letter which Catherine wrote to her mother that Don Giovanni Tantucci and Fra Bartolommeo Dominici also had the same illness. Monna Lapa longed desperately for her daughter, who had now been away from her for months—and so far away, in a strange and enemy country, God knows in what terrible and strange dangers: naturally the old mother was wild with anxiety. So she got someone to write to Catherine for her. The daughter's reply is most touching, childishly respectful and tender—but nevertheless one cannot help wondering whether poor Lapa was as greatly consoled by the letter as she felt in duty bound to appear, when she received the epistle.

Four of Catherine's letters to her mother have been preserved, and the key-word to them all is patience—the virtue which Catherine has called the very marrow of piety, but which her hasty mother obviously lacked natural talent for. In her letter from Genoa she greets her beloved mother in the sweet Jesus Christ and tells her how greatly she longs to see in her a true mother, not only of her body, but of her soul. "I think that if you loved my soul more than my body all exaggerated tenderness in you would die, and you would not suffer so much when you lack my presence in the flesh. You would find consolation, and you would be able to bear the sorrow I cause you for the glory of God, when you thought that I was seeking grace and strength for my soul in working for the glory of God." She reminds her of Mary, the loving mother, who for the glory of God and the salvation of mankind gave her beloved Son to death on the cross—and was later left by the disciples who had to go out on her Son's errands. "I know that you wish me to obey the will of God. It was His will that I should go, my absence was ordained by the secret plans of Providence, and has not been without the most valuable results." The length of her absence was not caused by the will of man, but the will of God, and if anyone says anything else it is a lie. "Remember what you did for temporal gain when you let your children go far from you to win riches, and now that it is to win eternal life you suffer so much that you say you will die if I do not reply at once." It is because the flesh in which she has clothed Catherine is more dear to her than her soul, which her child received from God. But beyond the consolation of religion Catherine can finally console her mother with the fact that they are already on the way home, and if it had not been for all the sickness among the company they would have been home before.

But Stefano Maconi's mother also longed impatiently for her son and worried about him just as much as Lapa did for her daughter. And presumably Corrado Maconi's wife was not so used as Lapa to seeing her children going their own ways far from home and loving parents. Catherine replied to a letter from Stefano's mother, calling the woman who could easily have been her own mother, her "daughter". She demands no less of her than that she must overcome her natural maternal love which wants to possess her children for its own material reasons. "Children, and other creatures, must only be loved out of love for Him who created them, not from self-love or love for the children. You must never offend God for their sake.... A mother who loves her children in the wrong, worldly way, often says, 'I have nothing against my children serving God, but they must serve the world too.' ... Such people try to make laws and rules for the Holy Spirit." As consolation Catherine assures his mother that she has taken good care of Stefano and will continue to do everything she can for him until her last hour. "You, his mother, bore him once; I shall give him and you, and all your family, a new birth in ceaseless prayer, tears and zeal for your salvation."

Such are the paradoxes of Christianity that it is completely possible that both mothers agreed that Catherine wrote nothing but the purest truth. But to live and feel in accordance with what one knows to be the truth, when it becomes difficult and painful, is another matter: our hearts, which are of flesh and blood, refuse to obey. When Catherine went to Rome for the last time Lapa accompanied her, although she was so old, and it is good to know that the mother was not parted from her daughter in the last days of Catherine's life. But before

Stefano Maconi could join those who were gathered round Catherine's deathbed, he had many difficulties with his mother, who would not let him leave Siena.

In spite of the illness which prevailed among her travelling companions the people of Genoa crowded to the Palazzo Scotti to see Catherine. By now she was far too famous to enjoy anything resembling the peace of private life—her wasted body, and her soul which now was only able to rest with the Beloved when she was in ecstasy, had never a moment's peace from importunate guests who expected her to cope with their sorrows and difficulties, or who came merely to satisfy their curiosity, filled with the very human wish to be able to say, "I too have met this celebrity whom everyone talks about." In spite of the fact that one after another of her secretaries, Neri, Stefano, Bartolommeo, became unable to work because of illness, a stream of letters issued from Catherine's lodging—with good advice, encouragement, spiritual direction, or in reply to letters which she had received. The woman who had once had no other wish than to live the life of a hermit was now as occupied with the problems of her time as any ruling queen, and obediently she took upon her thin shoulders everything which she knew her Bridegroom laid upon her.

She considered herself His unworthy little servant, sinful, secretly full of self-love, which she considered to be the root of all the misery of the world. What she had achieved, God had achieved in spite of having to use such a miserable tool— for she could not possibly doubt that great things had been achieved by her as a tool in the hand of God.

Late one evening a man dressed as an ordinary priest came to Palazzo Scotti and asked to be taken to Catherine Benincasa's room. He entered, and Catherine fell at the feet of the Vicar of Christ. The Pope told her to stand up, and late into the night the two of them sat alone talking. When Gregory left her he had been "strengthened and edified".

He had landed at Genoa after a stormy journey from Marseilles—the crossing had been so bad that it had taken sixteen days. In Genoa Gregory was received with bad tidings; from Rome came the news of a rising, and the Florentine armies had beaten those of the Pope in several battles. The Doge of Genoa had refused to join the league, and had promised friendly neutrality. The French cardinals did everything they could to persuade Gregory to go back to Avignon. They interpreted the storm they had met at sea as a warning sent from God, and they exaggerated the rumours of the various misfortunes as much as they possibly could.

Gregory called together a council, and was on the point of giving in to his cardinals. But he knew that Catherine was in town, and his conscience would not allow him to make any decision before he had asked her advice. In order not to cause any scandal the head of the Church, immediately after the council, put on a simple priest's robe and went alone to the Sienese woman to let her decide his fate and the fate of the Church for many years to come.

On October 29th he sailed to Leghorn, and on December 5th he landed in Corneto in the Papal States. He decided to remain there for Advent and to celebrate his first Christmas in his own kingdom in Corneto.

XVIII

CATHERINE TOO EMBARKED in Genoa for Leghorn, the port of
Pisa. She too almost suffered shipwreck on the way, for there
was a storm and raging seas. Her companions and even the
pilot on board were afraid, but Catherine remained as calm as
usual: "What are you so afraid of? Do you think that you
have to save yourselves?" and to the pilot: "Turn over the rud-
der in God's name, and sail with the wind heaven sends us."
The next morning they came safe and sound into harbour
and the monks and priests sang a *Te Deum*.

In Pisa Catherine once again had to make a stay of some
weeks. While he was in Leghorn the Pope had received Pietro
Gambacorti and the ambassadors from Lucca, who tried to
negotiate a peace with Florence and the league. But the news
from the fronts regarding the league's war against him had
angered Pope Gregory so much that the negotiators of peace
had not much of a chance.

In Pisa Catherine was joined by her mother and Tommaso
della Fonte. As soon as she knew that her daughter was on
her way home Monna Lapa was willing to face any danger
and to make the long journey so that she might be as soon as
possible with the child she had missed so terribly.

It was probably from Pisa that Catherine wrote to the Pope
in Corneto to try to give him courage. She begs him to show
firmness, strength and patience; Christ has chosen him to be
His Vicar, to work and fight for His honour, for the souls of
men and for the rebirth of the Church. "You know well, Most
Holy Father, that when you took the Church to be your wife

you agreed to suffer opposition, pain and antagonism for her sake." "Peace, peace, Most Holy Father, and may Your Holiness be pleased to receive your sons who have displeased their father. Your goodness will triumph over your pride and wickedness... and Father, no more war of any kind.... I hope that Our Lord will work so strongly in you that your and my desires may be fulfilled. I desire nothing in life but the glory of God, your peace, the re-birth of the Holy Church and a life of grace for all God's creatures." For the wretched town which has always been the beloved daughter of His Holiness (she must mean Pisa) she begs for peace and forgiveness. "They know that they have sinned, but the force of circumstances made them do things which they now regret." Finally she begs for his blessing for herself and her great family.

But it was not until 1377 that she finally came home again to Siena.

Stefano Maconi had been sent on ahead. Among other things he was to arrange a *ridotto*—a little room which was to serve as a chapel for Catherine. Catherine had brought with her from Avignon the Pope's permission to have Mass said for her at a portable altar, wherever she might be staying. The three priests who were always to be among her travelling companions were now Fra Raimondo, Fra Bartolommeo Dominici and Dom Giovanni Tantucci.

The knowledge that Siena was now in collaboration with the enemies of the Pope must have cast a shadow over her joy at meeting her old friends again. During the absence of his "mamma" Francesco Malavolti had let himself be tempted back to his old sinful ways. She wrote to him and begged him tenderly to think of his true happiness.

On January 17, 1377, Pope Gregory XI made his entry into Rome, riding on a white mule. The Romans, who had remained loyal to the Vicar of Christ in spite of all the attempts to win them over to the other side, and in spite of all the misery they had suffered at the hands of his unworthy deputies, were wild with delight. Showers of flowers and confetti greeted the true lord of the town on his arrival. Throughout the night there was dancing in the streets, which shone from the light of thousands of torches and lamps. Even the French cardinals in the Pope's retinue were moved....

But the war continued, and news of towns which had been conquered and plundered with orgies of murder and cruelty streamed in from all over Italy. Early in the spring Catherine was in the new convent, Santa Maria degli Angeli, which she had founded in the old castle of Belcaro—the gift to her of Nanni di SerVanni—and from Belcaro she again wrote to the Pope in Rome. She compares him with a cellarer, because he has been allotted the keys of the Church which administers the blood of God's Son; and with a mother, because it is he who has to feed all the children of the Holy Church with the milk of divine love. And therefore peace, peace. The mild and amiable Word of God did not let Himself be hindered by our ingratitude, so, for the sake of Christ's love, follow in His footsteps. It seems to her that the devil has this world in his power, not by his own will, for he is powerless, but through our help because we obey him. The evil aroma arising from the degenerate priests and monks, and the wars which are waged by Christians against Christians, are the same as war against God. So cleanse the Church, create peace, think of the spiritual and not the temporal gains, she says to the Pope yet once again. She longs to see him, but affairs which are of importance for the Church prevent her. Peace, peace, for the sake of the love of the crucified Christ, and not war; that is the only solution.

From Belcaro she wrote a letter on Maundy Thursday to all the prisoners in Siena. To her beloved sons in sweet Jesus Christ,

Catherine, God's servants' servant and slave, speaks of our sins against God—not of their greater or smaller sins against the community. According to her way of seeing it, what they need is to be reconciled and at peace with their Creator, and this they need neither more nor less than she herself needs it, or the Pope needs it, or any of the great ones of this world, to whom she has written and is to write later, with always the same message: Be converted. Her letter to the prisoners seems to be full of an even deeper concern for their salvation; it is written with even more earnestness and a more urgent wording than usual. "Sin has caused the death of Christ. God's Son did need to follow the way of the cross, for the poison of sin was not in Him, and He possesses eternal life, but we wretches had lost it because of our sins, and between God and us was war." Rebellion against their Creator had made men weak and sickly, so that they could not swallow the bitter medicine which was essential for the cure of their faults. God had to give up His Son; His Word and His endless mercy made the divine nature one with our human nature. Christ came to suffer that we might be healed; our doctor was our Saviour who healed us with His blood. She compares Christ with a wet-nurse who swallows the bitter medicine which her infant is too small and too weak to take—the infant must take it through the nurse's milk. In the milk of divine love, we, the poor children of God, receive the bitter medicine which is Christ's suffering on the cross, the only remedy for our mortal illness—sin. She compares Christ, too, with a knight who has ridden out to fight for us; for our sake He came down from Heaven to fight and triumph over the devil. The crown of thorns is His helmet, His flayed flesh His mail, the nails in His hands and feet His gauntlet and spurs. So we should follow our Knight and take new courage in our trials and difficulties. "Bathe in the blood of Jesus Christ. . . . Then you will be able to bear your misery with patience, for in the memory of this blood all that is bitter becomes sweet, and all burdens are lightened."

Obviously the communities of the Middle Ages had to protect themselves against crime. The punishments which the criminals were given were often brutal and cruel—imprisonment for a fixed period was as yet unknown: when people were thrown into prison they lay there to await their sentence. They could be condemned to pay fines and damages, to be outlawed or banished, or to physical punishment such as whipping, torture or death. But although most people accepted the official cruelty as the fitting reward for criminals, they hoped at the same time that the criminals would be converted and escape eternal punishment. Even victims of brutal crimes usually felt horror when their enemies refused to receive the Church's help and went to their death hating God and man. But even the most terrible criminals were offered spiritual help—every government regarded it as a duty to give priests and monks free admission to the cells of the condemned and to follow them on their last journey to the place of execution. Even the two robbers whom Catherine's spirit followed on their journey in the cart while her body lay unconscious in the home of Alessia Saracini, were accompanied by priests who tolerated the sinners' blasphemy and curses during the slow torture, and received a princely reward when the two condemned men gave in to the prayers of the ecstatic virgin, and immediately turned towards the priests, willing to be reconciled with their Creator before they went to meet Him.

The Riformati government in Siena was just as sensitive about its worthiness as most governments. They had therefore condemned the young Niccolò di Toldo of Perugia to execution because this offspring of a foreign nobility had spoken flippantly and derisively in his cups of the citizens who governed in Siena. But Tommaso Caffarini had free access to the boy in prison and tried to reconcile him with his bitter fate. Niccolò refused point blank to be reconciled. He was wild with rage and despair over the crazy justice of this wretched government who wanted to take his life for such a trifle. No, he would not make his confession—he had not confessed since as a young boy he had for the first and last time received Holy Communion; and he would not go to Communion now, he would not bow himself to the will of God if it were God's will to take his life from him in the very flower of his youth. . . .

So Catherine went to him. She wrote to Fra Raimondo in Rome of this matter, certainly the best-known, and the most often misunderstood, in the strange life of Catherine. It is the story of how a woman, still young, of unusually attractive personality, tames a passionate and despairing young man who rebels against his hard fate and against all the powers of heaven and earth which have caused it. But Catherine had already tamed so many wild and despairing men, and what she did for Niccolò she would have done for any soul whose future in eternity wavered in the balance between Heaven and hell. Consciously or unconsciously di Toldo had perhaps been influenced by the knowledge that his guest was the young woman who by sheer spiritual strength had moved the papal seat from Avignon back to Rome; or it may have been the aura of holiness which surrounded this girl, both mother and sister to any and everyone in the world who was in need. We know the story of his conversion solely from Catherine's description, and she saw in it only the mystery of God's grace, and the cleansing power of Christ's blood. What she writes to Raimondo is a song of praise to the heart of God's Son.

"O heart, O cup which runs over and intoxicates and satisfies the desire of all love! You give joy, you throw light over reason, you fill our minds and capture them so that it is impossible to think of anything else, to understand or to love anything else but the good and gentle Jesus. O blood, O fire, love without end, how my soul would rejoice if I saw you [Raimondo] annihilated in it! I wish you to be as one who scoops up water with a ladle to pour it out over others. Yes, pour the water of holy desire over the heads of your brothers who are united with us in the body of the Church ... and beware of the spells of the devil, for I know that he would like to prevent you." On various occasions before Catherine had warned Raimondo against a certain weakness in his nature. She tells him of her meeting with Niccolò to rouse his courage in all situations, however frightening, and his continued perseverance, if necessary until he sees blood flowing—his own or another's—blood which will be spilled from tender and loving desire.

"Now I know that I shall never again flinch or rest. I have held a head in my hands, and felt a sweetness which the heart cannot understand, the mouth speak of, the eyes see nor the ears hear. God has truly shown me secrets which are more holy than all that has gone before, and which it would take too long to describe.

"You know that I went to visit him, and he gained such great strength and power that he made his confession in the right state of mind. He made me promise for the sake of God's love I would be with him when the day of execution came, and I promised. The next day before the bells rang for the first time, I went to him, and that consoled him greatly. I went with him to Mass, and he received Holy Communion, which he had always avoided. His will was one with God's holy will and submitted to it. He was only afraid of one thing— that his courage should fail in the crucial moment. But God's immeasurable goodness fired such love and longing in him

that he could not have enough of God's presence. He said,
Stay with me, do not go from me and I will be good, I will
die happy. And he leaned his head against my breast. I was
filled with joy, for it seemed to me that the perfume of his
blood mixed itself with mine which I long to be able to pour
out for my beloved Bridegroom Jesus. This desire grew in my
soul, and when I realised that he was afraid I said to him:
'Courage, beloved brother, for we shall soon go to the eternal
marriage feast. You go to it washed in the blood of God's
Son, with the sweet name of Jesus for ever in your mind, and
I shall wait for you at the place of execution.'—Oh, my father
and my son, then his heart was freed from fear, the melancholy in his face changed to gladness, and in his gladness he
said: 'Where does it come from, such great mercy? Oh, my
soul's joy promises to wait for me at the holy place of
execution.'—See what a light had fallen on him—he called
the place of execution holy! And he added, 'Yes, I shall go,
cheerful and happy, and it seems to me that I must wait a
thousand years when I think that you will be waiting for me
there.' And he said many other things which were so beautiful that I rejoiced at God's goodness."

So she waited for him at the place of execution, kneeling
in ceaseless prayer, and she laid her own neck on the block
"but I did not receive what I desired." Passionately she prayed
Our Lady to give him light and peace in his heart at his last
moment, and for herself she prayed to be allowed to see that
he arrived at his final goal. She was as though drunk with joy
at the gracious promises, so that she saw nothing, although
there was an enormous crowd assembled.

Niccolò came, peaceful as a lamb, and he smiled when he
saw that Catherine stood there waiting for him. He asked her
to make the sign of the cross over him, and she whispered to
him: "My dear brother, let us go to the eternal marriage feast,

to enjoy life which shall never end." She bared his throat, and when he laid his head on the block she knelt beside him. He said nothing but "Jesus, Catherine", and then his head fell into her hands.

"Then I fastened my eyes upon the Divine Goodness and said: I will. Immediately I saw, as clearly as one sees the sunshine, Him who is God and Man. He was there, He received the blood. In this blood was the fire of holy desire which grace had put into his soul, and this fire was swallowed up in the fire of God's mercy." She saw that Niccolò was as though drawn into the treasure chamber of mercy, his pierced heart into Christ's breast, so the great truth was made clearly apparent—that Christ receives a soul entirely because of His mercy, and not because of any merits of the soul itself. But as the soul of Niccolò entered the mystery of the Holy Trinity it turned and looked at her, as the bride does when she has come to the house of her bridegroom and with bowed head acknowledges those who have accompanied her, as a last sign of gratitude.

Catherine remained there, with deep peace in her soul and a great longing to follow the dead youth to her heavenly Bridegroom. He must therefore not be surprised, she writes to Raimondo, that she longs to be annihilated in the fire and blood from the wound in Christ's side. ". . . And now no more remissness, my beloved son, for in that blood is our life, Jesus."

XIX

IN THE SUMMER OF 1371 Catherine and her "family" were living in the country south of Siena. At that time she had apparently formed small groups of her spiritual children, which she left in several places to work for her goal, peace between men and peace between men and their Maker, through penitence and prayer. Her mother and her old friend Cecca she left in Montepulciano—Monna Lapa had a granddaughter and Cecca a daughter in the convent of St. Agnes. Late in the summer she herself was in the impenetrable fortress of the Salimbeni, Rocca di Tentenanno, on the top of the mountain which dominates the river Orco. With her were Raimondo, Tommaso della Fonte, Fra Santo, Lisa and several other friends.

The lady of the castle, the widowed Countess Bianchina, had sent for Catherine in the hope that she would be able to put an end to a feud between two nobles, Agnolino and Cione, who were the heads of two branches of the Salimbeni family. She wrote to them and visited Cione in his castle, and finally arranged a reconciliation between the Abbot of St. Antimo and his old enemy the dean of Montalcino. But a short while after, Raimondo went to Rome with a message from Catherine to the Pope. It was therefore Fra Santo who later described to him how she had driven out a demon from one of the Countess Bianchina's servants. Catherine's friends had warned the lady that Catherine was very unwilling to have anything to do with the possessed—they said it was because she was so humble. They advised the countess to have the poor wretch taken to Catherine without warning her, and then they felt sure that the virgin's tender heart would be moved when confronted by the woman. But when the possessed woman was brought to Catherine, who was just about to go out on one of her errands as peacemaker, she turned to Bianchina: "May God forgive you, what have you done? Do you not know how often I am tortured by demons—why do you bring others to me when I suffer so much myself from their attacks?" But she went over to the possessed woman: "So that you shall not undo the good work which is already begun, lay your head on the breast of this man, and wait till I come back." Obediently the wretched women went over and laid her head on Fra Santo's breast. But through her mouth the evil spirit swore and cursed at his enemy who had made it impossible for him to come out of the room, although the door was wide open. The spirit then entertained the interested listeners by naming each place Catherine passed on her way out and home again. But it could not get the woman to lift her head from the breast of the pious old hermit, and when Catherine came home again and commanded him to loose his hold on the poor woman and never come near her again, he had to obey. Fra Raimondo heard this story later from over thirty people who had been present.

Once she had stepped into the ring, Catherine fought like a valiant knight against the demons as long as she was at Rocca di Tentenanno, where innumerable insane and possessed people were brought to her. Some arrived in chains and were so wild and unmanageable that six or eight men could not always cope with them. Catherine used to sit on the grass on a terrace outside the fortress, and she always said to the warders on these occasions: "Why have you put this poor creature in chains? In Christ's name, free him." Even those who raged the most became quiet immediately, and when Catherine had held the poor creatures' heads in her lap, prayed for them and wept for them, they became well again. Not only the demons which had tortured the sick men took flight, but the lice which often swarmed over their filthy bodies also left them, to the fear and horror of her family. Catherine only laughed. "Don't bother yourselves about them, these lice will not come onto you." She was right, as usual.

The Salimbeni had always been disturbers of the peace, and time and again had been at open war with the republic of Siena. So Catherine's long stay with one of their family wakened mistrust in the Sienese government—they knew of course that Catherine disapproved profoundly of many of their policies. She wrote an indignant letter of reply to the "Defenders" and Siena's Capitano del Popolo. Once again she reminds them that men who are to guide and lead others must first be able to guide themselves. "How can the blind lead the blind, or the dead bury the dead?" "Yes, my dear gentlemen, he who is blind, whose intelligence is darkened by mortal sin, can know neither himself nor God, and can neither see nor correct the faults of those who are under him, or if he tries to correct them it is through the darkness and imperfection which is in him." She tells her dear gentlemen how they ceaselessly punish innocent men and let the guilty, who have deserved punishment a thousand times, go unpunished. They complain of unworthy priests and monks, but let themselves be fooled by them, and persecute those who are good and righteous servants of God. "With regard to my return home with my spiritual children, I have heard that all sorts of doubts and accusations have been concocted, but I do not know whether I ought to believe this? If you were as interested in your own welfare as we are, you and all the inhabitants of Siena would have nothing to do with such groundless doubts and passions, and not listen to such stories. The only thing we always try to obtain is your spiritual and temporal welfare, and we offer God our pious desires with tears and sighs, to prevent the Divine Justice descending upon us with the punishment we deserve because of our imperfections. I have so little virtue that I can do nothing, except in an imperfect way; but those who are perfect and desire nothing but God's glory and the soul's salvation do good deeds, and the ingratitude and ignorance of the people of my own town shall not prevent us from striving after their salvation until we die.... I see that the devil is furious because of the losses which, by the grace of God, this journey has cost him, and will cost him in the future. I came here to tear these souls out of the hands of the devil. For this end I would sacrifice a thousand lives if I had them. I shall therefore move and act as the Holy Spirit wills me."

She writes to a citizen of some importance in Siena in the same vein: "Whether the devil likes it or not, I shall use my life to the glory of God and the salvation of souls, to improve the state of the world, and especially of my native town. The citizens of Siena should be thoroughly ashamed of themselves if they think that we are staying with the Salimbeni to forge secret alliances ..."

But Monna Lapa had again become impatient, and Catherine had to write to her mother begging her to be patient and think of Mary, the great example of an unselfish mother. "You know so well, my dearest mother, that your worthless daughter is here on earth only to do what her Creator decrees. I know that you are pleased when you see that I am obedient to Him."

But the mother of Fra Matteo Tolomei, who was by then a Dominican monk, was even more impatient. It was she who a year or two before had come to Catherine and begged her to save her shameless son and light-minded daughters. Now she sent Fra Matteo a furious letter commanding him to come home at once from the fortress of the Salimbeni, the arch-enemies of the house of Tolomei, and threatened him, if he did not obey, with his mother's curse. In her letter to Monna Rabe, Catherine takes it for granted that she has deep religious experience—she speaks of the ladder of perfection, which is Jesus, and only at the end warns her solemnly that purely natural love for her children has led her astray and made her demand that her son should fail in his duty in the world to hurry home to her.

Tommaso Caffarini relates how while she was at Rocca di Tentenanno Catherine suddenly discovered that she could write. Quite by accident she came upon a jar of red colour such as was used for the drawing of initials. She had learned to read several years before, and had already dictated hundreds of letters to her secretaries, so it would not be surprising if one day she suddenly wanted to try and see if she could write herself.... But in a letter to Raimondo in Rome she says that she had learned to write while she was in ecstasy, and that this gift had been bestowed on her as a consolation in a time when she had many very difficult trials. The learned French Dominican Père Hurtaud, who has edited the *Dialogue*, expresses his doubt of the whole story—especially as no letters written by Catherine's hand have been preserved, and he is not sure that the letter to Raimondo has not been altered by the copyist. The question remains open. It does not seem unlikely that Catherine one day discovered that she herself could do what others do every day, nor that she received this ability as a special gift from God. Caffarini says that the first thing Catherine wrote with her own hand, with the red colour, was a verse, a prayer to each of the three Persons of the Trinity to fill her soul with holy love, guard her against evil thoughts, and help her in all her actions. No translation can give any idea of the loveliness of this little prayer in her own musical Tuscan dialect.

She certainly needed heavenly consolation. Pope Gregory had become completely dependent on the Sienese virgin, who was so much more manly and courageous than himself, and now he was extremely annoyed because she had wasted all these months in the valley of the Orco, which she could have used so much more profitably for him if she had gone to Florence. In October 1377 the Florentines had won a great victory over the Pope's mercenary army, and when ambassadors from Florence once again failed to arrange a peace on conditions favourable to the republic, the Florentines decided to disregard the interdict. Mass was said publicly in all the churches in the city, and the attitude of the Florentines to the Pope was extremely bitter.

The Pope's position was terrible. His temporal possessions had been reduced to Rome and a few strips of land just outside the city. He was in great financial difficulties—he even tried to borrow money from the Queen of Naples. But the obstinacy which often accompanies indecision made Gregory refuse all attempts to make peace with the Florentines under conditions which could be honourable for both sides. He was moreover so lacking in judgment that he tried to make Bernabò Visconti arbitrator at the proposed peace conference— the very man whose tyranny and intrigues started all the misery.

Catherine wrote to the Holy Father and humbly begged his pardon for the fault she had unintentionally committed. She sent the letter to Rome with Fra Raimondo. Arriving there he was re-instated in his old position as prior of the convent of Santa Maria sopra Minerva. Catherine was only to meet her best friend and most affectionate son once again, and to be with him for a few weeks when she came to

Rome some years later. For three years he had been her confessor, and their mutual respect had created riches in the souls of the brother and sister who so generously exchanged their mystical experiences.

Fra Raimondo had come nearer than anyone to understanding this strange woman and the intense life she led, hovering on two wings, as she herself had once expressed it, over the abyss between time and eternity; she touched both shores, but was never allowed to lie down to rest on either of them. Raimondo had loyally done everything he could to meet all the needs of an extraordinary soul; he gave her permission to satisfy her ceaseless hunger for the supernatural nourishment of the Sacrament; he let his penitent follow her own inspirations as often as she convinced him that she had been given a deeper insight into the ways which her heavenly Bridegroom had chosen for His bride. Catherine loved with deep tenderness all those whom she called her sons and daughters, whether they were young men and women or people much older than herself; but they all expected her to strengthen and console them, they all depended on her. Raimondo was the only one who had been able to give her any human consolation.

Catherine was thirty, and the fresh loveliness of the dyer's young and healthy daughter from Fontebranda had disappeared. Her body had become a fragile, almost transparent, vase, lighted from within by her burning soul. But although Catherine was a sick woman—in spite of her indomitable energy when the Lord sent her out on His errands—it was just at this time, during her stay at Rocca di Tentenanno, that she awakened a violent erotic passion in a man. A young monk who had become her disciple was seized with the wrong kind of love for her and fell in love with her selfishly and passionately. When his desire proved to be powerless against her love for him, which was completely spiritual and full of tenderness for his soul, he was in despair, and one day in church he tried to kill her. He was disarmed by some who were standing near. But then he fled, threw off his monk's habit and returned to the fortress of his fathers. Here he succumbed completely to his despair. Two letters which Neri di Landoccio received while he was at Rocca di Tentenanno, from someone who did not sign them with his name—"for I do not know what my name is"—are perhaps from this man. It is not that he doubts or scorns religion—he has just lost the taste for all those things which once filled his soul with happiness; he can feel neither peace nor light. "I have been turned from the table because I have clothed myself in darkness ... God in His mercy give you grace, perseverance and a holy death."

We hear later that this escaped monk finally went into the woods and hanged himself. And Catherine, who prayed with all her might for the son she had lost, how much did she know about it? Against her will she had been the cause of his destruction. She never said so. Some lines in a letter to Neri perhaps concern the suicide: "Do not be afraid, God does not wish that the same should happen to you as to that other." Neri di Landoccio dei Pagliaresi was of a melancholy nature, and if the letters to him from the unhappy writer are from the monk who hanged himself, he and Neri must once have been friends.

XX

BEFORE STARTING on his journey to Rome, Fra Raimondo had a visit from Catherine's old friend and correspondent, Niccolo Soderini from Florence. Messer Niccolo was fairly optimistic: the Florentines really wanted peace. The four or five men who wanted the war to continue could be rendered harmless if everyone else would work together, irrespective of parties, and have them banished. The best thing would be for the leaders of the Guelph party to put themselves at the head of the action against the war-mongers.

One morning, after preaching at the High Mass in Rome, Raimondo was called to the Pope. The Pope said that he had been informed that if Catherine went to Florence the Florentines would make peace. Raimondo was strongly against his "mamma" being sent on such a dangerous mission, and offered to go himself. "Not only Catherine, but all of us are willing to do anything Your Holiness demands of us, even though it might lead to a martyr's death." But the Pope was not impressed. "I will not send you, they might murder you, but I do not think they will do anything to Catherine—she is a woman and they have great respect for her." The next morning Raimondo had to appear before the Pope to receive credentials for Catherine. She was to go to Florence as the Pope's ambassador.

In December 1377 Catherine was once again in Florence. This time there were no priests in her company—the town lay under an interdict. She had only a very few companions, the faithful

Alessia and two other Mantellate, Stefano Maconi, Neri, and Fra Santo, the old hermit. Niccolo Soderini housed the Sienese visitors in his home. But another leader of the Guelphs, Pietro Canigiani—also an old friend of Catherine's from her first visit—made a collection among the men and women of his party to build a house for her.

Catherine was often present when the parties had their meetings, and friends and enemies were in agreement about one thing: this woman was unusually well versed in everything concerning the Church, was very learned, and had a brilliant intuitive understanding of things. Otherwise they were in strong disagreement: her supporters considered her a holy virgin, a visionary to whom God had granted special revelations. Her enemies called her a hypocrite, a shameless female, or a witch.

Ever since she had been a very young girl Catherine had been used to meeting violent opposition, misunderstandings and slander. First in her own family, when she refused to allow herself to be married as they had planned; later among her sisters in the order because many of them did not like her ecstasies and exaggerated love for the poor and the sick—they suspected her of hypocrisy. Poisonous tongues had talked of her friendship with the brothers up at San Domenico, and murmured that when it came to the point it was not so certain that the holy virgin was a virgin. Her burning zeal for the conversion of sinners had infuriated sinners who had not the slightest wish to be converted—this impertinent young woman practically forced people by violence to cease their wandering down the broad and pleasant way to hell and shoved them onto the way of thorns which leads to heaven. Well-meaning people were always criticising her travels over Italy, not to speak of those in foreign lands—even to the Papal court in Avignon, at the head of a company of priests and monks, young and old men and women and God knows who else besides. . . . They considered that a virgin consecrated to God should stay at home in her cell, say the daily Office, do good in secret, and otherwise hold her tongue. As for less well-disposed critics, all with their private reasons for being upset and annoyed—when they saw a young woman, the daughter of respectable but quite ordinary people, mixing herself up in affairs which concerned governments and prelates, stepping into the arena where complicated party interests and matters of state were decided by force of arms—what could they say, but that in spite of all her fine words about humility and the love of Christ, conversion and all kinds of spiritual things, they realised that behind all the pious words and excuses for daring to give advice to men who held the fates of countries and peoples in their hands, was an unbending will; and beneath all the fine words they heard a tone of steely determination.

Now she should really learn to know the passions of men fired by political fanaticism and violent disagreements between party groups. Even many of the Guelphs were greatly put out because Catherine was in the town and was present at the party meetings—it was unpardonable of the Pope to give a woman the authority to come here and mix herself up in their affairs. Canigiani had to put up with the scorn of his party because he admired and loved Catherine. This did not prevent him from letting his young son, Barduccio, join Catherine's family. Barduccio was extremely young, fragile in health, but with an unusually lovable and pure mind. He became one of her secretaries, and when she left Florence Barduccio accompanied her and was with her until her death.

At the same time the Guelphs were fully aware of the prestige they gained through their connections with Catherine. They used it to slake their thirst for revenge against their old enemies, and once they began to condemn the "war-mongers" to banishment, many more than the original six or eight were driven from their native town. But Catherine was neverthe-less full of hope. The Florentines had again accepted the inter-dict, they no longer forced the priests to celebrate sacrilegious Masses and services, and it seemed to her that this was the first sign that the republic really wanted to return to the Pope's community. She wrote to all the monasteries where she had friends among the monks and nuns and asked them to pray for peace and God's grace.

At the beginning of 1378 a peace conference started in Sar-zana. The Pope was represented by three French cardinals, Flo-rence by five ambassadors. Venice, France and Naples had also sent ambassadors, but Bernabò Visconti came in person. But before the conference had achieved anything came the mes-sage that Pope Gregory XI had died suddenly on March 27th. The conference broke up, and it did not look as though peace were any nearer.

A Florentine chronicle tells us how, on the night of March 27th, the guards at the Porta San Frediano heard someone knocking at the gate and a voice shouting: "Open at once for the bearer of peace!" But when they drew back the bolts they saw no one. Nevertheless the news flew over the town: "The olive branch has come, peace is established." Some thought that the invisible messenger was an angel of God, others that it was the soul of the dead Pope who regretted his hardness towards the Florentines.... It was not long before the whole of Christendom discovered that the death of the Pope had not brought peace to the war-weary world. Quite the contrary....

On April 18 the cardinals in conclave chose the Archbishop of Bari, Bartolommeo Prignano, as Pope. He took the name of Urban, the sixth who had chosen that name. Catherine had met him in Avignon, when he was Archbishop of Acerenza. At the court in Avignon, where all the vices of the

world, greed, pride, lust and lies, flourished profusely, the Nea-
politan was like a pillar of virtue. He was old, born in 1318.
As the Pope's Vice-Chancellor he had shown also that he was
far from being afraid of work and was a competent adminis-
trator. Catherine knew that she could depend on him to try
with a firm hand to root up all the weeds which were over-
running the Church of Christ on earth, and carry out the
reforms which were so sadly necessary. But perhaps right from
the beginning she had her doubts as to whether he could show
himself merciful when it was necessary. The prior of the Carthusians at Gorgona wrote to Catherine: "It is said that the new
Holy Father is a terrible man, and he frightens people with
his words and deeds. He seems to have complete faith in God,
and therefore fears no man, and it is obvious that he will uproot
the simony and love of luxury which has flourished in God's
Church." With regard to the outlook for peace, the prior writes
that the Holy Father tells everyone that he wants peace, but it
must be a peace which is honourable for the Church. He does
not demand money, but if the Florentines want peace, they
must come forward openly and honestly, without any lies. In
other words, for the new Pope it was a question of spiritual,
not temporal values—exactly what Catherine had begged his
forerunner to remember. Urban VI had never been greedy for
temporal reward. But when he spoke of spiritual values he did
not mean quite the same as Catherine. He demanded that the
Florentines should declare themselves guilty and humble themselves as he ordered, prompted by his own pride and his idea
of what the honour of the Church demanded.

Catherine remained in Florence. She had decided that she
would not leave the town until peace was made. But the
Guelph party which was in power continued to persecute
their public and private enemies. In vain Salvestro de' Medici, who was himself one of the heads of the Guelph party

and Gonfaloniere della Giustitia—the Flagbearer of Justice—
begged his companions in the government to use their power
with discretion and avoid arbitrary and unjust decisions. All
the lawlessness practised by the other members of the government became at length intolerable, and on July 22 Salvestro led his countrymen to rebellion. The guilds mustered to
arms and were joined by the enraged mob. It was civil war.

The course of the civil war was the usual one—once the
passions of the masses are roused, the people attack any and
everyone, guilty and innocent alike, without discrimination.
The palaces of well-known Florentines were stormed and
plundered, whether they belonged to the tyrannical rulers or
to those who had fought against tyranny. The houses of Pietro
Canigiani and one of his sons were plundered and burned,
the prisons were broken open, the monasteries stormed. Those
citizens who were known to belong to the peace party had to
save their lives by escaping from the town. Hordes of furious
rebels streamed over the Ponte Vecchio towards Niccolo Soderini's house on the west bank of the Arno. They were going to
seize Soderini, and they would also seize the Sienese witch
whom he harboured. "If we get hold of her we'll tear her to
pieces, burn her alive. . . ."

Catherine was in the garden behind the house. The garden
was on a hill, so she could see right over the town. It seemed
to her that devils sailed on their wings under the clouds, which
were lighted from the flames of burning houses. It was a night
full of blood and fire. She prayed to Him whose blood is the
only remedy against man's thirst for the blood of his fellow-
men, whose fire of love is the only cleansing fire which can
consume the fire of self-love on earth—the same fire which
now dyed the heavens red over Florence. And when the men
who came to murder her stormed into the garden, swinging
swords and clubs, and shouting, "Where is the damned

woman—where is Catherine?" she went to meet them. "I am Catherine. Do what God allows you to do, but do not touch my companions." The leader of the band was so confused that he started to put his sword back in the sheath, and when Catherine knelt before him he began to tremble and begged her to go away; but Catherine repeated, "Here I am. Where do you want me to go? I have always longed to suffer for God and His Church, so if you have been appointed to kill me do not be afraid to do so. Only you must leave my friends untouched."

The man turned and ran, and soon all his followers too had disappeared. But the danger was not over yet. Soderini's house was not considered safe. Raimondo, who heard the story from an eye-witness, Ser Cristofano di Gano Guidini, says that the Soderini were frightened and advised her to leave the town, Catherine would not. The tailor Francesco di Pippino and his wife Monna Agnese proved to be the most courageous of her friends. She had got to know them the first time she was in Florence, and had exchanged letters with them. They now opened their home to her and her companions. But whether it was because she was worried about her friends or for other reasons, some days later she left Florence, but not Florentine ground. She found a place of refuge in a lonely wood, where some hermits lived. It is generally thought that this brotherhood was the community of hermits in Vallombrosa, founded by St. John Gualbert, the man who had spared the life of his deadly enemy because it was Good Friday, and later rushed into the nearest church and fell before the feet of the crucified Christ, as though drunk with this new adventure—the adventure of forgiveness. And the Saviour leaned down from the cross and kissed the boy.

But flight was against Catherine's nature, and it was not long before she returned to the town. Soon she did not even try to hide the fact that she was in Florence, where the waves of passion still rose so high.

Just after she had been attacked in Soderini's garden she wrote a long letter to Raimondo. In it she speaks of the longing of her soul to give its life for Christ and His Church. Let us never look back at what hindrances and persecutions we might encounter in the world, but hope steadfastly in the light of our holy faith that we shall be able to cross this stormy sea with courage and perseverance. "I tell you that to-day I shall begin a new life, so that not even my old sins will be able to take from me the happiness that it would be to die for Christ Crucified. . . . I burned with desire to suffer for the glory of God and the salvation of souls, for the reform and welfare of the Holy Church. My heart almost burst with the desire to give my life, and this desire was both sweet and painful— sweet because I had become one with the Truth, painful because it tore my heart to see this insult to God and this crowd of demons which darkened the sky and blinded men's understanding, for it seemed as though God let them do as they wanted for the sake of justice and vengeance. I sighed because I was afraid for the misfortune this would be if it became an obstacle in the making of peace." So she understands that it was perhaps for the best that her desire to suffer martyrdom was not fulfilled. Nevertheless there is a note of disappointment in her description of the feelings with which she went to meet those who came to take her life with swords and daggers. This is one of the most revealing of Catherine's letters; it shows that she was never granted peace in her soul. When she met her heavenly Bridegroom in Holy Communion she was carried away in ecstatic visions and mystical bliss, but she was always thrown back into the bubbling cauldron— the world which bleeds from all the sores made by the passions of men and their misfortunes. And in spite of her triumphant trust in Christ, in spite of her unselfishness and assurance when she went on her Bridegroom's errands, the young woman with her quick intelligence understood quite clearly that in the maelstrom of world politics into which she had been thrown the most vital interests of the parties she had tried to reconcile were in fact often completely irreconcilable.

Finally she gives Raimondo a message for the Pope: "I must beg you to ask Christ on earth not to let peace be delayed because of what has happened. On the contrary—say to him that he must work even faster to bring about peace, so that he can be free to occupy himself with the great plans he has for the glory of God and the rebuilding of the Church. For these events have not altered anything, and the town is now quite calm. Tell him to hurry, in the name of mercy, for it is the only way that an end can be made to the innumerable offences which have been committed against God. Tell him that he must have mercy and sympathy for the souls which are in darkness. Tell him that he must free me from this prison, because if no peace is made I feel it impossible to leave the town, and I long to come away and taste the blood of the holy martyrs, to visit His Holiness and meet you again, so that I can tell you of the wonderful things God has done in these days to delight our souls, intoxicate our hearts and increase our hope in the light of our holy faith. I end now. Remain in the holy and sweet joy of God. Sweet Jesus, Jesus Love."

From Florence too she sent her first letter to Urban VI. She begins as usual, but, with an eloquence unusual even for her, she praises love, the perfect love of the good shepherd who gladly gives his life for his flock, unhindered by love of himself. Catherine compares justice combined with mercy with a precious pearl. Justice without mercy would be dark, cruel, more like injustice than justice. But mercy without justice would be like salve on a sore which should be cleansed

with the red-hot iron; if the salve is applied before the wound
is cleansed it only makes it smart, and does not heal it. But
a leader must never relax, even though his subordinates oppose
a thousand times his attempts to improve them. The guilt of
the rebels does not detract from the virtue of him who tries
to lead them back to the right road through pure and true
love. He does not seek friendship with his neighbour for his
own sake but for God's sake. "He desires to do him the
service which he cannot do God, for he sees and understands that He who is our God does not need us. Therefore
he strives zealously to be of use to his neighbour, and especially his subordinates who have been entrusted to him." With
perfect honesty she speaks of the abuses which flourish in
the Church and of the sins of the worthless servants of God
who bring up their bastards to sell the blood of Christ, behave
like tinkers, throw dice with their consecrated hands, and
practise simony, usury and innumerable other sins. "Oh, Father,
give a crumb of consolation to the servants of God who die
of grief and cannot die." To complete the reform for which
she has sighed so long she advises the Pope to surround himself with many holy men who are not afraid of death—he
must not worry whether they are of noble or common birth,
but only whether they are fitted to be shepherds for the
lambs. He must create a college of cardinals, firm as pillars,
who will be able to support the Pope's work, of reforming
the Church. (She presumably already knew that the Pope
had begun the badly needed reformation in the Church itself,
with boundless energy and complete lack of tact.)

She prays for the Florentines: "I pray and beseech you to
lay it to your heart for the sake of Christ Crucified that you
must have mercy on the sheep who are outside the fold—
surely because of my sins. Out of love of the Blood which
you have command over, do not hesitate to receive them with

true mercy and goodness. May Your Holiness triumph over your hardness and treat them well, and in this way you will win them back to the fold. And if they do not approach with true and perfect humility, may Your Holiness overlook their hardness and the faults caused by their weakness; do not demand of the sick more than they can achieve. Ah, woe, woe, have mercy on all the souls which founder, do not think of the offences which have occurred in this town.... The Divine Goodness has seen to it that the great evil did not bring even greater evils after it. Now your children have become calm and beg you for the oil of mercy. Overlook the fact, Holy Father, that they did not beg for it in the most seemly manner, not with the broken-heartedness which they should feel for their misdemeanours and which Your Holiness demands. Oh, do not turn them away, and you will see that in future these children will prove themselves better than all the others."

As soon as peace is made, Catherine begs the Pope to raise the banner of the crusade. "You see yourself that these infidels incite you." The threats of the Turks in the Mediterranean countries had now become intolerable. While France and Italy were drained by endless wars, not only their shipping but also their islands and coasts suffered ceaseless attacks from the infidel pirates. Her first letter to Urban VI ends with repeated prayers for mercy, mercy, mercy, and then she asks him to accept her love and grief as excuse for having dared to write to him and give him advice.

She sent him another short letter not long after: "Oh, Most Holy Father, be patient when they give you advice, for they do not say anything to you except for the glory of God and your own welfare, as a son should if he is really fond of his father. He cannot bear to see anything done which might bring shame or injustice on his father, and he watches zealously, for he knows that his father is only human, and has such a large family to look after that he himself cannot see everything. If his true-born sons do not watch over his honour he will often be betrayed. So it is with Your Holiness; you are father and lord of the whole of Christendom, Holy Father; we are all under your wings. You have authority over all things, but the range of your eye is limited as is all men's, and therefore it is necessary that your children keep watch with honesty and without slavish fear, and do all that can serve the glory of God and your honour, for the safety of the souls which are under your care. I know that Your Holiness deeply desires to find helpers who can serve you, but then it is necessary to be patient with them. . . ."

It appears that a certain Fra Bartolommeo (perhaps Bartolommeo di Dominici) had brought the Pope's anger on his head because he had expressed himself too frankly. He was very unhappy because he had aroused the Pope's anger, and Catherine begged Urban to turn his wrath against her if he thought he had a right to correct and punish. "I think it is my sins which are the cause of his fault, and therefore I ought to take the punishment for him." Whichever of her sons it was who had aroused the irritable old man's wrath, Catherine, like a loving mother, was immediately prepared to excuse him and take on herself the guilt of something which most probably was just as much the Pope's fault as the offender's.

On Sunday, July 18, a messenger from the Pope rode into Florence bearing an olive branch. As the news—"Peace at last"—spread over the town the Florentines broke into wild jubilation. While the bells pealed from the Cathedral and the Palazzo Vecchio, Catherine wrote and told her children the good news. She put a leaf of the blessed olive branch in her letter.

But she had been too optimistic when she wrote to the Pope that the Florentines had become more peaceful. Only two days after the peace had been made a new rebellion broke out. This time it was the working people—"il Popoli Minuti"—who had neither political status nor political rights, who rose and streamed through the town to burn and plunder. Anarchy reigned for three days, and then the revolt was crushed with an iron hand.

The peace treaty was finally signed on July 28. The fine demanded by Urban was about an eighth of what Pope Gregory had claimed. But the Florentines had to promise that all laws which were in conflict with the Church would be annulled and that the churches and monasteries which had been plundered should be compensated. The interdict was withdrawn, and Catherine's prophecy that once the Florentines were reconciled with the Holy Father they would be his most loyal sons was fulfilled. When, shortly after, the great catastrophe came upon the Church, the Florentines stood firmly at Pope Urban VI's side.

Catherine left Florence a couple of days after the peace treaty was signed to return to Siena—that is to say, before the news could have reached Siena. She had brought one of her most difficult missions to a successful close. But there is a certain note of sadness in the letter of farewell which she sent to the governors and the Gonfaloniere from Siena. She had wished to celebrate the feast for the holy peace with them—this peace which she had been willing to work for, even though it cost her her life. But the devil had sown so much unjust hatred against her, and she did not wish to be the cause of more sins. So she preferred to leave. . . .

The Florence which she left behind her had become a new city. Many of the men who had been most important were no longer there; some had been banished, some killed. Some of these had been her friends, some her enemies. And she could not help being full of anxiety for the future. The terrible thing which she had foreseen "when the Pope really begins to reform the Church" might happen at any moment. The Pope was in Tivoli with the four Italian cardinals. The French cardinals and the cardinals from Limousin who for months had represented the ever-growing opposition to Pope Urban, had gone to Anagni, and it was not to be expected that any good would come of their conferences.

XXI

IT WAS A FACT which was not to be denied—Bartolommeo Prignano had been elected Pope under circumstances which were both confusing and shameful. Pope Gregory XI was quite clear about the fact that there were many dangers threatening the future, and therefore had given precise instructions in his will regarding the coming papal elections. An ordinary majority should have been sufficient to make the vote of the conclave valid, and the fortress of St. Angelo, which was the key to the district round St. Peter's Church and the Vatican, should be given to the new Pope after the approval of the six cardinals in Avignon had been obtained. But the really decisive factor was the attitude of the Roman people, *Popolo Romano*—the ordinary people of the eternal city.

"True-born sons of the murderers of St. Peter and St. Paul" the other Italians called them. For several generations they had been deserted by their bishop, who was also their lawful temporal prince; so the Romans had become accustomed to taking the law into their own hands—and this was true not only of the workers in Trastevere and the citizens who lived in the narrow, crooked streets between the deserted Forum and the river, but also of the barons in their fortified houses inside the city walls, or in their great fortresses on the hills outside the town. The attempts of Cola di Rienzi and Cardinal Albornoz to bring law and order back to the city were nothing but interludes in the rule of the papal legates, most of whom were Frenchmen. Because they were French the Romans mistrusted and hated them, and at times they had ample ground

to mistrust and hate them. During this period the old imperial city, which had been conquered time and again throughout the centuries, became more and more depopulated and
ruined. Inside the wide area within the city walls great por-
tions of the old city became waste land, overgrown with
grass and bushes. White buffalo grazed among the ruins of
buildings which had half sunk into the ground—once they
had had their own history, which was now forgotten, although
there were legends attached to them about the terrible things
which were supposed to have happened there in the old days,
and of ghosts which wandered at night between the sunken
arches and the underground tunnels. Churches dedicated to
saints and martyrs of long ago stood roofless and gradually
crumbled to dust; in the ruins the grass grew between the
remains of broken pillars. Along the paths across the desolate
ground a few ancient monasteries lay behind their garden
walls; or some poor peasant, living in a ruin of the great old
days in a couple of rooms covered by a roof of rushes from
the marshes, tried to cultivate the ground. Outside the city
walls lay the Campagna, ravaged by malaria and bands of
robbers: otherwise lifeless. Only the small groups of pilgrims
who, in spite of everything, were determined to make the
dangerous pilgrimage to some ruined sanctuary, wandered over
the paths, looking anxiously at the motionless rider who tended
his flock of white buffaloes or grey sheep, carrying a long
spear instead of a shepherd's crook.

Pope Urban V had come to Rome in 1367, but in spite of
the warnings of St. Birgitta he returned to Avignon after
a sojourn of less than three years, and he died in Avignon a
couple of months later—of poison, according to the Italians.
Rumour had it that Pope Gregory XI too was on the point of
forsaking Rome for his beloved Avignon, when he died suddenly. Often before this the Roman people had done their

best to take a hand in the papal elections—their contention was that as the Pope was also their bishop and temporal prince they had a right to have a word in the matter of the election. It was more or less certain that a French or Provençal cardinal would leave the graves of St. Peter and St. Paul as quickly as possible; and the Romans did not intend to allow themselves to be treated in this way any longer.

Of the sixteen cardinals who met at the conclave on April 7, 1378, only four were Italian. It was Wednesday of Holy Week, and the hysterical mob who poured into St. Peter's Square shouted at the tops of their voices, "Romano le volemo"—we will have a Roman. They had been strengthened by bands of wild-looking men from the Sabine mountains, shepherds, or robbers, or both. Before the doors of the room where the conclave were to sit had been closed, some of the mob forced their way in and began to shout at the tops of their voices that they would murder the whole college of cardinals if they did not choose a Roman cardinal. Cardinal Orsini, who was himself Roman noble, went over to the screeching mob and ordered them to leave. After a while the Vatican was cleared of all those who had no business to be there, the doors were sealed, and the conclave could begin their business: but all the time they could hear the shrieks and threats from the square outside the window, where the milling crowds yelled, "Romano le volemo!"

During the night the cellars of the Vatican were broken into, and the following morning most of the mob were dangerously drunk. When the cardinals took their places after Mass the tocsin was ringing; it seemed as though the disturbances had spread over the whole of Rome. Terrified, the cardinals decided to hurry through the election before the mob broke in and murdered them. The Cardinal of Limoges stood up: "Gentlemen, as it is not God's will that we can agree upon a member of the Holy

College we must choose one from outside. It seems to me that the most worthy is the Archbishop of Bari; he is a holy and learned man, of ripe age. I propose him freely and voluntarily." Almost all the cardinals voted in agreement—some of them somewhat hesitantly. Only Cardinal Orsini suggested that there might be some doubts as to the validity of the election as they had not been given complete freedom of choice. But his objections were overruled, and Bartolommeo Prignano was chosen as Pope by an overwhelming majority.

If he was not a Roman he was at least an Italian. A message was sent to him, and in the meantime the Holy College went through the election ceremony again and elected him—this time in the chapel—so that no doubts could arise as to the free and correct character of the election. Cardinal Orsini went to a window to inform the excited crowds outside: "Habemus Papam"—we have a Pope. At the same moment the doors were broken down and drunken men armed with sticks and stones forced their way in. Several of the cardinals were wounded and threats were shrieked at them: If they had not chosen a Roman they would be torn to pieces. . . .

Not only the cardinals, but the whole retinue of priests and servants, felt their lives threatened, and a certain curate turned towards old Cardinal Tebaldeschi, who was a Roman noble, and begged him to save all their lives. Although the upright old man protested, a degrading comedy was now performed: they put a white mitre on Cardinal Tebaldeschi, threw a red cape over his shoulders, and lifted him up to an altar. In vain he cried: "I am not the Pope, it is the Archbishop of Bari who is our Pope", his voice was drowned in the confusion; but the crowds who recognised him were satisfied.

When Bartolommeo Prignano arrived at the Vatican the building had been cleared of most of those who had forced their way in. Some of the cardinals tried to persuade him not to receive the tiara, but in vain. He had been chosen by a majority of votes, as Pope Gregory had decreed in his will, and even though the cardinals had chosen him in a panic—there was no doubt of the fact that if they had chosen a French Pope they would immediately have been in danger of their lives, and it would moreover have been the greatest misfortune for the Church in the long run—there was no one at the time who uttered the slightest doubt about the validity of the election. On the contrary, some of the cardinals had already hastily left the Vatican to seek refuge in places they considered safer; six made their way to Castel San' Angelo where Pierre de Got, brother of the Cardinal of Limoges, was commander, and where the garrison was largely composed of Frenchmen. But now they all came back to the Vatican to do homage to the new Pope. His most ardent supporters at this time were the Spanish cardinal Pedro de Luna and Cardinal Robert of Geneva—or at least they were the most loud-voiced in their vows of loyalty to Pope Urban VI. The day after his election the cardinals who were still in Avignon were informed, and in due course they paid their respects to the new Pope by letter. On May 8th the results of the election were sent to the German Emperor and all the Catholic princes.

But it was not long before the first signs of catastrophe appeared. The cardinals in Avignon wrote to the French king and other Catholic princes that they were not to accept any declarations sent out in the name of Pope Urban VI. They were supported by their Provençal colleagues in Italy. During the first months of the summer the opposition against the harsh reformer who had been made Pope increased. But as yet it was still an underground movement.

If the Pope had any idea of what was going on, he at any rate paid it no attention. As the prior of the Carthusians at Gorgona had written to Catherine, Urban trusted in God and feared no man. He was convinced that he had been chosen because he was to pull up the weeds and plant the garden of Christ's Bride with beautiful and sweet-smelling flowers, to use Catherine's favourite simile. He started his programme with indomitable energy. He drove all the bishops who were idling in Rome back to their bishoprics, he sent out a number of bulls at lightning speed, and thundered against the luxurious and voluptuous lives of the cardinals. A sermon which he preached on the words "I am the good shepherd" was a searing attack on the worldliness of the higher clergy. Towards the poor he was kind and generous, but the Roman nobility, who had been used to considering themselves as the Holy Father's trueborn, if not always obedient, sons, were deeply offended because the Pope showed them no consideration.

It was against Urban's nature to show consideration for anyone, and decisions which were in themselves both good and wise led to nothing because he was so harsh and lacking in tact and the ability to understand men. It was too much for weak men, of more or less good will, who knew in their hearts that the Pope was right and that they ought to cooperate with him, when the Pope demanded, with harsh and angry words, that they should immediately change their way of life and give up all the small comforts they had grown accustomed to, in order to live in a state of self-denial suitable for the strictest ascetic. They were agreed that it was time for a reform within the Church. But if this were reform... And the language he used when he broke into a rage! "Shut up!" he said to the cardinals. He shouted "Pazzo!"—Idiot—to Cardinal Orsini, and "Ribaldo!"—Bandit—to the Cardinal of Geneva. His electors began to regret their choice bitterly.

In the hottest part of the summer the Pope with the four Italian cardinals moved up to Tivoli. The opposing cardinals, thirteen in number, also left the town and gathered in Anagni. The Pope, who eventually realised that danger was afoot, sent the Cardinals Orsini, Brossano and Corsini to negotiate with them. Only faithful old Cardinal Tebaldeschi remained with the Pope. The ambassadors returned to the Pope from Anagni without having achieved anything.

In August the French and Provençal cardinals sent a letter addressed to "the Bishop of Bari", and a declaration in which they went through all that had happened on the election day. They said they had only chosen Bartolommeo Prignano to avoid certain death. The thirteen cardinals therefore declared him an unlawful pope. They then put themselves under the protection of Count Gaetano of Fondi. The Count had been papal deputy in Anagni and Campania, the port of the Papal States which bordered on Naples. But the new Pope had taken this honour from him and appointed another in his stead. He therefore considered himself to be mortally offended by the Pope. A short while after, the cardinals moved to Fondi— further from Rome and nearer Naples—where the Queen— Joanna—also had a grudge against the man who had once been her subject, and also, in the distant past, when she was a relatively innocent young woman of nineteen, her spiritual director. The conspirators hoped to win her over to their side.

It was just at this time that Catherine had completed her mission in Florence and started her journey back to Siena with her faithful friends. She spent the hot days of August on a farm belonging to her beloved sister-in-law, Lisa Colombini, a few miles from the town. With bitter sorrow she heard the terrible news from Rome: her friends, first and foremost Raimondo, kept her informed of all that went on. The news filled her with a terrible feeling of guilt. She, who had been given such wonderful graces by her Lord, should have done so much more—prayed much more earnestly, practised stricter self-denial, been more eloquent, written more and better. She collapsed under the weight of her own inadequacy and became ill again. Then one morning she crept into the little country church, so broken that she did not dare to approach the altar's Sacrament. But a new vision came to her which filled her with courage and zeal—it was as though she once again experienced the cleansing bath of Christ's burning love.

It seemed as though her tremendous energy could be even greater. After her return to Siena she kept three secretaries at work—they wrote letters for her to nuns and monks who asked her advice in things spiritual, to friends in all the towns where she had been, to people in power in the Italian towns, and to the powers-that-be in foreign countries. She used all her talents to convince them that Urban was the lawful Pope, to whom all Christians owed their loyalty. For the schism was not to be avoided. At the beginning of September the three Italian cardinals went to Fondi—there were only three now, as old Tebaldeschi was dead. It was rumoured that Pope Urban was to create a number of new cardinals—there was no doubt that he would choose men after his own hard heart. So no time was to be lost if the fatal papal elections of April were to be annulled. The King of France let it be known that he would support the election of a French Pope. On September 20th the cardinals in Fondi elected Robert of Geneva; there was one vote against, and the Italian cardinals refused to vote. The new Pope called himself Clement VII. (But when Giulio de' Medici became Pope and took the name of Clement he was called the Seventh; the schismatic pope of Avignon was not counted on the list of the Popes.)

The rival Pope was a brother of the reigning prince of Genoa, related to the French royal family and several other reigning royal houses. This naturally influenced his career in the Church—he was created cardinal while he was still very young. But as long as he was a prelate in France he had maintained an unstained name—that he had to run his house on luxurious lines was considered only natural; a man is forced to live up to his social position; even people who otherwise condemned the luxury of the prelates were agreed on this. He was a handsome man, with a most winning manner, and was well liked by his countrymen. But for the Italians he was the "Butcher from Cesena"—he had not protested against the terrible reprisals taken by the mercenary soldiers of Gregory XI against the rebellious towns in the Romagna and Umbria.

A day or two before the rival Pope was elected, Catherine had sent Urban a letter full of consolation and good advice. She points for consolation to the Eternal Truth which loved us before we were created. The soul which has freed itself from the mists of self-love sees this truth and understands that God wishes for nothing but what is of value to the soul. Such a soul receives with respect burdens, calumny, scorn, injustice, offences and defeat, and bears everything with patience, because it only seeks God through the salvation of the soul. (She makes a variation on her usual phrase "the glory of God and the salvation of souls"; for the Pope the glory of God consists in the salvation of souls.) Such a soul is patient, but not indifferent when its Creator is offended. Through its patience a soul is deprived of its self-love and clothed in divine love. The light of eternal truth will arm us with the two-edged sword, the sword of love and hate—hatred for vice and love of virtue, for this virtue is the bond which attaches us to God and love of our neighbour. "Oh, Most Holy Father, this is the sword which I beg you to take in your hand. Now is the time to draw it from its sheath, and to hate vice in yourself, in your children, and in the Holy Church. I say 'yourself', because in this life none dare say that he is free from sin, and love should begin with oneself." She encourages him to continue with his reforms, and tells him how she suffers from the present state of affairs. "When I look at the places where Christ should be the very breath of everything, I see before you, who are Christ on earth, a hell of abominations. All are infected with self-love. It is this self-love which causes them to rise in rebellion against you, so that they will no longer support Your Holiness." She advises him to surround himself with true servants of God who will advise him faithfully and honestly without passion, and without listening to the poisonous advice of self-love. "I would rather not say any more, but go into the battle myself, to suffer agony and to fight at your side to the death, for truth, for the glory and majesty of God, and for the reformation of the Holy Church."

Catherine had foreseen the schism. When she received the news of it, she must have known that her longing to throw herself into the tumult of battle would soon be fulfilled. She certainly knew in advance that this would lead her to the goal she desired—complete unification with her heavenly Bridegroom whom her soul had longed for so long. Soon she was to enjoy the eternal blessedness which consists of the sight of God As He Is, seen without the veil of our flesh and blood. Soon there was to be an end of her fluttering back and forth over the abyss between heaven and earth, and her eagle soul should find rest on the Bridegroom's breast. But she had still much to do here on earth. Because she knew the time was approaching when she should depart from this life, she had to write her last will and testament for her spiritual children.

XXII

SHE WENT OUT to Fra Santo's solitary dwelling somewhere outside the gates of Siena, intending to remain there some days. She asked her secretaries to listen intently when she was in ecstasy, which was more often now than ever before, and write down all she said. During these periods of ecstasy her body always became stiff and without feeling, sight or hearing, but sometimes words streamed from her lips, and she had on occasion dictated letters while in this condition. Now she knew that the whole of the spiritual knowledge which had been poured into her soul when, transported from this world, she talked with her Lord, would be revealed again to her in a concentrated form which she was intended to give to her children as their inheritance.

Raimondo understood the importance of this book, the *Dialogue*, for he begins the third part of his book on Catherine—the story of her death—by telling how the book came into being. As a suitable quotation from the Bible he used as a motto for this part a quotation from the Canticle of Canticles: "Who is she that cometh up from the desert, flowing with delights, leaning upon her beloved?"

In a long letter to Raimondo in Rome, Catherine told him how the book came into existence and sketched the main themes of it for her understanding confessor. On St. Francis' day, that is to say, October 4, she had felt terribly depressed at the thought of the Church's great misery, and because of something Raimondo had written to her of his own unhappiness: "So I asked a serving-woman of the Lord to offer her tears and her sweat before the face of God for the Bride of Christ and for her spiritual father's weakness." It is Catherine who is the serving-woman. The Saturday after, the Virgin Mary's day, she was in her usual place at Mass. Because she knew the truth about herself, she blushed for her imperfections before God, but soon lost all knowledge of herself through her passionate desire. She fastened the eyes of her understanding on the Eternal Truth, and as she offered herself and her father (Raimondo) for the Church, she turned to God and asked for four things.

First she prayed for the Holy Church, and God condescended to be moved by her tears and her desire, and said to her: "My very dear daughter, see how her face is soiled with vice and self-love, how it is swollen with the pride and avarice which approaches her breast. But cast your tears and sweat over it and draw from the well of My divine love to wash her face, for I promise you, her beauty will never return to her through the sword, violence or war, but through peace—through the humble and persevering prayers of My servants, and their sweat and passionate desire. In this way I will fulfil your longings, and My Providence will never fail you."

And although this prayer for the Church of Christ included the whole world, this woman still had other special requests to make. But God showed her with what great love He had created mankind and how none can escape Him, however many there may be who persecute and offend Him by all kinds of terrible sins: "Open the eyes of your understanding and look at My hand." She looked, and saw the whole world shut in His hand. And God said to her: "You must know that no one can escape me. All things belong to Me because of My righteousness and mercy, and because they have come from Me I love them with indescribable love and will be merciful unto them, and My servants shall be My tools."

In the same way Julian of Norwich in her *Revelations of Divine Love* had seen the world lying in the hand of Christ, a small, dark object resembling a nut. And He had said to the English hermit that this little thing was "everything created", and that He loved it. Both the visionaries had perhaps got this picture from some lines in one of the hymns in the breviary:

> Beata Mater munere
> Cuius Superbus Artifex
> Mundum pugillo continens
> Ventris sub arca clausus est.

(O Mother blessed with gifts, in the ark of whose womb He was contained, the Divine Creator who holds the universe in His closed hand.)

But in the book itself Catherine prays first for herself. For how could she achieve anything for the Church or for her neighbour if she did not receive God's grace? As in the Old Testament fire fell from heaven and consumed the sacrifices on the altar, the Eternal Truth must send the fire of His mercy, the Holy Spirit, and let it burn up her sacrificial gifts of desire and longing. For by ourselves we can achieve nothing which is perfect. Catherine quotes (rather freely) St. Paul's words: "Though I speak with the tongues of angels, though I give all I possess to the poor, my body to be burned in the fire, though I know the future—and have not love, so is all the other as nothing." For her these words meant that temporal actions are insufficient both as expiation and as a means of obtaining grace, if they are not sprinkled with the spices of love, the divine love which God gives us gratuitously.

Catherine calls the manuscript "the book" or "my book". It was Raimondo who first gave it a title and called it the *Dialogue*. The first Latin translation, by Cristofano di Gano

Guidini and Stefano Maconi, had been called by the transla-
tors the *Book of Divine Learning*. Since then the various transcriptions and unprinted editions in several different languages
have gone under several names. But Père Hurtaud chose the
most appropriate when he decided to call his French translation *The Book of Mercy*. The undercurrent beneath the waves
of shifting ideas in these conversations between the Eternal
Father and her whom He calls His very dear daughter, and
His much loved child, is the belief in God's mercy. With her
heart crushed by compassion Catherine begs for mercy—for
all this world which sin has laid waste, for all Christians and
heathens and the infidel too. And finally, when the Eternal
Father compresses all He has taught His daughter into a few
sentences, He says: "I have told you that I will show the world
mercy so that you can see that mercy is the sign by which I
am known." God is inseparable in His being, but *we* must
speak of Him as we experience His actions in different ways:
thus St. Thomas speaks of one of God's qualities which is neither love nor goodness, nor righteousness, nor providence, but
which perfects all God's perfections, which is the root of all
His actions towards that part of His creation which He has
given the ability to think and judge—His mercy.

In the *Dialogue* the Lord repeats for Catherine all that He
has taught her before of the knowledge of God and the knowledge of one's own ego and the way to perfection: "Your service is of no use to Me, it is by serving your neighbour that
you can serve Me." The soul which has once experienced the
bliss of being united with God in love, which has reached the
point where it only loves itself in God, will expand and embrace
the whole world with its love. Once it has won for itself the
virtue which brings a life of grace it will work with the utmost
zeal to help its neighbour. But this is an inner virtue; outward
action, physical work, diligent penitence, self-chastisement and

all kinds of self-denial are nothing more than tools of virtue—God is not interested in them for themselves. On the contrary—they can be an obstacle on the way to perfection if the soul begins to love penitential exercises for their own sake. One must do penitence from love, with true humility and perfect patience. And it must be done with understanding, that is to say with a true knowledge of God and one's own self.

That the soul knows itself means among other things that it understands the great honour that was done to men when they, through no merit of their own, were created in God's image. In the mirror of God's goodness the soul sees how badly it has degraded and crippled itself by love of the wrong things. When she saw herself in this mirror Catherine realised that her guilt was so great that it was enough to have caused all the misery of the world and the Church which she wept over. Therefore she begged God that His vengeance might fall on her head, but His mercy over His people. "I will not go from Your presence before I have seen that You will have mercy on them. What would it help me if I knew that I was sure of my own blessedness, if Your people are to be given to death, and darkness shrouds your Bride, for my sake and no one else's?" So she prayed for the Holy Church and for all men, calling on the love which caused Him to give His Word, His only Son, so that He might be a mediator between Him and us. "O abyss of mercy, we are Your image, and You became our image when You united Yourself with man and unveiled the eternal divinity in the dark clouds of Adam's degenerate flesh."

When she saw that she had been given a new and deeper understanding of the love which caused the redemption by Christ Crucified, Catherine was filled with holy joy and prayed again for the whole world—although if the Holy Church should regain the outward beauty which is an expression of its eternal inner beauty, the whole world would be saved, for it would draw all men to itself so irresistibly that it would lead to the conversion of all men, both Christians and heathens. But when Adam rebelled against God the old royal road which led innocent man from earth to heaven was destroyed. An abyss opened between the two kingdoms, and through this abyss runs a dark and tumultuous river—all the unreal, fleeting things to which mankind's contorted desire aspires. For we cannot live without desire; our soul's actions are desire, holy or unholy. So when mankind had rebelled against God it immediately rebelled against itself; the flesh rebelled against the spirit and mankind drowned in the dark and bitter waters of sin. Because these waters lack solidity, none can live in them without drowning. These waters are the joys and honours of this world: in all eternity they stream past and are carried away in the current. Man thinks it is the things he loves which float, but in reality it is he himself who is swept by the stream towards the end of his life. He would like to stop, to keep his hold of this life and the things he loves, so that they are not washed out of his reach. He reaches out blindly to whatever he happens to touch, but he cannot tell the difference between the valuable and the valueless. Then comes death and takes him from all he loves, or Providence takes a hand, and even before his death he may be robbed of all his beloved worldly treasures. And because he has run after unreality he has followed the way of lies and is the child of the devil who is the Father of Lies. And so he is carried forward to the gates of lies and eternal damnation.

God made a bridge over this abyss when He gave the world His Son. For God, who created us without our having anything to do with it, demands of us that we should work with Him for our salvation. We are all bound to work in the vineyard where God is the husbandman. We have all been given our little vineyard, but the way in which we cultivate it is of great importance for the prosperity of our neighbour's vine-yard. Out in the country Catherine had certainly seen how a piece of earth overgrown with weeds and infested with insects was a source of infection for the neighbouring fields. In fact all our vineyards are a part of the Lord's great vineyard, the Holy Church, and we are all bound to work here too.

But because it is through the grace which God gives us that we are able to work with Him for our salvation, Catherine prays for light. This too she is given, and then she sees how one can receive and increase the grace which God gives freely. It is the old teaching of the mystics on the *Via Purificativa*, the way to cleanse the soul, the *Via Illuminativa*, the way to enlightenment of the eternal truths, and the *Via Unitiva*, the way to unification with God in love.

She develops the bridge symbol in several ways. The soul steps onto the bridge by three steps. Sometimes, according to her, the steps mean the three grades of intimacy with Christ, which are also expressed by the kiss on His feet, the kiss on the wound in His side and the kiss on His mouth. Then she lets the three steps mean three stages towards perfect union with God: slavish fear of God's punishment is what leads most souls to the bridge. The next step is the faithfulness of a servant who follows his kind lord through love, even though this love is still imperfect, because the servant thinks of his reward—the blessedness which God gives His faithful servants. This leads to the third step, where the soul loves God with the love of a son—for what He is, not for His gifts. At another time, the three steps become a symbol for the qualities of the soul—memory, intelligence and will. With an interpretation, entirely her own, of a phrase in the Bible, Catherine declares that when these three qualities of the soul run together in the desire for unity with God, Christ will fulfil His promise: "When two or three are gathered together in my name, I am among them."

She compares memory with a pitcher full of the impressions which we obtain through our emotional life; fill it with nothing, and the empty pitcher is easily broken, or it emits a shrill clang if anyone knocks it. Or fill it with reality, the love of God, and, like a pitcher filled with water from the well, it can take a knock without being broken or emitting a loud noise. For none here on earth can escape suffering and blows, and the pursuit of nothingness also brings hard blows and great bitterness for the soul: those who follow the devil have to bear his cross, and there are many who become martyrs for the devil too. But for a heart which is full of God, suffering is sweet, for we know that it is sent to us by love, so that we shall gain by it. For a soul cannot live without loving. It must have something to love, for it was created of love.

No place or position in the world exempts us from the law of love. None may make his inheritance, his office, his authority, marriage or children an obstacle which hinders his attainment of this unity with God. All visible and sensual things are created by Him and are good in themselves; it is only if we love the created things more than the Creator that they become the tools of our damnation. Ceaselessly the devil tries to tempt us to this wrong kind of love, but it is we who condemn ourselves, because we are willing to be led astray. The devil has no power over us if we do not voluntarily give in to his temptations.

The contents of the book came from Catherine's lips during a series of visions and take the form of thoughts which are often repeated or which reappear constantly in new forms. Her mind is like the waves of the sea which break inwards over the same problems and then wash back again, then break again. The comparisons and symbols, some of them old favourites from earlier visions and letters, are repeated or given new meaning. No translation can do justice to the beauty,

tenderness and pathos she expresses in her lovely Tuscan dialect, and which have made the *Dialogue* one of the masterpieces of Italian literature as well as a milestone in Catholic
thinking.

God speaks to His daughter of the presumption of judging
one's neighbour, and explains to her how it is possible to work
for the conversion of sinners, calling evil by its rightful name,
but yet leave the judgment of them to God. He particularly
warns Catherine against judging unworthy priests and monks.
To wage war on the Church because its bad servants sin is
itself a great sin. God who raised up His priests and clothed
them in power and dignity will judge them Himself, and however wretched they may be they are still the ministers of the
sacraments which nourish the life of grace in us. But Christ
says, "My priests shall be high-minded men, not hired apprentices. They must not sell the grace of the Holy Spirit, which
is Myself, for rewards."

In the *Dialogue* God speaks too of the degeneration within
the Church, and expresses Himself so uncompromisingly regarding bad priests and monks that some of the French transla-
tions which appeared at a time when anti-clericalism in France
was at its most violent, simply omitted these chapters in
Catherine's book. She compares good priests and monks with
suns which give life and warmth to the whole of Christendom. But woe to the priests and monks who are proud, practise simony, and intrigue to win honour and power among
men. They waste the riches of the Church, which should be
used for charitable work and for the upkeep of ecclesiastical
buildings, on themselves and their concubines and bastards, or
on their relations for whom they have exaggerated love. Instead
of feeding Christ's lambs they flay them and use their dishon-
est earnings for gambling and drinking. Nevertheless God says
the same to us as His Truth says in the Gospel: "Do as they

tell you, continue to keep the commandments they preach, but do not imitate their actions."

But it almost broke Catherine's heart to see so many abominations in the Church, and the great misery caused by them. God looks down with indescribable tenderness and consoles her: "Daughter, your refuge is to do honour to My name and offer ceaseless prayers, like incense, for the wretches who have deserved to be condemned for their crimes. Your refuge is in My only Son, Christ Crucified.... In His pierced heart you will find love for Me and your neighbour.... Fill yourself at the table of the cross, and bear with your neighbour with true patience, and bear patiently too all the pain, fear and toil, from whatever side they may attack you. In this way you shall win grace and escape the leprosy of the time."

Catherine's prayer is an answer to these words: "O eternal God, Your servants beg for mercy; answer them. As though I did not know that mercy is so divine that You cannot deny it to those who pray for it! They knock at the door of Truth, Your only Son, for they have recognised in Him Your infinite love towards mankind. If they knock at this door with passionate love, You will not, You cannot, refuse to open to those who pray ceaselessly. Open, therefore! Expand and melt the hardened hearts of Your creatures, not for the sake of those who knock, but for the sake of Your infinite goodness and for the sake of Your servant who prays to You for them.... And what do they demand of You? The blood of Your Truth, which is also the gate. They desire the blood with which You have washed away the stain of Adam's sin. It belongs to us, this blood, for You have made us a bath of it. You cannot, You will not refuse it to those who pray for it...."

"Eternal Father, all things are possible for You. Although You created us without our assistance, You will not save us unless we help. Therefore I pray You, re-create their wills so that they wish for what they do not wish for: I ask this of Your infinite mercy. You have created us out of nothing. Now that we exist have mercy on us. Re-make the vessel which you created in Your own image and likeness. Bring them back to Your grace through the grace and blood of Your Son, the beloved Jesus Christ." And, moved by her prayers, God condescends to explain to her how His providence is mercy, and nothing but mercy. To open the eyes of her understanding so that she may see this truth, He condescends to explain to her how He has heard her prayer for a soul which has gone from this life. It was finally saved for the sake of the love which it always had for the Mother of Jesus.

This part of the *Dialogue* is obscure, and it has never been made clear for which soul it was that Catherine had prayed so persistently. Perhaps the suicide from the summer before in the Orco valley? It is possible, but it may be another. Although world politics had now become Catherine's field of action, she was still the same Catherine from Fontebranda who put the whole energy of her soul and the whole of her passionate personality into the salvation of the two wicked old women, Cecca and Andrea; the tearing of the souls of the two robbers out of the claws of the devil on the way to the place of execution; and the saving of the soul of Niccolò di Toldi, who rebelled against the righteousness of God because he was the victim of the injustice of men.

In her beautiful final prayer Catherine pours out her thanks for the treasures with which the Holy Trinity has filled her heart: "O eternal Trinity, You are a bottomless ocean. The more I throw myself into the ocean, the more I find You, and the more I find You the more I will search. I can never say of You—It is enough . . . As the hart longs for the running water of the spring, my soul longs to escape from the dark prison of my body to see You in truth . . . For in the light with which

You have illuminated my intellect I have seen and tasted Your bottomless depths, O Eternal Trinity, and beauty of all that is created . . . O Eternal Trinity, You are the Creator, I am Your creature. In my redemption through the blood of Your Son I have recognised that You love the beauty of Your creatures. O abyss, O Eternal Divinity, bottomless ocean! Oh, what could You give me that is better than Yourself? You are the fire which burns eternally, and never dies. You are the fire which consumes self-love, You are the fire which melts all the frost and illumines all things, and it is in this light that You have taught me to know Your truth."

With this outburst of burning gratitude she became silent. Stefano Maconi, who wrote most of her revelations—although Neri di Landoccio and Barduccio Canigiani had also written parts of them—stopped here. According to the custom of that time he added a few words to ask the reader to pray for him who had written. Stefano's "signature" is always the same: "Pray to God for your useless brother."

The book was finished on October 13, written without a break in four or five days. The division into chapters and sections has been arranged by the transcribers and publishers. In Catherine's lifetime it was only circulated among her friends and disciples. But after her death it became known in wider circles, and transcriptions were made for monastery libraries both in her own and other orders. It was recognised that her teaching was inspired by the Holy Spirit, and not what she had learned from theologians. On the contrary, Catherine became recognised as a teacher of divine knowledge—as her disciples had always considered her to be.

Ser Cristofano di Gano Guidini tells us that he had just obtained a new and beautiful transcription of the Latin translation of the *Dialogue*, revised by Stefano Maconi, when he was visited

by a French Cardinal of the Dominican order. He came with
Fra Raimondo, who was now the Master General of the order.
The Cardinal had met Catherine in Avignon many years before
and had been deeply impressed by the remarkable personality
of the Italian Mantellata. In the meantime Raimondo had told
him so much about her that his interest in Catherine had been
re-awakened. When Cristofano let him see the copy of the
Dialogue, the Frenchman began to read here and there in it,
and became so interested that he begged Ser Cristofano to
give him the book. He would preach the teachings of Catherine to his own people; schism or no schism, the faithful in
France should be nourished with the spiritual food which had
been prepared by the woman who had flung the most violent
accusations at the rival French pope in Avignon. Ser Cristofano had to let the Cardinal have the book. "I did not have it
in my house more than a single night." But, as he remarks, he
had the original, so he could easily get a new transcription for
his own use.

XXIII

AFTER HAVING, so to speak, disposed of her effects, Catherine started on her journey to Rome. But this time she had written beforehand to Raimondo and asked him to obtain a written order from Urban VI to leave Siena and come to Rome. For not only had many of her townspeople taken exception to her frequent journeys, but many of her sisters among the Mantellate had also done so. They considered that a virgin dedicated to God should keep in her cell and do good in secret. And although she had not a trace of guilty conscience on this ground, as she had never travelled anywhere except in obedience to God and His Vicar, she did not like to annoy her neighbours unnecessarily. The Pope sent her a written order, and Catherine was free to start her journey.

This time she travelled with a great company. With her were the faithful friends Lisa, Alessia and several other sisters, her dear sons Neri di Landoccio and Barduccio Canigiani, the old hermit Fra Santo, who had now been her steadfast companion for several years, and a number of priests, among them Fra Bartolommeo Dominici and the Augustinian, Fra Giovanni Tantucci from Lecceto. There were many others too, and even more wanted to accompany her, but according to Raimondo Catherine would not allow it. Although many of her companions had left comfortable homes, the whole company had promised voluntarily to travel as beggars, trusting in God's providence to supply them with alms on the way.

Lapa was to remain in the house in the Via Romana where she had lived since the old home in the Via dei Tintori had been broken up. But it was arranged that she should follow, when her daughter had arranged a house in Rome. Stefano Maconi also remained in Siena, most probably because his mother intervened—later at any rate she opposed him when he wished to join Catherine in Rome.

The company arrived in Rome on the first Sunday in Advent, November 28. The town Catherine came to was a town under arms. The Romans were besieging San Angelo, which the French garrison was holding for Clement. This meant that the Pope could not move into the Vatican, and so Urban lived at Santa Maria in Trastevere. In the country outside the city walls too, armies were on the march.

Catherine was immediately received by the Pope, who was overwhelmed with joy at meeting her again. He asked her to make a speech to the assembled cardinals, first and foremost about the schism, which had now become a fact. She did so in such a way that everyone was greatly moved. She encouraged them to show courage and determination, and brought forward many reasons for this. She explained how God's providence watched over each individual in a special way in these times which brought such great suffering on Holy Church. Therefore, she said finally, they should not let themselves be frightened by the schism, but persevere and work for God without fear of men. When she finished her talk the Pope seemed extremely happy. He summed up what she had said, and added to the cardinals: "See, brothers, how guilty we must appear to God because we are without courage. This little woman puts us to shame. And when I call her a little woman [*piccola donzella*] I do not do so out of scorn, but because her sex is by nature fearful; but see how we tremble while she is strong and calm, and see how she consoles us with her words. How could the Vicar of Christ be afraid even though the whole world rise against him? Christ is stronger than the whole world,

and it is impossible for Him to fail His Church." With these
words he encouraged himself and his brothers, praised the saint
in her Lord, and granted Catherine and her company his blessing and indulgence.

A day or two later Urban suggested that Catherine and another
virgin, also called Katherine, should go as his ambassadors to
Queen Joanna of Naples, who now openly supported the
schismatics. This other Katherine was the daughter of St. Birgitta and had come to Rome to arrange several matters connected with the convent in Vadstena which her mother had
founded. But St. Karin of Vadstena, as the Swedes call her,
blankly refused to visit Queen Joanna. The last time the Swedish girl had met the Queen of Naples was when she was on
her way to Jerusalem with her mother and two of her brothers. For a while it seemed as though the many-times-married
Joanna was listening to Birgitta's advice and thinking of beginning a better life. But at the final audience when they were to
take their leave, after Birgitta and her two younger children,
Karin and the serious young Master Birger, had approached
and kissed the Queen's foot, as the custom demanded, the
eldest brother went boldly forward and gave the Queen a
resounding kiss on the mouth. The Swedish knight was a man
of great beauty—his mother's pride and sorrow, for she knew
all too well that she was guilty of too much forbearance with
this favourite child; she had been far too patient with his pride
and frivolity. Unfortunately it has not been recorded whether
he appeared before Joanna in the same costume which had
once caused Pope Urban V to say something about its being
almost too magnificent, although the Pope must have been
used to seeing people spending enormous sums of money on
their clothes. On Herr Karl's chest the golden chain of knight-
hood glittered, and his cape of azure blue was lined with

ermine—not merely the skins, but the small white animals were stuffed so cunningly that it looked as though they sported and tumbled about his tall and magnificent body every time he moved.

The Queen immediately fell violently in love with the handsome Swede. And although she was married to her fourth husband, and Herr Karl had a wife in Sweden, Joanna swore that she would marry Karl Ulfsson—they must arrange to get rid of their unwelcome partners. Birgitta was almost out of her mind with fear; for once her iron will could not achieve anything against the infatuated queen. She stormed heaven with prayers: God must save her son from falling into this mortal sin. Her prayers were heard. Herr Karl suddenly fell ill with a high fever, and two days later he died in his mother's arms. Long weeks followed during which all Birgitta's prayers were for her son's soul. Finally she was granted a vision in which she saw that Karl had been raised out of purgatory because Christ's mother had prayed for him. In spite of his sinfulness Herr Karl had always had great love for the Virgin Mary.

Karin Ulfsdotter was now a woman of about forty, but she was obviously convinced that there was no misdeed so terrible that Queen Joanna would not commit it. If she and Catherine of Siena went to Naples they risked being taken in ambush on the way, and killed. Raimondo agreed with Karin; he considered Queen Joanna an utterly depraved woman, and was stubbornly set against his "mamma" meeting her. Only Catherine scorned her friends' lack of courage. "If Agnes or Margaret or Catherine of Alexandria had been so afraid they would never have won the crown of martyrdom. Have not all good virgins a Bridegroom to watch over and care for them? It seems to me that these doubts show lack of faith more than the virtue of forethought." But Urban thought over what Karin had said and let the idea drop.

While she was still in Siena Catherine had written to Queen Joanna—a passionate plea for the lawful Pope, Urban, to whom all Christian princes owed their loyalty. From Rome she sent the Queen a letter which was even more outspoken. She addresses the letter to her "dear mother in Christ". (Joanna was by then a woman of fifty-one and married for the fourth time.) Catherine now writes to this woman on her favourite theme, self-love opposed to the love for God as He has revealed Himself in Christ Crucified. "Oh, dear mother, you must love the Truth, you must submit yourself to the Holy Church—for otherwise I will never again call you mother or turn towards you with respect. From being a queen you have been made a servant and the slave of something which is nothing. . . ." Because she has left the breast of her mother, the Holy Church, people weep over her as over one who is dead; she has chosen lies instead of truth, and listened to the advice of men who are incarnate devils. How can they prove it when they say that Urban VI is not the lawful Pope? They cannot, they lie abominably. If it is true that Urban VI was not lawfully elected they deserve to die a thousand times, for if they elected him from fear and afterwards set him up as the lawful Pope, and caused us to support them in doing homage and promising obedience to one who had not the right to receive it, no punishment is hard enough for them. The man whom they tried to present as the Pope, the high-minded old Cardinal Tebaldeschi, protested loudly and declared that the Archbishop of Bari was the Pope. And who is it they have chosen as Pope in his stead? A criminal wretch (no Italian had forgotten the massacre in Cesena), a devil, who does the devil's work. But if she still has any doubt of the validity of Urban's election, Catherine begs Joanna at least to remain neutral until she has discovered the truth. "Oh, I say to you in the deepest sorrow, for I wish with my whole soul that you may be saved, that if you do not change, and turn from this error and all the others, the Highest Judge will punish you in such a way that it will fill all who think of rebelling against the Church with terror. Do not wait for Him to strike, for it is hard to withstand God's justice. You must die, and you do not know when."

Joanna paid no attention to Catherine's warnings, nor to those of the Pope. In April 1380, a day or two before Catherine's death, she was excommunicated by Urban VI. Her subjects, who had never been particularly fond of their self-willed ruler, thereupon were freed of all their duties towards her. As the kingdom of Naples was a vassal of the Holy See, Urban gave it to Charles of Durazzo, a relation of Joanna's first husband. Charles believed, or chose to believe, the rumours which blamed Joanna for having had a share in the murder of her first husband. To avenge his relative Charles had Joanna killed in a manner which was far from dignified—she was strangled in her bed.

Catherine and her companions settled down in a house near Santa Maria sopra Minerva. As they had all vowed voluntary poverty they lived on alms. But although she seldom had less than twenty-five in the household Catherine gladly received all those who came to stay with her whether for a short or long time—the Sienese naturally wanted to avail themselves of the influence their Popolana had with the Pope to obtain indulgences or audiences, or to visit the old sanctuaries of the apostles and martyrs with one who they were sure was in close contact with the Lord of all the saints. Catherine depended on God's providence, and they never suffered want, but always received enough to meet their modest demands.

But however modestly they lived, the wise virgin, as Raimondo called her, demanded that the house-keeping should be ordered and that all should have time to make their pilgrimages and visit the churches of Rome. So she arranged that all the women in the company should take a week at a time to look after the house and prepare the meals, and if they lacked bread or wine or fuel, whoever was in charge that week was to say so to Catherine, so that she might go out and beg or send some of the others to do so. But one day when it was Giovanna di Capo's week she forgot to tell Catherine that they had almost no bread. Only when the company were about to sit down to their meal did Giovanna think of it and, filled with shame, she had to say so to Catherine. For once it looked as though Catherine were cross: "God forgive you, Sister, how could such a thing happen? Have we no bread at all?" Yes, there was a little, said Giovanna, but it was so little as to be almost nothing. "Let the family come to table," said Catherine, "and tell them from me that they are to begin and eat the little we have." The family was ravenously hungry, for they had fasted the whole morning, so they began to eat with hearty appetites. But the scrap of bread—bread is the chief sustenance of the Italians—was more than sufficient; they ate bread before the soup, and with the soup; and when the men had eaten and the women came to the table there was still more than enough. After the meal they were able to give away a lot of bread to the poor. Throughout the mealtime Catherine had knelt in her chamber in prayer.

On November 29 Pope Urban solemnly excommunicated Cardinal Robert of Geneva and a number of other cardinals, prelates and princes who supported him—also the military leaders of the troops which the rival Pope had collected in the hope of taking Rome by storm and getting rid of Urban. The three Italian Cardinals, Corsini, Orsini and Brossano, and the Spanish Cardinal de Luna, had not yet openly joined the Clementists.

It is possible that a letter from Catherine to the three Italians caused them to hesitate. She begins by telling them that if they come out of the darkness in which they live she will call them her fathers, but not if they do not change their opinions. The Sister of Penitence speaks sharply and to the point to the cardinals, as one who has authority. Even her favourite theme of the two kinds of love, the one life-giving, the other bringing death, is turned into a violent attack against these men who have been invested with the greatest responsibility and the highest dignities in the Church, but have become traitors through love of temporal things. Not that all that God has created is not good in itself, but how sinful and stupid our flesh is which clamours for and becomes attached to the transitory goods of this life! Our life and the beauty of youth are as short-lasted as the beauty of a flower; once it has been plucked no one can preserve it. So it is with our life on earth when the Highest Judge lets death pluck us, none knows when. She reminds them that it is their duty to be examples of pure and holy life—and they have become as hired apprentices, ungrateful and untruthful. For it is a lie to say that they elected Urban out of fear—the comedy with Cardinal Tebaldeschi was played through fear. "Perhaps you will ask me, 'Why do you not believe us? We know the truth about this election better than you, for we were present and made the election.' I answer that I have seen you depart from the truth in so many ways that I cannot believe you when you try to convince me that Urban VI is not the lawful Pope." If this were true, they have tried to seduce her and all Christians into idolatry, and they themselves have been guilty of idolatry and were heretics when they crowned Urban VI (Orsini had put the tiara on his head) and received simoniacal marks of favour from his hand, if they doubted that he was the lawful Vicar of Christ. If they had only elected him through fear, "how could you partake in such an election, even though you were in danger of your lives?" But "you could not even take a well-earned correction, let alone a hard word of accusation. Then you became obstinate; that is what has made you rebellious. Yes, we know the truth. Before Christ on earth corrected you, you were ready to acknowledge him as the Vicar of Christ and did homage to him. But the last fruits you have borne show what kind of trees you are." She begs them with great eloquence to return to the fold, and promises to pray for them. Finally she uses a very human argument: "In the eyes of religion we are all alike. But humanly Christ on earth is an Italian, and you are Italians. You cannot be led astray by patriotism as are those from the other side of the Alps." "Do not believe that I wish you any evil when I hurt you with my words; care for your salvation is what makes me write. I would sooner have talked to you personally if God had allowed it; but His will be done: you deserve punishment more than words." Even Catherine's usual excuse for her boldness in speaking to those who are so much above her in wisdom and rank—she begs for forgiveness because she only thinks of the salvation of their souls—is exceptionally short and meagre in this utterly crushing letter to the three Italian cardinals who have become traitors to God and the Holy Church.

Catherine had advised Pope Urban most urgently to collect around himself a lifeguard of the most worthy, righteous and pure of God's servants—the same advice as she had given his predecessor. The Pope listened to her advice, or perhaps he had himself had the same idea. Now he wrote to the prior of the Carthusians at Gorgona and asked him to arrange for Masses to be said and prayers offered in all the monasteries in Tuscany for the Pope's cause. He commanded the prior moreover to appear in Rome before the end of the month, for the Pope wished to consult with him and other holy and pious monks regarding the problems of the times. Catherine sent her own letters with the Pope's bulls: she wrote to most of her old friends in the various monasteries, and also to the prior of Gorgona.

Almost all of them came to Rome. But the English hermit of Lecceto, William Flete, refused point blank to leave his solitary dwelling in the woods, although Catherine told him and his friend Fra Antonio di Nizza that woods and solitude could be found round Rome if they could not manage without them. Fra Antonio decided to answer the Pope's call, but Catherine wrote to him expressing her deep displeasure with Fra William. "I sigh from the bottom of my heart over his stupidity, for he does not seek the glory of God and the good of his neighbour with noticeable zeal." She has heard that two servants of God (William and Antonio) have had a revelation from God that if they left their solitude they would risk losing the glow of their faith and would not be able to put themselves whole-heartedly into their prayers for the lawful Pope. Catherine remarks: "The glow of your faith cannot be very ardent if you risk losing it by changing your dwelling. It seems as though God cares about places, and is only to be found in solitude and no other place in the day of need."

But the learned Oxford theologian did great work for Urban's cause through the letters he sent home to England. It was largely through him that England remained steadfastly loyal to Urban, while Scotland became Clementist.

Urban was always loyal to Catherine. He always thought seriously over what she suggested and advised, and he did not turn against her or become sulky, as Gregory XI had done at times when it seemed as though he had got himself into a difficult position through following her advice. The obstinate and headstrong old man never seems to have been offended at anything she wrote to him; he obviously felt real fatherly love for "this little woman" whom he allowed to lead him, and honoured her as the chosen spokesman of his Lord and Master. Gregory insisted that Catherine should undertake the dangerous mission to his enemies in Florence; he "did not think" they would do anything to her. Urban immediately gave up his plan to send her and the Swedish Karin as his messengers to the Queen of Naples as soon as Karin refused because of the far more unlikely dangers to which she thought they might be exposed. Catherine and Urban looked in exactly the same way at the most important questions of their time—the cleansing of the Church and the re-awakening of faith among all Christian peoples. She was not blind to his faults; her letters show this all too clearly. And Catherine of Siena had been dead several years, and Urban had become worn out by the wars and treacheries of the Clementists, and was probably suffering from acute hardening of the arteries, when he developed into the dreadful old man whose insane suspicions and devilish cruelty shook even the most ardent of his supporters.

In spite of his consistent loyalty to Catherine he soon demanded of her that she should make the greatest sacrifice possible for her, humanly speaking. She had looked forward greatly to being with Raimondo again. Perhaps she was no more fond of him than of any other of her spiritual sons, she was so indescribably fond of them all, each in his own special way—"the melancholy Neri, and the joyous Stefano, the angelic Barduccio, the faithful old Fra Santo, and the unstable Francesco Malavolti". But Raimondo was the only one of her sons who could ever be compared spiritually with his mother. He was the grown-up son with whom she could have a comradeship of the soul. And now when she had not been more than a

couple of weeks in Rome Pope Urban had decided to send
messengers to King Charles of France; they were to try to
persuade him to break with the schismatics, in spite of the
fact that he had been one of the first to encourage them. The
Pope was to send three men, and Raimondo was to be the
leader.

The story of his leave-taking from Catherine must be told
in his own words:

When I became acquainted with the Pope's plan I talked about
the matter to Catherine. Although it cost her much to renounce
my presence, she immediately advised me to obey the Pope's
commands and wishes, and said to me: "Father, do not doubt
that this Pope is the lawful Vicar of Christ, whatever scandal
the schismatics may invent about him. I wish you to face anything to defend this truth, just as you would face anything to
defend the Catholic faith."

This confirmation of a truth which I already knew strengthened my determination to fight with all my strength, whatever the schismatics might do, so that to this very day I have
never ceased to work assiduously for the defence of the lawful
Pope, and when I have come into dangers and difficulties these
words of Catherine's have always been my consolation. So I
did as she advised me and bowed my neck under the yoke of
obedience.

But because she knew what was to happen she wanted to
talk to me during these few days before I left of the revelations and consolation she had had from Our Lord. And she
spoke to me in such a way that none of the others who were
in the room could hear anything. After our last conversation,
which had lasted several hours, she said to me: "Go now and
work for God, but I do not think that we shall meet again in
this life or talk to each other as we have done now." This
prophecy was fulfilled. I went to France and left the saint in
Rome. When I returned she had already been taken from this

earth to heaven. Never before had I enjoyed the grace of listening so long to her holy conversation.

I think it was because she wanted me to understand that
this was a last farewell that she went with me to the ship when
I sailed. When the boat had put off she fell on her knees and
prayed, and then she made the sign of the cross with her hand
as though to say, "Son, go in safety, protected by the holy sign
of the cross, but in this life you will never see your mother
again."

Christmas was approaching—the first which Catherine was
to celebrate in Rome. As a Christmas present Catherine sent
the Pope five oranges which she had candied and covered
with gold leaf. (Oranges were at that time a novelty in Italy;
according to tradition the first orange tree was brought to
the country by St. Dominic, who planted it in a garden beside
the monastery of Santa Sabina.) The Christmas present was
accompanied by a letter which she had written "desiring to
free you from the bitter agony which rages in your soul.
May the cause of this agony disappear so that you know
nothing but the sweet pain which makes the soul strong and
passionate. It is the pain which springs from the love of God—I
mean the sorrow and pain caused by our own faults." She
develops the theme of the difference between the bitter and
the sweet pain, and gives the Pope a recipe for making candied
oranges. Catherine, who was such a good cook, finds it seemly
to draw some good spiritual maxims from it: "This fruit tastes
bitter at first, when we bite it with holy desire in the mouth,
but when the soul has become willing to suffer unto death
for the love of Christ Crucified, then it tastes quite sweet. I
have often noticed this with the oranges, which seem sharp
and bitter at first. When one has taken out the inside, and
allowed the orange to absorb boiling water, the bitterness
disappears, and then one fills them with good and nutritious

things and covers them with gold on the outside. What has become of the bitterness which is so unpleasant to human taste? It is drawn out by the fire and the water. Most Holy Father, it is just the same with a soul which understands the love of virtue. The beginning seems bitter, for the soul is still imperfect, but if it uses the remedy, which is the blood of Christ Crucified, then the water of grace which is in the blood will draw out the physical bitterness which causes our dislike. And as the blood can never be separated from the fire, because it is poured out of the fire of love, we can say that water and fire take away the bitter taste of self-love, and so constancy fills the soul with good things—the patience combined with the honey of humility which conserves our knowledge of our own self.... When the fruit is filled and finished, the outside must be covered with gold. This gold is the purity which shines radiantly from burning love, and it manifests itself through faithful and patient service of our neighbour."

Catherine had come a long way since the time when she was a little girl in her father's house in Fontebranda and played her games before God, in the serious and preoccupied manner of children when they play. But the pale and emaciated woman whose body was almost annihilated by supernatural experience and supernatural problems, must sometimes have shown a glimpse of the same small girl who played before God, smiling delightedly at her own strange ideas and inventions.

XXIV

Catherine wrote to Stefano Maconi that she longed to see him break the bonds which he obviously was unable to loosen and which kept him in Siena. "The blood of the great martyrs who went so ardently to their deaths here in Rome, who gave their lives from love of life, is still boiling, and invites you and others to come here and suffer for the glory and majesty of God; and for the Holy Church." "The bonds" were possibly the illness his brother suffered from, but he was better by this time, and Catherine expressed the hope that Madonna Giovanna had been consoled so that Stefano would soon be able to "say farewell to the world".

But Stefano remained in Siena another year—his loving mother would not let him escape. Maybe he had changed a little since the time when his only wish had been to be with his "mother" always. Although in his letters to his friend Neri di Landoccio he is always talking of their wonderful mother and of his longing to sit at her feet. He kept Catherine and her friends informed of what went on in Siena. Her native town stood firmly on Pope Urban's side, and Stefano thought that if ambassadors from the "anti-demon", Fra Fondi—whom in a somewhat confused simile he calls the rival Pope—were to set their feet inside the gates of Siena, the street urchins would stone them. Moreover, through Stefano Catherine kept up a lively exchange of letters with her friends in Siena, and she naturally kept in constant touch with her native town through all the Sienese who came and went in her house in Rome.

Her mother had come to Rome some time in the New Year of 1379. Now Monna Lapa—Catherine's family called her "Nonna", grandmother—was to be allowed to remain with her daughter as long as Catherine lived. It was not very long.

The Tyrrhenian Sea was infested with pirate ships and the galleons of the schismatics, but Raimondo travelled safely as far as Pisa. Catherine's first letter reached him while he was there. Lovingly and earnestly, she encouraged him to carry out with bravery the task which had been committed to him in the service of the lawful Pope; he must seek from the Source of wisdom and light for wisdom and light to perform his actions. Without light a man may say too much or do too little. But at the end she could not retain a sigh: "I do not want to say things to you which would be hard to say or write, dear Father. My silence ought to express what I wanted to say. I end. I long greatly to see you return to this garden and help me to pull up the rank weeds. Rest in the sweet and holy joy of God. Sweet Jesus, Jesus Love."

Raimondo and his companions sailed to Genoa and continued their journey overland. But in Ventimiglia a Dominican monk from the neighbourhood came and warned Fra Raimondo—he knew that an ambush had been laid for them, they would be taken prisoner, and Raimondo at any rate would certainly be killed. They returned to Genoa, and Raimondo sent a message to the Pope and asked for further instructions. The Pope told him to remain in Genoa and preach against the schismatics. But Catherine took an unfavourable view of her dear confessor's carefulness: "My very dear Father in Jesus Christ, I Catherine, Christ's servants' serving-woman and slave, write to you in His precious blood, full of longing to see you grow out of your childhood and become a grown man.... For an infant who lives on milk is not able to fight on the battlefield; he only wants to play with other children. So a man who is wrapped in love for himself only wishes to taste the milk of spiritual and temporal consolation; like a child, he wants to be with others of his kind. But when he becomes a grown man, he leaves behind him his sensitive self-love. Filled with holy desire, he eats bread, chewing it with the teeth of hate and love, and the coarser and harder it is the better he likes it.... He has become strong, he associates with strong men, he is firm, serious, thoughtful; he hastens to the battlefield with them, and his only wish is to fight for the Truth; he is happy and praises himself, like St. Paul, for his adversities when he has to suffer for the sake of the Truth.... Such men always find peace in the centre of the storm; they taste great sweetness in bitterness. They barter poor and wretched wares for eternal riches...." But "you were not yet worthy to fight on the battlefield, and therefore you were sent behind the lines like a little boy; you fled of your own free will, and were glad to do so, because God showed mercy for your weakness.... Oh bad little Father, what happiness it had been for your soul and mine if you had cemented a single stone in the Church of God with your blood, out of love for the precious Blood.... We have truly reason to complain when we see how our wretched deeds have lost a great reward for us. Oh, let us lose our milk teeth and cut instead the strong teeth of hate and love. Let us take our coat of mail, the breastplate of holy faith, and rush onto the battlefield. With the cross before and behind us we cannot run away...."

Raimondo was obviously deeply moved when he read this letter. He was afraid that he had lost Catherine's love and respect. She wrote a long and detailed letter in reply to a letter from him. Filled with grief she accuses herself—she too could so easily have shrunk from martyrdom: "I am convinced that God is the same for me as He was for the martyrs, that His power is no less, that He can and will provide me with all I need. But because I do not love Him I do not rely completely upon Him; the physical fear which I know I possess shows how lukewarm my love is, how the light of faith is dimmed by my presumption and my faithlessness towards my Creator. I acknowledge and do not deny that this root is not yet weeded out of my soul completely, and it is this which delays the work which God has entrusted to me and prevents me from reaching the great goal which God intended for me when He let me start this work. . . ." She begs Raimondo in the most touching words to pray for himself and for her, that God may annihilate their old selves and re-create them, so that they may receive the ability to love perfectly and be strong and faithful. "It seems to me, from what I have understood from your letter, that you have suffered from terrible inner strife. The snares of the devil and your own sensitiveness have made you think your burdens were too heavy for you to bear, and that I had measured you with my own yardstick. And you thought that my love for you had diminished; but in this you are wrong, and you show that my love has grown, while yours has diminished, for I love you as I love myself. I had hoped so ardently that God's goodness would add to you that which was lacking. But it was not to be so, for you decided to throw off the burden which chafed you, and to fall into weakness and unfaithfulness. All this I see clearly, and I wish I had been the only one to see it. So you can see that my love for you has increased and not diminished. But how explain that your ignorance of my love could cause you the smallest grain of suffering? How could you ever think that I desired anything but life for your soul? What has become of the faith you have always had and ought to have? What has become of your conviction that everything that happens is according to God's providence, not only in great matters but in the smallest trivialities?

"If you had been faithful you would not have been full of doubt and faint-heartedness towards God and me. But like an obedient son you would have done all that you could, and if you could not proceed on your two feet you would have continued your way on your hands and knees. If you could not travel as a monk you could have travelled as a pilgrim. If you were penniless you could have begged. Such filial obedience would have done more for the cause, for God, and for the souls of men than all the carefulness and forethought in the world." At the same time she is convinced of his will to serve God and His Vicar, the lawful Pope, and she too has not the ability to bring to a successful conclusion the works she has undertaken, partly because those with whom she works lack zeal, but first and foremost because of her own sins. "Oh, we see in agony of soul how our sins against God rise and overpower us. I live in sorrow, and pray God in His mercy to take me from this dark life."

The news from Naples was worse than ever—yet another reason for Catherine to grieve over the fact that he had shirked his duty. She had some slight hopes of this meeting he was to have with the French King, but God's will be done. An embassy to the King of Hungary had been talked of, but now the Pope had decided that Raimondo and his companions should not go. So she returns to her sorrow for Raimondo and herself: they must be as though dead to everything except the Church's and the Pope's cause. "Be strong and kill yourself with the sword of hate and love, then you will not hear the insults and abuse which the enemies of the Church throw at you. Your eyes will not see anything which seems impossible, or the sufferings which may follow, but only the light of faith, and in that light everything is possible; and remember God never lays greater burdens on us than we can bear." As a cure against the misery of the times Catherine encourages Raimondo again to go to the Source from which all perfection and holy recklessness spring—all that his spiritual daughter desires with the whole of her fiery nature for her beloved son and father.

It seemed to Catherine that the blood of the martyrs in Rome was still boiling. She had arranged her household expressly so that it should be easy for her family to visit the sanctuaries of the saints and martyrs, especially during Lent. The custom of keeping the "stations" gave another opportunity for great solemnities: every day during Lent the priests from all the parish churches in Rome went in solemn procession to a chosen church—some of them were so dilapidated that they were only opened on this one day of the year—in order to celebrate the Mass with all the pomp and magnificence they could contrive. Catherine was more active than ever; she wrote letters and talked with people, she carried out all kinds of charitable actions, but in her letters from Rome she speaks again of the "cell of self-knowledge" which is built in the depths of the soul—and not by human hands. She advises the friends who have made her their spiritual leader to retire to this cell and never leave it, however busy with outward duties they may be. Few saints have lived such a busy life, or been so occupied with the problems of their time, as Catherine of Siena, but she was absolutely sure that the most important work she had to do was to pray ceaselessly, to suffer gladly and to receive with the humility of love the messages and advice which her divine Bridegroom gave her when she was in ecstasy.

XXV

IN THE MEANTIME it seemed as though the schism would lead to a great war. Most of the Christian countries were still loyal to Pope Urban VI. The German Empire, Hungary, Poland, Norway, Sweden and Denmark acknowledged him as the rightful Pope. Some time later the young King of England, Richard II, drew up a document, *Rationes Anglicorum*, which he in vain challenged the University of Paris to refute. It had not yet come so far that the schism divided nations internally, and split the monastic orders into parties and factions, rival princes declaring themselves for Urban or Clement, bishops and their chaplains supporting different sides, and the religious orders dividing themselves in favour of Urban or Clement. It was not the first time there had been schism in the Church, but it had never meant so much before: on previous occasions everyone had known that the rival Pope had been set up by the German Emperor or some political group, and politics and force of arms had decided on the support given to the Pope or his rival. But this time the reason for the schism was really a problem concerning the Church: had the election of Urban VI been valid or not? Even people of good will, even saints like St. Colette, who reformed the order of the Poor Clares, and the Dominican St. Vincent Ferrer supported the Pope in Avignon. St. Vincent indeed ended by acknowledging that he had made a mistake and denied the authority of the Avignon Pope from the pulpit: the rival pope at that time was Benedict XIII, who had once been the Cardinal Pedro de Luna.

The Master General of the Dominicans, Fra Elias of Tou-louse, went over to the Clementists, and, not long after, the Dominicans in the countries loyal to Urban were given a new Master General, Fra Raimondo of Capua. The three Italian cardinals had retired to Tagliacozza and demanded that a general council should be held to decide the question. Cardinal Orsini on his deathbed in the summer of 1379 repeated this demand. Cardinals Brossano and Corsini as well as Pedro de Luna ended by joining Clement's party.

The Tuscan republics would have nothing to do with the rival French pope. But they were in no hurry to help Pope Urban with either money or troops, although both the Pope and Catherine wrote urgently to both the governments and several men of influence in the various republics. Catherine knew well enough that peace cannot be created in Christ's Church by the sword, violence, and bloodshed. But the schism led to consequences which had to be met with force of arms.

On April 17 the rival Pope in Avignon sent out a bull in which he gave most of the Papal States in Italy in fee to Duke Louis of Anjou—the man whom Catherine had once visited in his castle in Villeneuve-lez-Avignon to persuade him to become one of the leaders of the crusade planned by Pope Gregory. The rival Pope commanded him to go as quickly as he could and occupy his Italian territories. This was neither the first nor the last time that Robert of Geneva tried to divide up North and South Italy by the sword into prizes for the princes he wanted to win over to his cause; and each time he urged them to hurry off and occupy them.

A Clementist army of mercenary soldiers under the command of Louis de Montjoie, the rival Pope's cousin, was in the Campagna outside Rome. The French garrison at St. Angelo was holding out against the Romans, who had besieged the fortress since the preceding autumn. So the Pope was unable to move into the Vatican, and the troops he had were not enough to guard the town while so many of them were needed for the siege of the fortress of St. Angelo. One of Montjoie's officers, therefore, managed one day to force his way into Rome with a handful of men and storm the Capitol, where several hundred citizens were gathered in consultation. They were massacred, and the enemy managed to retire before the Romans had recovered from the shock. The people took their revenge on the foreigners in the town, and murdered many of them. Catherine felt herself entitled to demand of her Tuscan countrymen that they should come to the help of the lawful Pope with money and soldiers.

The Pope took into his service a certain Alberigo di Balbiano, a professional condottiere, famous for his abilities as a military leader. His army of four thousand infantry and as many cavalry was, of course, also an army of mercenaries, but his picked troops were Italians who called themselves the "Compania di San Giorgio" and had sworn to give their lives to driving all the foreign troops out of Italy.

The fortress of St. Angelo surrendered to the Romans on April 27. The victors poured into the fortress and immediately began to demolish it. Urban's hope of taking it over came to nothing. But two days later Count Alberigo attacked the French camp at Marino, killed most of the men and took Montjoie and his officers prisoner. "The Holy Church and the Pope could begin to breathe a little more freely, and our saint found some consolation", writes Raimondo.

According to Raimondo, it was Catherine who advised Pope Urban to go barefoot from Santa Maria in Trastevere to the Vatican, to take up residence beside the grave of St. Peter. An enormous crowd of people, wild with joy, followed the thanksgiving procession. Many considered that they could thank the

Seraphic Virgin from Siena for the victory. Like Moses in the Old Testament she had plucked victory for her people from heaven, with her hands, which she held up in ceaseless prayer.

A day or two later, on May 6, she wrote to the government of Rome. Since the days of Cola di Rienzi Rome had remained a republic under the Holy See, and chosen its own government, the Seven Flagbearers, one from each district of the town. There were moreover four "good men" whose duty it was to attend to what we would call social services. Catherine exhorts them to show gratitude to God who has saved their city from the danger which threatened, and, besides her usual advice regarding love for oneself and love for Life, she offers particular advice regarding the sins of ingratitude: blasphemy, swearing, scandal, and wicked attempts to ruin the names and reputations of one's neighbours. Only men who have learned to love God humbly and sincerely can govern their fellow-men with righteousness and human love, remain faithful to Christ in His Church, and faithfully protect the honour and happiness of their neighbours. As a suitable object for their neighbourly love she names the wretched soldiers who were wounded at Marino. She accuses the government of ingratitude towards Senator Giovanni Cenci, who was chiefly responsible for the taking of St. Angelo. Not only has he received no sign of their gratitude, but envy has caused him to be an object of slander and all kinds of scandal. "You offend God and hurt yourselves, for this town greatly needs wise, thoughtful and conscientious men." She reminds them that she is a stranger in Rome, so they must understand that when she gives them advice it is not because she supports any particular party, but only because she is concerned for their welfare.

Catherine wrote three more letters that day. To Count Alberigo di Balbiano and the officers of the Compania di San

Giorgio she speaks of gratitude to God who gave them victory and perseverance in the good fight—in other words perseverance in the fight against the enemies who persecute the Holy Church and the Vicar of Christ. (Some time later Alberigo abandoned Urban's cause—when it came to the point he was after all a condottiere.)

King Charles of France was in reality the head of the Clementist party: he was naturally eager to reinstate the papacy in Avignon and to have a French Pope, even though he were a rival Pope. Catherine wrote to him and hoped against hope that perhaps some of her eloquence could make an impression on this man whom Raimondo called Pharaoh. She had more reason than ever for writing of self-love as the principle of evil, the root of all the evils which were practised against God and one's neighbour. She repeats all the arguments for the validity of Urban's election: the interlude with Cardinal Tebaldeschi was the outcome of fear, they tried to say that the election of Urban was caused by fear, but they proclaimed to the whole world that they had elected Urban VI, honoured him, crowned him, and asked him as their overlord for favours and advantages—did they not deserve eternal punishment if they did this from fear? She condemns the schismatics in the most searing words she can find and ends by reminding the King that he has the "source of wisdom", the University of Paris, at his right hand. The University had at first acknowledged Urban, but in May 1379 it submitted to pressure from the King and went over to Clement's party. But Pharaoh's heart remained hardened, and before long Charles's policy celebrated a triumph: Clement returned to Avignon and took up residence in the papal palace.

When the news of the loss of St. Angelo and the rout of his army at Marino reached Clement in Fondi, he and the cardinals who supported him withdrew as fast as they could to

Naples and put themselves under the protection of Queen Joanna. It is possible that they were still in Naples when the Queen received a letter from Catherine, which, according to one of the copyists, was dictated by Catherine while in ecstasy on May 6.

She begged Joanna to have mercy on her soul and body: "How cruel is the soul which offers its enemy the sword with which it is killed! For our enemies have no weapons to use against it, however much they want to. Only the will can commit a crime; neither devils nor any other being can force it to commit the smallest sin if it is not willing. Therefore the sinful will which submits to the temptations of the enemy is a sword which kills the soul when it is offered to the enemy by the hand of free will. Which is more cruel, the enemy or the person who is wounded? We are the more cruel, for we agree to our own death." She quotes a proverb which was current in the Middle Ages: "It is human to sin, but devilish to persist in sinning." Again she warns the Queen: if Joanna does not return to the true faith, death may take her suddenly. "Oh, do not wait for the time when perhaps no time will be granted you! Do not force my eyes to stream with tears for your wretched body and soul!"

The Neapolitans were furious at having to have the schismatic Frenchmen in their town. Led by their Archbishop, they were ardent supporters of their countryman, the Pope in Rome, and there was a limit to their love for their Queen. They rebelled, and Clement and his followers were so terrified that they hastened to embark and sail for France. At Whitsun 1379, almost at the same moment that Urban VI took up residence in the Vatican, the rival Pope reached his goal after a stormy and dangerous journey, and moved into the papal palace at Avignon. This was to be the headquarters of the schismatics for nearly seventy years.

The military defeat of the Clementists gave Joanna food for thought. She sent ambassadors to Urban in Rome, but soon recalled them, before they had achieved anything. It seems that while her ambassadors were in Rome Joanna wrote to Catherine and gave her to understand that she intended to return to Urban's party. Catherine then sent the Queen her last and most outspoken letter. For the first time she does more than hint that she knows quite well what kind of self-love it is which keeps the much-married woman from repentance and the search for God's grace, and, when repeating her warning that her traffic with schismatics and heretics may cost her not only her eternal life but also her physical life, Catherine is cruel enough to remind her that she is no longer young. She has ruled her people wisely and well for a long time and seen to it that they have lived in peace (no small achievement in Joanna's time), but now her fall from grace has brought them discord and war; they fight among themselves like wild animals. It should break the Queen's heart to see the misery she has brought over her people, both physically and spiritually.

She sent this letter with Neri di Landoccio to Naples. He had also with him a number of letters to titled ladies of the court, with whom it seems Catherine had had contact. In one of the letters, to a high-born lady whose name is not given, she emphasises that she must use her influence over the Queen to convert her. The other letters all concern spiritual things. But Catherine's opinion was that politics are never anything but the product of a person's religious life: if the ladies lived lives of sincere piety they would naturally be against the schism.

Yet another of the sons who were nearest to her heart had left her. And Raimondo was to remain in Genoa. The Pope had again had plans of sending him to the King of France. Then came the news that the King of Aragon had imprisoned Urban's ambassador to the Spanish King, and once again Raimondo's courage failed. But Catherine was resigned—she must accept the fact that she could not measure him by her own yardstick. And her last letters to him show that she loved him as much as before. If he had not in him the iron of which martyrs are made, she knew for certain that Our Lord Jesus Christ had determined him for other work in His vineyard, and knew that there he would do his uttermost.

However busy she was with politics, Catherine always found time to write to her private friends; it must have been a great consolation for her, knowing as she did how few of the great ones of this world would listen to her attempts to convince them, if her advice did not coincide with their worldly interests. But she wrote tender and intimate letters to the tailor Francesco Pippino and his wife, Monna Agnese—good friends since her first visit to Florence. To Ristori Canigiani, the brother of her "youngest son" Barduccio, she gives advice as to how he can serve God in the position he has in the world, as a married man, father and head of a great family. But whatever his position in the world, he wished to serve God to the best of his ability, and Catherine advised him practically and tenderly. She sent a warning to the pious wife of the tailor— Agnese wished to practise strict self-denial, but Catherine begged her to guard against any exaggeration: "The blessed Christ is our peace, He who made Himself a mediator between God and us." "Read in the sweet book which is He" (the New Testament), and the doubt which she and her husband have felt after reading some new prayer-books will disappear. If there is anything in these books which is against the teachings of the Church and the saints, leave them alone.

She naturally exchanged letters regularly with Stefano Maconi and with Neri, who was absent on the Pope's and her errands.

When Andrea di Vanni, the painter who had once painted a sketch of her as a young girl on a pillar in the Dominican church at home, was chosen as Capitano del Popolo in Siena in 1379, Catherine wrote him a long letter, saying that she longed to see her friend become a just and good ruler. Yet another of her letters to Andrea di Vanni was most probably written in the autumn of 1379.

XXVI

In January 1380 Catherine moved into a somewhat larger house near Santa Maria sopra Minerva, the street which is now called Via di Sta. Chiara. She wrote to Neri that she hoped to be home in Siena again for Easter. But it is possible that she had a presentiment that it was not to be so. "In Your nature, Eternal Divinity, I have learned to know my own nature", she whispered in one of the prayers which one of her disciples wrote down while she prayed in ecstasy. "My nature is fire."

It was almost burned out. The thirty-three-year-old woman was so emaciated as to be almost a skeleton; the skin seemed to cling to the bones. Monna Lapa maintained that Catherine was not only so thin that she looked like a shadow, but she had also grown much shorter than she used to be. The mother's heart must have bled when she looked at this daughter who had once been so lovely and so strong. The Blessed Sacrament was now her only food. She could not manage to swallow anything else, not even a little water, although her breath was like hot air from a glowing furnace. Once again, and for the last time, the hidden fires were to leap up, and then the soul consumed the long-suffering body and flew off to become one with the "Love which moves the sun and all the stars."

Her death-agony began when the Romans at the beginning of January rebelled against the Pope and threatened to take his life. Broken with sorrow at this new horror, Catherine could do nothing but pray her Bridegroom not to allow such a terrible crime to occur. While she prayed, she saw with her inner

sight how the whole town was flooded with devils who tried
to incite the people to patricide. They screamed at the virgin:
"Damned woman, do you dare to stand up against us? Do not
doubt we shall see to it that you die a terrible death." She
never replied, only continued to pray, for the people and for
the Pope. After some days she had a vision, and with her inner
hearing she heard her Lord answer: "Let this people who daily
mock My name fall into this sin. Then I will take revenge and
crush them, for My justice cannot let Me tolerate their abominations any longer." "O most merciful Lord, You know how
almost the whole world has risen in fury against Your Bride
whom You bought with Your precious blood. You know how
few there are who support and protect her. You must know
how usurpers and the enemies of the Church long for Your
Vicar to be overthrown and killed. If this misfortune happens,
not only this people but the whole of Christendom and Your
Church will suffer terribly. Turn Your wrath from us and do
not despise Your people whom You have redeemed at so high
a price."

Several days and nights passed in this way. Catherine begged
her Lord insistently to have mercy on His people, but the Lord
answered that for the sake of justice He could not hear her prayer,
and devils threatened and raged at the saint. She prayed so intensely
that she said afterwards that her body would have fallen to pieces
if the Lord had not bound it with His strength as the cooper binds
hoops round a barrel. According to what Catherine wrote to Raimondo about those days, her visions and locutions were almost
entirely intellectual; they practically never took the form of
pictures or sounds. Finally she triumphed with her prayers. She
had answered her Bridegroom: "Since it is impossible for Your
justice to be denied fulfilment, let the punishment of these people fall on my body. Lord, hear Your servant-woman—I am willing to drink this cup of death and suffering for the glory of Your

Name and for Your Church. I have always wished for this, as Your Truth can witness, and from this wish sprang the love which the whole of my heart and the whole of my soul have felt for You."

After this prayer, which she made in her thoughts, not in words, the voice of her Lord in her soul was silent. But she knew by the silence and peace which filled her that her prayers had been heard.

From this time the troubles in the city began to diminish, and after some days Rome was once again more or less peaceful—no Roman had ever known it completely peaceful. But this spiritual battle had worked complete havoc with Catherine's body. She looked like a corpse as she lay and rested on her bed of rough planks. Her children were in despair, for they had given up all hope that their beloved mother could live. But each morning she got up and walked the whole way from her house to St. Peter's. The only relaxation she allowed her tortured body was that the Mass which was celebrated daily at her private altar was now said as late as at terce— about nine o'clock. She remained in prayer at the tomb of the apostles until vespers, and then went home and fell on her bed, unable to move.

In the entrance to the old basilica of St. Peter's, there was a mosaic of Giotto's, called "Navicella"—St. Peter's ship. Catherine must have seen it hundreds of times, sometimes with deep thoughts, sometimes without noticing it. But when she received the vision which assured her that her heavenly Bridegroom had accepted her prayer to sacrifice her life, the impression of this mosaic may have helped to decide the pictorial form of her vision.

Sexagesima Sunday fell on January 29. Catherine was on her knees in St. Peter's, where she had remained motionless for hours. But suddenly at vespers her friends saw that she collapsed, as though an overwhelming burden had been laid on her shoulders and crushed her body with its weight. When they tried to help her to her feet she was so weak that she could not stand. Supported by two of her sons she was more carried than led home. When they lifted her onto her bed it looked as though she were dying.

Tommaso Caffarini's description is repeated by William Flete: "As Catherine knelt at the tomb of St. Peter that Sunday at vespers, while the winter evening began to creep in over the city, she felt how Jesus Christ laid the whole weight of His Church, *la Navicella*, on the thin shoulders of His faithful bride."

And the crushing pain was sweet too—indescribably sweet. It meant that He had accepted the sacrifice she had offered Him in love and desire. It meant too that He would soon come and lead her from "this dark world" to the land of her desire and eternal union with Him.

The following evening Catherine dictated a letter to Pope Urban. In a momentary pause between shattering spiritual experiences, visions of God's majesty and the terrible power of the evil ones, racked by spiritual and physical pains, Catherine sent this last short message to the man whose virtues and faults she had measured with perfectly clear insight, and to whom she firmly and steadfastly believed that God had entrusted the office which she considered the greatest and most important on earth. The letter, with its mixture of tenderness and anxious predictions based on Urban's character, of sound common sense and deep spiritual insight, is wonderfully clear and purposeful. This time she does not call herself the serving-woman and slave of God's servants, but simply the poor, unworthy little daughter of her dearest and most Holy Father. She says how earnestly she wishes to see him follow in the footsteps of the great St. Gregory, so that, enlightened by the sweet light of Truth, he may guide his flock with such great wisdom that he may never need to reconsider any of his actions or commands. She has heard of the bitter and offensive answer which the Prefect of Rome has given to the Pope's ambassadors, and advises him to call a meeting of the leaders of the seven districts of the city and some of the nobles. "I beg you, Most Holy Father, continue to meet them as equals, as you have done up to now, and be wise and bind them to you with the bonds of love. When they come to you to tell of the decisions they have made in their councils, receive them with the greatest possible friendliness and explain to them what Your Holiness thinks most important. Forgive me if my love makes me say things which had been better unsaid, but I know that you ought to understand the character of your children, the Romans, who will be drawn to you and bound more easily by goodness than by hard words and power. You know, too, that it is most important for you and for the Holy Church to keep this people faithful and obedient to Your Holiness. For this is the seat of our faith's origin and its head. I beg you, too, be most careful never to make any promises which you are not quite sure you can keep, and so escape the difficulties which would follow such an action. Dearest, Most Holy Father, allow me to say these things. I hope that your humility and your goodness will make you receive these words without anger or scorn, because they come from a poor miserable woman—he who is humble does not allow the personality of the adviser to be an obstacle, he only thinks of God's glory, of Truth and his own salvation."

Finally she names an incident which occurred in Siena when the Pope's ambassador was there and caused great annoyance. (What this incident was is not known.) Catherine warns against measures which can cause bitterness in the feeble hearts of men. What the Pope needs is a man of peace, not a warrior, even though this man may have acted from a praiseworthy but exaggerated desire for justice. But Urban must remember that men are weak, and use a medicine more suitable for healing sickness. "Remember how ruin spread over the whole of Italy because of the wicked rulers who behaved in a manner which was harmful to God's Church; and yet they were not removed from their positions. I know that you know it. May Your Holiness understand what has to be done! Courage, courage, for God does not despise your desire and the prayers of His servants. I say no more. I ask humbly for your blessing. Sweet Jesus, Jesus Love."

It had been her intention to write to the three cardinals too, but now her physical pains became too violent. Exhausted, she remained silent. But after a while the demons began to attack her with terrible fury—she who was no more than a worm in the dust had dared to tear out of their claws all they had possessed so long, even inside Holy Church herself. In addition to the physical pain, there came too an agony of soul so terrible that she had to escape from her cell and seek refuge in the chapel in the house. Just as during that time in her youth when devils were allowed to persecute her, it seemed to her now that her own cell was the place where they had the most power over her.

She got up, but could not walk, and supported herself on Barduccio's shoulder. But she was immediately thrown down, and while she lay on the floor it seemed to her that her soul left her body. Not, as before, when her soul had escaped its cage of flesh and blood and enjoyed a foretaste of the blessedness of souls which have come into possession of the Highest Good; it seemed to her now as though her body did not belong any more to her, but to another. When she saw the grief of the boy who was with her she was astonished, but could use her body to speak to him and say, "Son, do not be afraid." But she saw that her tongue was as unable to move as her limbs; it was as though her body were lifeless. So she let her body lie there and fastened the eyes of her intellect on the abyss of the Trinity. Her mind was filled with thoughts of the Church's need and all that Christians everywhere in the world suffered and needed. She cried to God and begged confidently for His help for all those whose suffering and want she felt as if it were her own. She prayed too for each of her spiritual children separately. The devils were dispersed and she heard in her soul the voice of God's Lamb: "Be confident that I shall fulfil the desire of all My servants. I wish you to understand that I am a good Lord. I act as the potter who breaks up and re-forms his vases. Therefore have I broken the vase of your body, and I shall re-form it in the garden of the Holy Church. It will be different from what it was before." And the divine Potter broke her with grace and with words which she could repeat to no one—not even to Raimondo.

Her body began to breathe again; it looked as though life had returned. But when she had been carried down to a room on the ground floor, a new and terrible horror came over her. It was as though the room were full of demons, and she had to fight the hardest fight she had ever been submitted to, for they wanted her to believe that it was not she but an unclean spirit who lived in her body. She did not flinch from the fight, but the whole time her soul repeated with intense tenderness: "Deus in adjutorium meum intende, Domine, ad adjuvandum me festina"—God come to my help, O Lord hasten and come to my help—words from the daily Office which she had always loved.

The storm raged for two days, but her desire and her spirit never wavered; her soul was united with its goal, but her body was as though annihilated. On the day of the Purification of Our Lady God showed her the great dangers which threatened His Church, and told her to hear Mass before daybreak each day during Lent. It seemed impossible that a woman so ill could manage to do so; but for those who obey God all things are possible.

All this is described by Catherine in the last letter she sent to her friend Fra Raimondo, in Genoa. The letter is written about the middle of February, and she knew it would be a last farewell. Although she did not know what God would do with her, she was completely happy, not in spite of her sufferings, but as it were on a different plane in her soul—for at the same time she was filled with grief and anxiety over the miseries of the times, anxious for those she loved, and suffering intolerable physical pain. But these physical pains were perhaps a new way of winning the martyr's crown, for she knew that she would die of them and of the love of God and His Church with which her soul overflowed.

Anxiety for those she loved—she speaks to Raimondo of her anxiety for him, her father and her son, whom the beloved Virgin Mary has given her. Let him die from all personal feelings, and consecrate himself body and soul to the service of the Church. "Always be prepared in all situations. You will not be able to enjoy much of the solitude of the cell, but it is my will that you carry with you everywhere the cell in your heart, for you know that when we are enclosed in it the enemy cannot harm us." He must be a model for all priests. The voluntary poverty in which he has always lived, his generosity and kindness to the poor, must be ceaselessly renewed and rejuvenated in perfect humility. "Love the table of the cross and nourish yourself with the soul's food in holy vigilance and ceaseless prayer; say Mass every day unless you are absolutely prevented. Avoid vain and useless talk. Cast your weakness and slavish fear from you, for the Holy Church has no use for such servants."

She had already finished her letter to Raimondo with a loving farewell, in which she expressed her deep love for his soul and her hope that he might be like a candle set on a high candlestick, and that he might never retreat before persecution, but be brave, brave in Jesus Christ; and then she adds a kind of postscript. She has asked him for pardon for her many faults—disobedience, ingratitude, lack of respect, and also for this letter if it makes him sad, and she asks him not to be unhappy if they cannot meet, as long as they can pray for each other. He is to take in hand all her writings, and she begs him to pray for her and also to make others pray for her. She ended the letter, but then it seemed to her that there was something else she had to say, and the next day she had a couple of pages added. They dealt with her anxiety for Pope Urban—she could speak freely of it to Raimondo.

It is as though she were forced to do it, to say a little more about her longing to stand before the eternal Trinity, of her boundless love and anxiety for the Church on earth which she was soon to leave, and which was still so full of abuses and false servants. Christ had spoken of Pope Urban in her innermost soul: "I permit him to cleanse the Church with the violent means he uses and with the fear which he awakes in his subordinates, but others shall come who shall serve the Church with love, and they shall make her rich. He [Urban] shall be for the Bride what fear is for the soul, for the soul is first cleansed of its vices by fear, but later it is filled and adorned by love." "Say to My Vicar that he must try to make his nature milder and that he must be willing to grant peace to all those who are willing to be reconciled to him. Say to the cardinals, the pillars of the Holy Church, that if they really wish to compensate for all that has been laid waste, they must unite and stand together, so that they form a cape to cover their father's faults." She had been as though drowned in the divine mysteries in a way which she had never before experienced, and she was so overwhelmed that she was forced to get up and go down to the oratory in her house.

Then once again she was warned that the hour of her death was near, and while the demons threw themselves upon her and beat her body, her desire grew as a flame rises upwards, and she cried out to her Bridegroom: "O Eternal God, receive my life as a sacrifice for Your mystical body, the Church. I can give You nothing which You Yourself have not given me. But take my heart and squeeze it out over the face of Your Bride, the Church." And the Almighty looked mercifully upon her, and did as she asked him.

Rocked as though on the waves, between a bliss of which she had never dreamed and the fury of the demons, Catherine cried: "Thanks, thanks to the Highest, the Eternal, who has placed us on the field of battle. We have become victors through the power which triumphed over the devil, the lord of mankind. He has been overcome, not by our physical sufferings, and not by the virtues of mankind, but by the power of God. Yes, the devil is conquered and shall be conquered again, not by our struggles and our deeds, but by the fire from the bottomless depths of divine mercy."

The letter finishes suddenly here, without the usual ending—without even the words which had become Catherine's signature: "Sweet Jesus, Jesus Love."

XXVII

Obedient to the voice she had heard in her vision, Catherine got up each morning at dawn and went down to take part in the Mass in the oratory in her house. But when she had received Communion her friends had to carry her upstairs and lay her on her bed. An hour or two later she got up again and went on foot all the way to St. Peter's. It was as though her fragile body were upheld by supernatural power, and she still walked quickly and lightly. In the old days when she had run about in her own town on her numerous errands of mercy, no one had been so quick and light as Catherine. Now she was sent out on errands which she could not explain to her sons and daughters in words which they would be able to understand. They realised vaguely that their "mamma" had been chosen to carry out the work which is entrusted to the saints. With her physical and spiritual agonies she filled up in her flesh "those things that are wanting of the sufferings of Christ", as St. Paul expresses it.

He had once written to the Corinthians: "You are partakers of the sufferings" of Christ; but, he continues, "so shall you also be of the consolation." But the mystics who have experienced this have never been able to tell of the dark night of the soul and the radiance of the community of Heaven except in symbols borrowed from our own human life, agreeing sorrowfully that they are inadequate.

When Catherine came home in the evening she would immediately sink onto her hard bed and lie down, and it looked as though she would never be able to move again.

Her children stood round her bed full of consternation, and, broken with grief and sympathy, thought of the day when they would be motherless; for how long could this state of affairs last? It lasted until the third Sunday in Lent. After that she was unable to leave her bed: she could just manage to move her head and hands, but soon her body became paralysed from the waist down.

With secret horror her family had seen how her body sometimes looked as though it had been beaten by invisible hands. The sick woman told them that these pains were physical, but not natural: "God allows demons to torture me in this way." Tommaso Caffarini writes of her last days: "She bore everything with such a steady courage and cheerfulness that it was as though it was not she herself who suffered these terrible pains. She always spoke so calmly and lovingly that all who heard her were full of admiration. If one tried to describe her patience in words it would seem as though one were trying to disparage her rather than praise her. No one ever heard the smallest moan from her blessed lips. She said that her sufferings were not so great. No one ever heard her say a vain word; she always spoke of God's glory, of gratitude for the salvation of men, and of the eternal happiness of her neighbour. And although she suffered physically more than words can tell, the expression on her face was always as happy and good as an angel's."

On the Sunday of Holy Week Fra Bartolommeo Dominici, who was now prior of a monastery in Siena, came to Rome. He had some matters to arrange for his monastery, but the first thing he did was to hasten to Catherine's house. Completely unprepared, he found himself face to face with his mother on her bed of wooden boards. They had fastened a framework of planks round the bed, so that it looked as though she already lay in her coffin. She had shrunk so that she looked like a dried-up corpse: even her face had darkened and become so puckered that not a trace of her beauty was to be seen. He had had no idea that she was ill, except that he naturally knew that her health, with its constant shifting between exhaustion and moments of great activity, and back to exhaustion again, had always been something of a mystery for all who knew her. But this was a dying woman. Sore at heart, Fra Bartolommeo asked her, weeping, "How are you, Mother?" Catherine could not speak, but let him understand by eloquent signs how happy she was to see him. Then he bowed his head so that his ear was beside her mouth, and she whispered: By the grace of God, she was well.

It was the day before Catherine's thirty-third birthday, and Bartolommeo said "Mother, to-morrow is Easter Sunday. I would so much like to celebrate the Mass here and give Holy Communion to you and your spiritual children." Catherine whispered: "Oh, if only our sweet Saviour will allow me to receive Him."

On the morning of Easter Sunday Fra Bartolommeo returned to fulfil his promise. Catherine had confessed to him, and as a penance he told her to pray to God that He should allow her to be given strength to receive Him on the great day, as a consolation for herself and them all. The altar stood beside her bed, and Fra Bartolommeo began the Mass while Catherine lay motionless until after the priest had received Communion. Then she suddenly rose, went without help the few steps to the altar, and knelt with closed eyes. She received the Body of the Lord. Afterwards she remained motionless on her knees in deep ecstasy. But when she recovered consciousness her friends had to lift her up into her bed, and she lay as before, unable to move.

But during Fra Bartolommeo's stay in Rome Catherine was able to talk to him a little once or twice, and tell him how

God had allowed her to suffer for peace in the Church. "So that the Church may be liberated I suffer happily, and would gladly die for it if necessary."

When he had completed his commission, Fra Bartolommeo was unwilling to return home—how could he leave her when she was so ill? Catherine said: "Son, you know what a consolation it is for me to have near me the children whom God has given me. I should be so happy if Fra Raimondo could be here too. But it is God's will that I am to be without you both, and God's will be done, not mine."

She said to him that she knew that Fra Raimondo would soon be chosen as Master General of their order, and Bartolommeo must always help him and be obedient and loyal to him. When he begged her to pray God to make her well again she promised to do so. And the next day when he came to say good-bye, it seemed as though she were a little brighter—she managed to lift her arms and put them round her son's neck. But it was her last farewell to him.

It was perhaps Fra Bartolommeo's account, when he returned to Siena, which at last caused Stefano Maconi to hurry to his mother's deathbed. But there is a legend that he was kneeling in prayer in the hospital church of La Scala when he learned of her condition in some mystical way. So instead of the sons whom she missed being round her deathbed, she had Stefano back again, the fresh and noble young soul whom she had always loved especially tenderly. Now he was with her again, for ever; he took down the few letters she still managed to dictate, and listened to her when she was able to speak, with the old passionate affection.

Messer Tommaso Petra, a papal protonotary, had met Catherine in Avignon, and when she came to Rome he renewed his friendship with her. It was apparently one day in April that he came to visit her and found her on her hard bed in the little oratory where Mass was said for her. He said: "Mamma, it seems to me that your heavenly Bridegroom is calling you to Him. Will you not make your last will and testament?" Catherine was obviously astonished: "I? But I am only a poor girl, I possess nothing. I have nothing to make a testament of." But Messer Tommaso explained that he meant a spiritual testament with advice for her disciples to follow and live by when she had left this life. She replied that if God gave her grace she would do so willingly.

It was presumably Messer Tommaso, the old notary, who wrote down this spiritual testament while her family were present. It is a summing-up of all that she had tried to teach her disciples. In her earliest youth it had been given to her to understand how a soul which wishes to give itself completely and absolutely to God and to possess Him entirely, must pluck out of its heart all merely natural love for human creatures and all that is created, in order to love God only and all things in Him. This has to be the way of suffering, for it means that one must let one's eyes be blinded by the tremendous light of faith which engulfs all temporal and sensual things. But Catherine believes firmly that nothing can befall her or anyone which is not sent from God. The source of everything is His great love for all His creatures—never hate. She had therefore always tried to be obedient to God and to all those to whom He had given authority over her, for she was always sure that what they told her to do was God's will and necessary if her soul was to be saved and virtue grow in her. But the beginning and end of perfection is prayer—prayer with the lips at the appointed times, and ceaseless interior prayer, which means that we always remember God's goodness towards us.

She warns her disciples insistently that they must never condemn others or indulge in vain talk against their neighbours.

If we see them doing things which we know are great sins, we must nevertheless leave God to judge them—let us pray for them, humbly and piously, with real and tender sympathy.

She reminds them of Our Lord's words which St. John repeats: "Love one another. . . . By this shall all men know that you are my disciples, if you have love one for another." She speaks of the reformation of the Church: it is what she has fought and suffered for these last seven years. She thanks God because He has graciously let devils tempt her, as He once allowed Job to be tempted. But now she knew that her Beloved would soon free her soul from this dark prison so that she could return to her Creator. She was not sure of this, and if God still wished her to work on earth for Him, His will be done, but she thought that she would soon die. She asked her dearest children not to sorrow or lose courage, but to be glad if her sufferings ended now and she was taken to rest in the ocean of peace which is the eternal God, and to become one with her Bridegroom.

"And I promise you that I shall be with you always, and be of much more use to you on the other side than I ever could be here on earth, for then I shall have left the darkness behind me and move in the eternal light."

She gave each of her children special advice for the future. Sister Alessia should be the mother and head of her daughters, who were also her sisters in the Mantellata order. Her sons should have Fra Raimondo as their father and leader. One by one she called her disciples to her bed and gave them advice; some she said should go into one of the monastic orders, some be priests, some hermits. She had decided that Stefano Maconi should join the Carthusian order, Francesco Malavolti the Olivetans, and Neri di Landoccio should become a hermit. She advised the notary, Messer Cristofano di Gano Guidini, to enter the hospital of Santa Maria della Scala as a nurse. She

asked all her children to forgive her, because she had not been
a more perfect example for them, and because she had not
prayed for them so ceaselessly as she should. She also asked
their pardon for all the pain, bitterness and unpleasantness which
she might have caused them. "I did it from ignorance, and I
vow before the face of God that I always wished with my
whole heart that you might be saved and become perfect."
One by one her weeping disciples came forward and received
her blessing in God's name.

Catherine continued to live until April 29, the Sunday before
Ascension Day. Some hours before dawn it seemed to those
who stood round her bed that the death-agony had begun.
The rest of her companions were sent for, and when they
were all assembled she made signs that she wished to receive
the papal absolution *in articulo mortis*—absolution from guilt
and punishment. Fra Giovanni Tantucci gave it to her. Now
there was no other sign of life than the feeble breathing. The
abbot of Sant' Artimo, whose cause Catherine had once
defended in the city council of Siena, was present. He gave
his old friend the last anointing.

But after a while the unconscious woman began to be restless. She lifted her right arm and let it fall on the blanket
again and again, while she repeated: "Peccavi, Domine, mis-
erere mei." It looked to those who stood around her bed as
though she fought with terrible demons: her face darkened,
she turned her head from side to side and looked away as
though she would escape some awful sight. All the time she
murmured: "Deus in adjutorium meum intende"—God come
to my help. Suddenly she cried, "with holy recklessness": "My
own honour? Never! But the true glory of Christ Crucified."

She had fought and won the last battle. Those who watched
over her saw the white, dying face become radiantly happy,

her dim eyes suddenly shine like two stars. Greatly moved and happy, her children thought for a moment that God had worked yet another miracle and would let them have their mother back. The virgin smiled: "Praised be our beloved Saviour."

Alessia supported her head on her breast. But the restlessness which precedes death had come over Catherine—she made a sign that they should help her to sit. Alessia took the slender figure and sat her on her knee as though she were a little child. Her disciples placed before her her little altar, beautifully decorated with pictures and relics—it had once been given to her by a cardinal. But Catherine fixed her eyes on the crucifix in the middle, and before this picture of her Lord she made her last confession.

She praised God's goodness, but accused herself of lukewarmness and ingratitude: "You condescended to choose me as Your bride when I was still a child, but I have not been faithful to You; I did not seek Your glory so diligently as I should. I did not always let the memory of the grace You poured over this miserable being fill my thoughts: I often let my mind be full of other unseemly thoughts."

She repeated her self-accusations—she had not fulfilled her duties towards the souls whom God had entrusted to her to lead: "You sent me so many dear daughters and sons and told me to love them with a special love and lead them on life's way to You. But I was only a mirror for them, a mirror of human weakness, I have not lifted them up before You in persistent prayer, I have not been enough of an example for them."

"So the purest dove accused herself", say Barduccio and Tommaso Caffarini. Then she turned to the priest and asked to receive the absolution once again, for all the sins she had confessed and for those she had forgotten to confess. So she received the papal absolution for the second time.

Old Lapa, their dear Nonna, sat at her daughter's side. Humbly and sincerely Catherine asked for her mother's blessing. Poor Lapa, she tried to find some consolation in her great grief when she asked Catherine to bless her, and to attain a gift for her from God—that Lapa should not sin against God's will by sorrowing too greatly.

Catherine continued to pray till the last moment, for the Church, for Pope Urban, for her children. She prayed with such intense love that her disciples thought that not only their hearts, but the very stones must break. "Beloved, You call me, I come. Not through any service of mine, but through Your mercy and the power of Your blood." She made the sign of the cross and cried, "Blood, blood . . ." Then she bowed her head. "Father, into Your hands I commit my spirit." And as she said it, she gave up her spirit. Her face had become as beautiful as an angel's, radiant with tenderness and happiness.

It was about the hour of terce on April 29, 1380.

XXVIII

AT ABOUT THE HOUR OF TERCE on April 29 Raimondo was in his monastery at Genoa preparing for his journey to the Chapter in Bologna. He was to travel by sea to Pisa with several other monks, but the weather was bad, and he was not completely at ease. He went up the stairs to the dormitories and into his cell to put his few possessions into a sack. He stopped before the picture of the Holy Virgin in the corridor, bowed his head and repeated the Angelus in a low voice. A voice which he did not hear with his physical ears spoke clearly in his soul and said to him: "Do not be afraid, I am here for your sake, I am in heaven for your sake. I shall take care of you, I shall protect you, I am here for your sake." Greatly disturbed, he wondered where these promises of security came from. For a moment he thought it must be God's Mother—and then he thought that it could not be, he was too unworthy. He was afraid that this voice he had heard was a warning that he was in great danger; the schismatic pirates sailed all round the coast, and Raimondo knew how heartily they hated him because he had preached against them. Humbly he prayed that this warning might make him more careful and better prepared to suffer patiently whatever might befall him. "These ideas prevented me from entering into the great and mystical grace of Our Lord when He sent the spirit of His bride to help me against my weakness and despondency which the saint knew so well, but the Lord, her Bridegroom, knew even better. As this event seems to me to put me to shame and nothing to be proud of, I feel that I can safely write it down."

At the Chapter in Bologna where Raimondo was elected Master General of the Dominicans he heard that Catherine had died at precisely the same time that he heard the bodiless voice which consoled and encouraged him.

In Rome Stefano Maconi had carried the body of his beloved mother to the church of Santa Maria sopra Minerva. And as soon as the news spread over the town that the holy woman from Siena was dead, the Romans swarmed to the church. In wave upon wave the excited crowds pushed their way forward to touch the clothes or the feet of the dead woman. We are apt to think the way in which the faithful expressed their admiration for the saints was often most repulsive, from the earliest days of Christianity, when they dried up the blood of the martyrs and hid bits of their flesh and bones, right up to comparatively recent times. In their eagerness to acquire a relic of a popular saint they did not content themselves with tearing off bits of his clothes; they sometimes stole pieces of the body itself. To prevent such a thing happening to Catherine's corpse, the sisters of the convent put it behind the lattice in front of St. Dominic's chapel, and kept watch over it. "The crowd . . . who wished to do homage to her remains and to pray for her intercession, brought their sick to her. And God willed that they should not be disappointed."

Raimondo describes in detail eight miraculous cures which occurred in the days between Catherine's death and her burial. There were many others, but these he had himself been able to enquire into by examining those who had been healed, or who had been eye-witnesses of the miracles. But it is obvious that Raimondo especially enjoyed recounting the story of Semia, the widow of a Roman citizen. He had known her twenty years; she was simple and honest, a deeply pious woman. It is not strange that he tells this story *con amore*: Semia had seen in a dream Catherine's dazzling entrance into heaven, and afterwards she had been helped by supernatural means in her housework by the newly crowned saint, who while she lived on earth had so often taken upon herself to help ordinary people in the small difficulties of everyday life.

This Semia had always been in the habit of praying a great deal and making pilgrimages to the different pilgrim churches in Rome when she could get a free moment from her housework. Since her husband's death she had kept house for her five sons. The night before Catherine died she had got up as usual and prayed, and as the next day was Sunday and she wanted to go to Mass, she lay down again to sleep a little until it was time to get up for good.

But while she lay thus between waking and sleeping, she had a wonderful vision: she saw a boy of about ten, much more beautiful than anyone she had ever seen before, and he said to her: "You must not wake and get up before you have seen what I have to show you." Although Semia was very glad to see anyone so beautiful as this boy, she murmured: "Blessed child, let me get up, otherwise I shall be too late for the High Mass." But the boy took no notice, and then it seemed as though he took hold of her dress and led her to a room which resembled a church. Here she saw a tabernacle of silver, richly adorned with precious stones. Another beautiful boy opened the tabernacle, while four more carried in a chair magnificently adorned like the chairs that are used when a bride is carried to her bridegroom's home. She understood then that the boys were angels.

Out of the tabernacle stepped a young woman, radiantly beautiful and clothed all in white and glittering jewels. On her head she had three crowns, arranged so cleverly that all were visible, one above the other; one was of silver, the second of silver and red gold, the third of pearls and diamonds. The angel who had first appeared to her asked Semia: "Do you recognise the young girl?" Semia said: "She looks like Catherine of Siena, only she is much younger." (Semia had not seen Catherine before she came to Rome.) The girl in the vision smiled and said to the children: "See, she does not recognise me."

She seemed to float towards Semia: "Semia, do you not recognise me? I am Catherine of Siena, look into my face." But then the children lifted her into the chair and floated towards heaven with her.

As Semia watched, a throne appeared in heaven, and on the throne sat a King, crowned and clothed in radiance; in his right hand he had an open book. The boys put the chair down in front of the steps up to the throne. The young girl threw herself before the King's feet in adoration, and the King said to her: "Welcome, Catherine, my beloved bride and daughter." He told her to lift up her head and read in the book for as long as it takes to say a Pater Noster. The King let her stand beside his throne, and then Semia saw a procession approach—the Queen of Heaven with a great following of holy virgins. The new saint ran forward to kneel and adore, but Christ's Mother took her in her arms, bade her welcome and kissed her, and asked her to join the procession of holy virgins, who greeted her with the kiss of peace.

Semia assured Raimondo that she was sure she had seen this scene take place in heaven, and when she called out a loud greeting and prayer to the heavenly procession, she woke up and saw that the sun was already high—it was about terce, nine o'clock. Terribly ashamed of having slept too long, she hastened to light the fire, put on the saucepan with the dinner for her sons and hurried to the parish church, afraid she was too late for the High Mass. She said to herself that if she had missed the Mass she would take it for a sign that the dream vision was a trick sent by the old enemy of men, but if she came in time she would believe that she had been allowed to see this vision because her mother, Catherine, prayed for her. But when she got to the church they had sung the Gospel and were in the middle of the offertory. Disappointed, she went home again, sure that her dream had been a trick of the devil.

She started the housework, but suddenly heard the bells of a neighbouring convent ringing for Mass. She was so happy that she forgot to put the vegetables she had washed and cut up into the pan, but just locked the door and hurried off to the convent church. Her house was left empty. "So it was not Satan who tricked me, as I feared." But she was a little uneasy when she thought of the dinner for her boys, and prayed God to help her so that they would not be too cross because the dinner was a little later than usual.

Her sons stood outside the locked door when she returned, and, sure enough, they were cross and hungry. "My dear children, wait a moment, the food will be ready in a minute." But when she had unlocked the door and hurried in to the pan on the fire, the contents were bubbling; vegetables, meat and spices, everything was cooked exactly enough. She only needed to lay the table. The boys ate with a good appetite and said to their mother that to-day the food tasted better than usual. Semia was amazed at the strange things which had happened to her, and longed to be finished with the housework, so that she might run down to Catherine's house and tell her all about it.

It was many days since she had had time to visit Catherine. Semia knew that she was very ill, but like all Catherine's other friends she had often seen her lying apparently completely exhausted, only to come suddenly to herself again and begin to work and converse with her children. It did not occur to her that there was any difference this time. But Catherine's house was locked, and the neighbours said that she must have gone to church.

On the way home she passed Santa Maria sopra Minerva and was astonished to see great crowds of people outside. She asked what was the matter, and someone told her that Catherine of Siena was dead and her body now lay in the church. Semia pushed into the church and elbowed her way through the crowd till she came to the lattice. Tears streamed down her face and she shouted to the women round the coffin: "Oh, cruel women, why did you not send for me so that I could come to her deathbed?" She tore her face with her nails, while she sobbed out her story—how she had seen her mother step out of the tabernacle of her body, how she was carried to heaven by angels and received by our Saviour and all the saints; and how, by a miracle, while she was at Mass, the food had prepared itself at home.

On Thursday, in the dusk, at the hour of compline, they buried Catherine of Siena. Her body was still fresh and pure, unchanged; there was no smell of death, and her throat and limbs were as soft and supple as when she was alive. The stigmata, which she had prayed her Lord to allow to remain invisible in her lifetime, showed clearly on her dead body.

XXIX

CATHERINE OF SIENA was apparently first buried in the churchyard of Santa Maria sopra Minerva. People came there to pray for her intercession and many miracles were ascribed to the dead Sister of Penitence. But some years later Raimondo had her remains moved to a grave inside the church, where they would not be exposed to the weather and winds. It was perhaps during this first moving—or translation—that her head was separated from the body, put in a beautifully made reliquary, a bust of gilded bronze, and taken to Siena. It caused jubilation over the whole of Siena, both the town and its surroundings; and the reliquary was carried in solemn procession to St. Dominic's church. Immediately behind it walked the Mantellate, and among them was a very old woman, Lapa, the mother of the saint. One would like to know what her feelings were when this daughter whom she had loved so passionately, suffered for so bitterly, and so bravely tried to understand and follow, came home to her birthplace in triumph. This was in the spring of 1383.

Her body was moved again to the chapel of the Rosary, and finally laid to rest where it now lies, under the high altar in Santa Maria sopra Minerva.

Her last loving prayer to the men and women who had called her "Mother" had been: "Love each other; that is the sign by which people shall know that you are my disciples, the love which you bear each other." The flock of Caterinati remembered these words, which their mother had borrowed from her divine Bridegroom, as they remembered everything

she had said to them. They collected and copied her letters
and her book, they wrote down all they could remember about
her and worked for her honour, in the hope that one day she
would be solemnly declared a saint by Holy Church, the Bride
of Christ, for which she had lived and died.

As Master General of the Dominicans, Raimondo of Capua
had more than enough to do working in his mother's spirit
during the dark years of the schism and the perpetual inva-
sions of Italy by the French schismatics. Nevertheless he found
time to collect material for his book on the life of the Blessed
Catherine. He conscientiously gives the names of the sources
of all his information, some of whom had been eye-witnesses
of the miracles which took place in reply to her prayers, some
who had been present and seen and heard the different events
he describes—whether they were still alive at the time of writing or not. He worked on the book for fifteen years. Four
years later he died. His work as reformer of the Dominican
Order led him to Nuremberg in the autumn of 1399, and it
was there that he died. His body was brought home to Italy,
and buried in the Dominican church in Naples. He has never
been formally beatified, but the Dominican Order has always
honoured him as the Blessed Raimondo of Capua, and on the
five-hundredth anniversary of his death Pope Leo XIII officially acknowledged his cult.

When Raimondo finished his book Monna Lapa and
Catherine's sister-in-law, Lisa Colombini, were still alive; but
Alessia Saracini, Francesca di Gori and several other of the
sisters from whom he received his information were already
dead.

The first of her sons to die was her Benjamin, the young
Barduccio Canigiani. When Raimondo came to Rome for the
first time after Catherine's death, Barduccio appeared to have
consumption. To get him away from the Roman air, which

was notoriously unhealthy, Raimondo sent him back to the monastery in Siena, and there he died in 1382.

Fra Bartolommeo Dominici was moved from the monastery in Siena a short while after Catherine's death and given other responsible work in the order. In his place Catherine's old foster-brother and confessor, Fra Tommaso della Fonte, was made prior in Siena. He was the first priest who publicly set up a picture of Catherine in his church, so that the people could offer her their homage (this was before the Church had acknowledged her cult). His journals have been used to great advantage by both Raimondo and Tommaso Caffarini.

Neri di Landoccio was hindered in his vain errand to Naples, and returned to Rome too late to be present at his "mother's" deathbed. But he followed her advice and retired to a hermitage outside Siena, where he lived alone in prayer and contemplation; but he kept up his connections with his friends among the Caterinati, especially Stefano Maconi and Francesco Malavolti, until his death in 1406.

After the death of his wife and child, Francesco Malavolti entered the Carthusian monastery on Monte Oliveto, but after a while he changed over to the Benedictine order.

A little less than a year after Catherine's death Stefano Maconi entered a Carthusian monastery outside Siena. He was chosen as prior of his monastery almost as soon as he had finished his novitiate. He translated into Italian the biography of Catherine which Tommaso Caffarini had written in Latin, and worked with Ser Cristofano di Gano Guidini on a Latin translation of Catherine's *Dialogue*. Ser Cristofano was then a lay brother in the congregation of Santa Maria della Scala, and worked as a nurse and helper of the poor. Stefano was later chosen as Prior-General for the Carthusian order, and he succeeded in leading his order back to obedience to Rome.

Tommaso Caffarini, Catherine's fellow-citizen and one of her oldest friends, was sent after her death to the Dominican monastery in Venice. He too worked eagerly for his mother's honour. Among other things he succeeded in reorganising the third order of St. Dominic—the order to which the young Catherine had so passionately wished to be attached, and in which she had lived her strange life of mysticism and energetic practical activity. The rules which Tommaso Caffarini gave the order in Venice have to a great extent been followed by Dominican tertiaries up to our own day.

When complaints were made against the Dominican order for acting against canon law by doing public honour to a member who was not yet canonised, a council was held in Venice. The result was that in January 1413 the Dominican order was given solemn permission to celebrate a feast day for the Blessed Catherine of Siena.

In 1461 she was canonised by Pope Pius II—born Enea Silvio de' Piccolomini of Siena. She thereupon became St. Catherine of Siena for the whole Church. It was acknowledged that the life and teachings of the Sienese Popolana were worthy to be held as examples for all Christians, whether or not their life outwardly developed through actions and circumstances which resembled her own. For, as Catherine said, Christ taught us regarding Himself: I AM THE WAY. Therefore the way to heaven should be heaven for those who love Him.

Both Raimondo and Tommaso Caffarini maintained that Catherine lived and died as a martyr of the Faith. In the official language of the Catholic Church the expression "martyr" means a man or a woman who chooses to die a violent death rather than deny the Christian faith. But we have got used to using the expression in a much less precise way, and speak of people as being martyrs for any cause whatsoever for which they have suffered, voluntarily or involuntarily. (Sometimes also, very inaccurately, of people who suffer from misfortunes which they have definitely neither chosen nor wished to choose as their lot.) It is certain that Catherine voluntarily—and few women have ever had such an inflexible will—chose to suffer ceaselessly for all she believed in, loved and desired: unity with God, the glory and honour of His name, His kingdom on earth, the eternal happiness of all mankind, and the re-birth of Christ's Church to the beauty which it possesses when the radiance of its soul shines freely through its outward form—that form which was then stained and spoilt by its own degenerate servants and rebellious children. As Catherine expressed it: the strength and beauty of its mystical body can never diminish, for it is God; but the jewels with which its mystical body are adorned are the good accomplished by its sincere and faithful children.

The fact that the saints have been so willing to suffer, that they often in fact seemed to be in love with suffering and chose it as their inheritance on earth, is often looked upon by non-Catholics—that is to say non-Catholic Christians—as incomprehensible, and, in the eyes of many, extremely unsavoury. If God is goodness, if Christ died on the cross to save us from our sins, why should Christians have to suffer—and suffer not merely ordinary opposition, which may have an educational value for the sufferer, but, though innocent, suffer for others' sins? One thing is certain, that all the saints have maintained that they suffered for their own sins, although we cannot see it otherwise than that they suffered for the sins of others. It is only among the saints that we find any who have the right to say, "Nothing human is foreign to me." Nevertheless, we may all, at any moment, find that we have to suffer for what in our eyes are exclusively the sins of others. Two world wars, and their aftermath, spread over almost the whole of the world, should have made this truth understandable—emphatically understandable—even for the simplest and most self-satisfied of souls.

Since Jesus Christ redeemed mankind with His precious blood we can be saved if we are willing to let Him save us. But even St. Paul had to point out to the Colossians that Christ's sufferings sometimes overflow into our life, so that we in our flesh may be forced to "fill up those things that are wanting of the sufferings of Christ". There is nothing in the experience of man which shows that the raw material of human nature has ever changed. It is eternally dragged down by our desire for the things which escape our grasp, or if we manage to grasp some of them we find that we are still not satisfied. Satisfied desire produces new desire until old age puts a stop to the chase, and death ends all. We are shown frequent glimpses of our nature which remind us of our origin, and in whose image we were created. From the image of God in us we have creative energy, the spring of unselfish love—unselfish in spite of the shadow of egoism which is inseparable from all our impulses; the longing to create our world to an ordered pattern, to live according to the law, and to see our ideals of justice realised. (When West European man in the course of the last few centuries developed new and better tools with which to investigate the material world, and learned more and more of the apparently stable law between cause and effect in the physical world, he gave what he had discovered the name of one of the things which he had loved most dearly and hated most intensely, served most self-sacrificingly and betrayed most shamefully—he spoke of the "laws of nature".) We men have ceaselessly stained and crippled this image of God in ourselves: we have succumbed to our desire for power and flattery, to our passions, hate and revenge, lust and ambition. Or we have grown tired of what we achieved and fought for, and capriciously destroyed what we have created. We are afraid of change, and afraid of stagnation. We love old things and institutions, and will have something which is new and different. In the clash with our own human nature our most noble ideals and our boldest dreams of Utopia always crumble to nothing—until our last and boldest dreams of Utopia have put in our hands the weapon with which we are able to destroy our world completely if we will—and who can tell what the destructive instinct of mankind will shrink from doing? On that day which the Church has foretold from the beginning, when the Son of Man shall come again to judge the world with fire, it is perhaps we ourselves who will provide the fire.

St. Catherine's teaching on love for death and love for life is just as applicable to-day as in her life-time—neither more nor less so. Her extraordinary personality, so full of mystical activity, is timeless in its significance. It is not easy for us to understand her, but it was not easy for her contemporaries either. It is true enough that we have learned a good deal since her day: we know much more about the physical mechanism which can cause abnormal (that is to say unusual) symptoms and conditions in the human body, about the psychic energy which can cause one mind to affect the minds of others, even at a distance, even in opposition to the other mind. But we seldom see such unusual symptoms except in neurotics. Seldom or never do we see them in conjunction not only with a high degree of intelligence, but also with robust common sense, with unlimited ability to take upon oneself all kinds of hard work and trouble, with interest for the well-being of other people, and no interest whatsoever in one's own comfort or welfare. We have had terrible experience of the psychic power which can produce effects such as the possession by devils of a whole people. But we have less experience of the psychic powers which console and strengthen and fill our minds with peace, which encourage the despairing and drive out hatred and envy and the will to hurt others. Although, thank God, most of us have known someone with this psychic power, though perhaps it seemed to us to have only a small field of activity—a family, a circle of friends, at the best a people. But perhaps we are wrong; perhaps the power which proceeds from good men and women is too subtle for us with our limited abilities to understand. Perhaps its waves are like the light-waves and sound-waves of which our eyes and ears only perceive a small part.

The saints have always known that the power of good is something quite incalculable. When they renounced even pure and harmless happiness on earth, that they might have none of the hindrances interposed by care for their own or another's material needs, in their struggle to achieve unity with the Origin of life, they knew that if He filled them with His grace and mercy, His superfluous gifts—gifts bringing health and life—would overflow into the lives of other men—even to people outside the range of their knowledge, beyond their sight and the field of their activity. St. Catherine must often have felt discouraged when she saw no concrete results of her efforts for certain individuals, both men and women, through prayer and attempts at persuasion. But she never wavered; she gave of herself until her physical life was used up, in a fight whose final results she was as sure of, as she was sure that she would not see many victories on the battlefield of this world. But in fact Our Lord has never made any promises regarding the triumph of Christianity on earth—on the contrary. If we expect to see His cause triumph here, His own words should warn us: "The Son of Man, when he cometh, shall he find, think you, faith on earth?" He did not tell us the answer.

But these words should make those who talk of the bankruptcy of Christianity in our times a little more careful. We have never been given any promises of a world where all men and women willingly accept the teaching of Christ as their way of life. They have not even done so in a period when there were very few who doubted that He was the lord of heaven and earth; they still tried to escape Him or deliberately refused to listen to Him. For every man is born individually, and must be saved individually.

It is not given us to know what Christendom's final fate on earth will be. The gates of hell shall not overpower His Church, but those who wish to break out of it have full freedom to do so. The real question is: when the conditional reality which we call the material world withers away, who will have won real life in all eternity in the land of the living? Even the people of of our times, who have magnified mankind's ineradicable trust in the things which we can see, touch, and enjoy with our senses, and made their articles of faith out of materialism, self-aggrandising humanism, collectivism, or whatever one likes to call it—even they have caught a glimpse of how utterly worthless all material things are. In the light of the split atoms, solid objects become as it were transparent, evanescent. But who can say how mankind will react to the new discoveries it makes? We sorely need the wisdom of the saints.